The Romance of American

Communism

THE ROMANCE
OF AMERICAN
COMMUNISM

Vivian Gornick

BASIC BOOKS, INC., PUBLISHERS

New York

Excerpt from *American Hunger* by Richard Wright, copyright © 1944 by Richard Wright, copyright © 1977 by Ellen Wright, reprinted by permission of Harper & Row, Publishers, Inc.

Library of Congress Cataloging in Publication Data

Gornick, Vivian.
    The romance of American Communism.

        1. Communism—United States—1917. I. Title.
HX83.G6   335.43'0973   77-75248
ISBN: 0-465-07110-4 (cloth)
ISBN: 0-465-07111-2 (paper)

Copyright © 1977 by Vivian Gornick
Printed in the United States of America
Designed by Vincent Torre
10 9 8 7 6 5 4 3 2 1

*This book is dedicated to
the memory of Louis Gornick
and the spirit of Carl Marzani*

Let us acquit ourselves so that we shall not perish without having truly existed. . . . The worst thing that could happen to us would be to die without either succeeding or understanding.

—*Simone Weil*

ACKNOWLEDGMENTS

I wish to thank the Tamiment Library for letting me make use of its research materials and the Victor Rabinowitz Foundation for the financial assistance I received during the writing of this book.

CONTENTS

CHAPTER THREE

Living It Out: From Vision to Dogma and Halfway Back

CHAPTER FOUR

They Went Back into Everywhere: Varieties of Aftermath

CHAPTER FIVE

The Romance of American

Communism

CHAPTER ONE

To Begin With

BEFORE I KNEW that I was Jewish or a girl I knew that I was a member of the working class. At a time when I had not yet grasped the significance of the fact that in my house English was a second language, or that I wore dresses while my brother wore pants, I knew—and I knew it was important to know—that Papa worked hard all day long. One of my strongest memories of early childhood is that no matter what we were doing, my mother and I, everything in our Bronx apartment stopped dead at four-thirty in the afternoon and she began cooking supper. If ever I questioned this practice, or complained, or demanded that we continue what we were doing, my mother—whose manner was generally frantic and uncontrolled—would answer with a sudden dignity that stopped me cold: "Papa works hard all day long. When he comes home his supper must be on the table."

Papa works hard all day long. Those words, in my mother's mouth, spoke volumes, and from the age of reason on I absorbed their complex message. The words stirred in me, almost from the first time I heard them, an extraordinary resonance, one whose range was wide enough to compel my emotional attention throughout my subsequent life. To begin with, the words communicated pain and difficulty; my childish heart ached for my gentle father. The pain was frightening, and even as it began to flow inside me, like a liquid turning to a solid, I felt myself go numb. This emotion was awesome; it induced in me the sense of some mysterious force working on our lives, some force in which we were all caught: suspended, puzzled, moving blind. At the very same time, the mere articulation of the words in my mother's mouth produced a peculiar and relieving focus against the murkiness of that mysterious force, a focus which told me where and who I was: I was the daughter of Papa who worked hard all day long. Finally, the words said: We are all of us, here in this house, vitally connected to the fact that Papa works hard all day long. We pay attention to and respect that fact; we make common cause with it. This last, this oneness, this solidarity, produced in me pride and excitement; it dissolved the numbness and transformed the pain back into a moving, stirring, agitating element: something to be understood and responded to, something to be dealt with and struggled against.

My father stood upright on the floor of a dress factory on West 35th Street in New York City with a steam iron in his hand for thirty years. My uncles owned the factory. My father was Labor, my uncles were Capital. My father was a Socialist, my uncles were Zionists. Therefore, Labor was Socialism and Capital was Nationalism. These equations were mother's milk to me, absorbed through flesh and bone almost before consciousness. Concomitantly, I knew also—and again, as though osmotically—who in this world were friends, who enemies, who neutrals. Friends were all those who thought like us: working-class socialists, the people whom my parents called "progressives." All others were "them"; and "them" were either engaged enemies like my uncles or passive neutrals like some of our neighbors. Years later, the "us" and "them" of my life would become Jews and Gentiles, and still later women and men, but for all of my growing-up years "us" and "them" were socialists and non-socialists; the "politically enlightened" and the politically *un*enlightened; those who were "struggling for a better world" and those who, like moral slugs, moved blind and unresponsive through this vast inequity that was our life under capitalism. Those, in short, who had class consciousness and those *lumpen* or bourgeois who did not.

This world of "us" was, of course, a many-layered one. I was thirteen or fourteen years old before I consciously understood the complex sociology of the progressive planet; understood that at the center of the globe stood those who were full-time organizing members of the Communist Party, at the outermost periphery stood those who were called "sympathizers," and at various points in between stood those who held Communist Party membership cards and those who were called "fellow travelers." In those early childhood years these distinctions did not exist for me; much less did I grasp that within this sociology my parents were merely "fellow travelers." The people who came to our house with the *Daily Worker* or the Yiddish newspaper *Der Freiheit* under their arms, the people at the "affairs" we attended, the people at the *shule* (the Yiddish school I was sent to after my public-school day was over), the people at the rallies we went to and the May Day parades we marched in, the people who belonged to the various "clubs" and were interminably collecting money for the latest cause or defense fund—they were all as one to me; they were simply "our people." Of a Saturday morning, the doorbell in our Bronx apartment would ring, my father would open the door, and standing there would be Hymie, a cutter in my father's shop, a small, thin man with gnarled hands and the face of an anxious bulldog. "*Nu*, Louie?" Hymie would say to my father. "Did you see the papers this morning? Did you see—a black year on all of them!—what they're saying about the Soviet Union *this* morning?" "Come in, Hymie, come in," my father would reply. "Have a cup of coffee, we'll discuss it." I did not know that there was a difference between Hymie, who was also only a "fellow traveler," and my cousins David and Selena, who were YCLers, or my uncle Sam, who was always off at "a meeting," or Bennie Grossman from across the street who had suddenly disappeared from the neighborhood ("unavailable" was the word for what Bennie had become, but it would be twenty years before I realized that was the word). It was, to begin with, all one country to me, one world, and the major characteristic of that world as I perceived it was this:

At the wooden table in our kitchen there were always gathered men named Max and Hymie, and women named Masha and Goldie. Their hands were work-blackened, their eyes intelligent and anxious, their voices loud and insistent. They drank tea, ate black bread and herring, and talked "issues." Endlessly, they talked issues. I sat on the kitchen bench beside my father, nestled in the crook of his arm, and I listened, wide-eyed, to the talk. Oh, that talk! That passionate, transforming talk! I understood nothing of what they were saying, but I was excited beyond words by the richness of their rhetoric, the intensity of their arguments, the urgency and longing behind that hot river of words that came ceaselessly pouring out of all of them. Something important was happening here, I always felt, something that had to do with understanding things. And "to understand things," I already knew, was the most exciting, the most important thing in life.

It was characteristic of that world that during those hours at the kitchen table with my father and his socialist friends I didn't know we were poor. I didn't know that in those places beyond the streets of my neighborhood we were without power, position, material or social existence. I only knew that tea and black bread were the most delicious food and drink in the world, that political talk filled the room with a terrible excitement and a richness of expectation, that here in the kitchen I felt the same electric thrill I felt when Rouben, my Yiddish teacher, pressed my upper arm between two bony fingers and, his eyes shining behind thick glasses, said to me: "Ideas, dolly, ideas. Without them, life is nothing. With them, life is *everything*."

Sometimes I would slip off the bench and catch my mother somewhere between the stove and the table (she was forever bringing something to the table). I would point to one or another at the table and whisper to her: Who is this one? Who is that one? My mother would reply in Yiddish: "He is a writer. She is a poet. He is a thinker." Oh, I would nod, perfectly satisfied with these identifications, and return to my place on the bench. *He*, of course, drove a bakery truck. *She* was a sewing-machine operator. That other one over there was a plumber, and the one next to him stood pressing dresses all day long beside my father.

But Rouben was right. Ideas were everything. So powerful was the life inside their minds that sitting there, drinking tea and talking issues, these people ceased to be what they objectively were—immigrant Jews, disenfranchised workers—and, indeed, they became thinkers, writers, poets.

Every one of them read the *Daily Worker*, the *Freiheit*, and the *New York Times* religiously each morning. Every one of them had an opinion on everything he or she read. Every one of them was forever pushing, pulling, yanking, mauling those opinions into shape within the framework of a single question. The question was: Is it good for the workers? That river of words was continually flowing toward an ocean called *farshtand*, within whose elusive depths lay the answer to this question.

They were voyagers on that river, these plumbers, pressers, and sewing-machine operators. Disciplined voyagers with a course to steer, a destination to arrive at. When one of them yelled at another (as one of them regularly did) "Id-yot! What has *that* to do with anything? Use your brains! God gave you brains, yes or no? Well, use them!" he was, in effect, saying: Where will that question take us? Nowhere. Get back on course. We're going somewhere, aren't we? Well, then, let's go there.

They took with them on this journey not only their own narrow, impoverished experience but a set of abstractions as well, abstractions with the power to transform. When these people sat down at the kitchen table to talk, Politics sat down with them, Ideas sat down with them, above all, History sat down with them. They spoke and thought within a context that had world-making properties. This context lifted them out of the nameless, faceless obscurity of the soul into which they had been born and gave them, for the first time in their lives, a sense of rights as well as of obligations. They had rights because they now knew who and what they were. They were not simply the disinherited of the earth, they were proletarians. They were not a people without a history, they had the Russian Revolution. They were not without a civilizing world view, they had Marxism.

Within such a context the people at my father's kitchen table could place themselves; and if they could place themselves—compelling insight!—they could *become* themselves. For, in order to become one must first have some civilizing referent, some social boundary, some idea of nationhood. These people had no external nationhood; nothing in the cultures they had left, or the one to which they had come, had given them anything but a humiliating sense of outsidedness. The only nationhood to which they had attained was the nationhood inside their minds: the nationhood of the international working class. And indeed, a nation it was—complete with a sense of family, culture, religion, social mores, political institutions. The people in that kitchen had remade the family in the image of workers all over the world, political institutions in the image of the Communist Party, social mores in the image of Marxist allegiance, religion in the image of the new socialized man, Utopia in the image of the Soviet Union. They sat at the kitchen table and they felt themselves linked up to America, Russia, Europe, the world. Their people were everywhere, their power was the revolution around the corner, their empire "a better world."

To see themselves as part of an identifiable mass of human beings with a place and a destiny in the scheme of civilized life—when until now they had felt only the dread isolation that is the inevitable legacy of powerlessness—was suddenly to "see" themselves. Thus, paradoxically, the more each one identified himself or herself with the working-class movement, the more each one came individually alive. The more each one acknowledged his or her condition as one of binding connectedness, the more each one pushed back the darkness and experienced the life within. In this sense, that kitchen ceased to be a room in a shabby tenement apartment in the Bronx and became, for all intents and purposes, the center of the world as that center has ever been described since the time of the ancient Greeks. For, here in the turmoil and excitation of their urgent talk, the men and women at the kitchen table were involved in nothing less than an act of self-creation: the creation of the self through increased consciousness. The instrument of consciousness for them was Marx. Marx and the Communist Party and world socialism. Marx was their Socrates, the Party was their Plato, world socialism their Athens.

There are few things in life to equal the power and joy of

experiencing oneself. Rousseau said there is nothing in life *but* the experiencing of oneself. Gorky said he loved his friends because in their presence he felt himself. "How important it is," he wrote, "how glorious it is—to feel oneself!" Indeed, how impossible it is not to love ardently those people, that atmosphere, those events and ideas in whose presence one feels the life within oneself stirring. How impossible, in fact, not to feel passionately in the presence of such stirrings. For the people among whom I grew this intensity of feeling was transmitted through Marxism as interpreted by the Communist Party.

At the indisputable center of the progressive world stood the Communist Party. It was the Party whose awesome structure harnessed that inchoate emotion which, with the force of a tidal wave, drove millions of people around the globe toward Marxism. It was the Party whose moral authority gave shape and substance to an abstraction, thereby making of it a powerful human experience. It was the Party that brought to astonishing life the kind of comradeship that makes swell in men and women the deepest sense of their own humanness, allowing them to love themselves through the act of loving each other. For, of this party it could rightly be said, as Richard Wright in his bitterest moment did, nonetheless, say: "There was no agency in the world so capable of making men feel the earth and the people upon it as the Communist Party."

Who, who came out of that world could fail to remember the extraordinary quality these experiences embodied for all those living through them? You were, if you were there, in the presence of one of the most amazing of humanizing processes: that process whereby one emerges by merging; whereby one experiences oneself through an idea of the self beyond the self and one becomes free, whole, and separate through the mysterious agency of a disciplining context. In short, you were in the presence of the socializing emotion, that emotion whose operating force is such that men and women feel themselves not through that which composes their own unique, individual selves but rather through that which composes the shared, irreducible self.

To all this the Communist Party spoke. From all this it drew its formidable strength.

I was twenty years old in April of 1956 when Khrushchev

addressed the 20th Congress of the Soviet Union and "revealed" to the world the incalculable despair of Stalin's rule. I say "revealed" because Khrushchev's report compelled millions of people to know consciously that which many of them had known subconsciously for a very long time. The 20th Congress Report brought with it political devastation for the organized Left-wing. Coming as it did in the midst of one of the most repressive periods in American history—a period when Communists were hunted like criminals, suffered trial and imprisonment, endured social isolation and loss of work, had their professional lives destroyed and, in the case of the Rosenbergs, were put to death—the Khrushchev Report was the final instrument of annihilation for the American Left. Thousands of men and women in the Left walked about feeling as Ignazio Silone twenty-five years before them had felt: "Like someone who has had a tremendous blow on the head and keeps on his feet, walking, talking, gesticulating, but without fully realizing what has happened." And like Silone they, too, said to themselves: "For this? Have we sunk to this? Those who are dead, those who are dying in prison, have sacrificed themselves for this? The vagabond, lonely, perilous lives that we ourselves are leading, strangers in our own countries—is it all for this?" Overnight, the affective life of the Communist Party in this country came to an end. Within weeks of the Report's publication, 30,000 people left the Party. Within a year the Party was as it had been in its 1919 beginnings: a small sect, off the American political map.

For me, at twenty, the Khrushchev Report snapped the last thread in a fabric of belief that was already worn to near disintegration. In the previous three or four years I had often been in a state of dismay as I felt the weight of simplistic socialist explanation pressing upon my growing inner life. At fifteen I had been a member of the Labor Youth League (the Party's last incarnation of the Young Communist League), attending meetings in a loft on New York's Prince Street where the walls were covered with huge poster pictures of Lenin, Stalin, and (who could now believe it?) Mao, and where the Party organizer came weekly to deliver exhortations and assignments in a language that, increasingly, began to sound foreign to my ears: remote, very remote from the language of the kitchen which, itself, was beginning to be replaced by the language of Melville, Mann, Wolfe and Dostoevsky now sounding within me. As my interior language altered, and new kinds of thought challenged the once unquestioned, now vulnerable socialist ideology, shadows and confusions filled my mind. I began to feel a dreadful nagging pain developing at the edge of thought—sometimes like toothache, sometimes a sudden stab of fear, sometimes a quick wash of panic—about the "progressive" world. Its logic began to break down; injustices began to loom; discrepancies in behavior nagged at me; questions arose for which there were no longer ready answers. I found myself arguing with my relatives and my father's friends; the arguments produced anger and divisions instead of explanations and unity. It was no longer sufficient to be told "The Party knows what it's doing" or "Do you know better than the Soviet Union what is good for the workers?" or "They know better than we do what's going on. If they do thus-and-so there's a very good reason for it. Who are *you* to question those in a position to know what's going on?"

Now, in 1956, we sat in the kitchen: my mother, my aunt, and I. My brother was married and long gone from the house (not to mention the progressive world). My father was dead, and so was my uncle Sam. We alone remained—we three women—in this crumbling house to face the crumbling world outside the kitchen. Our men, our race, our politics: dead and dying, lost and gone, smashed and murdered. Hitler had destroyed half of our world, now Stalin had destroyed the other half. I was beside myself with youthful rage. My mother was desperately confused. My aunt remained adamantly Stalinist. Night after night we quarreled violently.

"Lies!" I screamed at my aunt. "Lies and treachery and murder. A maniac has been sitting there in Moscow! A maniac has been sitting there in the name of socialism. In the name of *socialism*! And all of you—all these years—have undone yourselves over and over again in the service of this maniac. Millions of Russians have been destroyed! Millions of Communists have betrayed themselves and each other!"

"A Red-baiter!" my aunt yelled back. "A lousy little Red-baiter you've become! Louie Gornick must be turning over in his grave, that his daughter has become a Red-baiter!"

And we stared at each other, each of us trapped in her own anguish. I, in the grip of that pain and fury that I can feel to this day (waking suddenly in the night now, twenty years later, having just read or heard some new report of inhumanity from the Soviet Union, I often find myself very nearly saying out loud: "All this done in the name of socialism. In the *name* of socialism"), and she, my aunt, her strong peasant face ashen with grief and survival, the world inside her and all around her dissolving in a horror of confusion too great to bear, too annihilating to take in.

And all the while, in the back of my head—even as my aunt and I were turning and turning, locked together inside this waking nightmare of human disintegration—I was hearing the felt sound of Ignazio Silone's voice saying: "The truth is this: the day I left the Communist Party was a very sad one for me, it was like a day of deep mourning, the mourning I felt for my lost youth. And I come from a district where mourning is worn longer than elsewhere."

All this happened a generation ago in a small world. An atypical world, many say: the ingrown world of the New York working-class Left. Certainly it is true that this world never *was* duplicated with any exactness anywhere else in the American Left. However, so far from being atypical, it was in fact archetypal. What was happening—in all its striking narrowness and intensity—in that kitchen in the Bronx in the Forties and Fifties—was happening simultaneously, in one form or another, in thousands of places not only in this country but over much of the Western world. The grief and rage that my aunt and I shared was heavy with symbolic weight; not hundreds, not thousands, but millions of people in this century had felt themselves come both to life and then to death through devotion to this ideology, this party.

Twenty years have passed since the time and the atmosphere I am remembering dominated not only my life but the life of the country. During that time innumerable people have written unceasingly about the Communist experience. Conservatives, radicals, ex-radicals, liberals, intellectuals, philosophers, historians, psychoanalysts—all have described, explained, defended, attacked, expanded, reduced, placed, and displaced the Communist experience. And yet: whatever the elements were of that world in which I grew, whatever its deepest subterranean currents, only rarely do I glimpse them, as I knew and felt them, in the volumes and volumes that have sought to interpret the experience; and almost never do I see before me the flesh and blood people, or feel on the page the fierce emotional pull of that life—awesome, hungering, deeply moving—they all led. That life which accumulated into those Large Events—war, revolution, nationhood, foreign policy, *realpolitik*—which all those books are forever chronicling; that life that, very nearly, reverberated with metaphoric meaning.

For, beyond the literal need of my parents' socialism lay a larger need to which Marxism ever spoke and which the Communist Party ever embodied: the need within the human spirit to say no to the judgment of man upon man that is the politicalness of life. Nothing in the twentieth century has spoken as compellingly— with such power and moral imagination—to this need as has Communism; nothing in modern times has so joined the need with the real and the ideal to produce a universe of internal experience as has Communism; nothing has so induced in men and women all over the world a commonly held dream of passionate proportion —one whose betrayal could never be forgiven, whose promise could never be relinquished—as has Communism.

It was this dream—this passion, this hook on the soul—that made of Communism the metaphoric experience that it was, causing people like my aunt to pass from vision to dogma, from exaltation to anguish, all the while remaining fixed in some truly terrible, truly awesome way on the object of the passionate dream.

What I remember most deeply about the Communists is their passion. It was passion that converted them, passion that held them, passion that lifted them up and then twisted them down. Each and every one of them experienced a kind of inner radiance: some intensity of illumination that tore at the soul. To know that radiance, to be lit from within, and then to lose it; to be thrown back, away from its light and heat; to know thereafter the ordinary greyness of life, black and lightless; that was to know a kind of exaltation and dread that can be understood only, perhaps, by those who have loved deeply and suffered the crippling loss of that love.

The ancient Greeks defined sexual passion as a disease: something that strikes from without and touches a source of human need so deep, so hungering that the rational and humane faculties are rendered helpless before the mad, distorting behavior that follows upon the attack, and are literally held in abeyance while the passion plays itself out, leaving the victim to recover as best he can. Homer's description of the love of Paris for Helen is confined within these terms. Helen touches in Paris his *capacity* for sexual love; once touched, that capacity suddenly realizes itself as a hunger of the soul; expressive life is now given to that which might have remained inchoate forever; the hunger flares up in Paris and burns steadily within him; it is all light and heat of such a high order that it is as though all other forms of love he has ever known become dim and cold in memory; this light and heat are all-consuming; Paris is soon addicted, given over to the hungry need; in time, Helen herself—the object, the cause, the origin of the hungry, burning need—becomes less real than the need itself; the hunger now has a life of its own, a life filled with stubborn power. At this point the nature of the force becomes clear: it is antisocial, fixed on itself, obeying internal laws that conflict with the laws of associativeness.

In the face of such pressure, such driving human need, it becomes absurd, almost, to speak of Paris' intelligence, character, moral or psychological development. The pressure, quite simply, is *there*: powerful, prehistoric, filled with the grief and longing of the primeval soul; beyond social time, beyond civilizing time, beyond tribal loyalties and the compassionate restraint of reason.

There are, it seems to me, a number of stable hungers in the human psyche, each one capable of flaring into passion once brought to expressive life. One of these hungers, beyond question, is the need to live a life of meaning. The motive force is the dread fear that life is *without* meaning. This fear-hunger speaks to a need not of the flesh but of the spirit, a need having to do with the deepest definitions of what it is to be human. And as with other human needs, it is possible to live an entire lifetime without encountering the people, ideas, or events which will trigger into conscious life this primeval hunger. But once met. . . .

Marxism was for those who became Communists what Helen was for Paris. Once encountered, in the compelling persona of the Communist Party, the ideology set in motion the most intense longings, longings buried in the unknowing self, longings that pierced to the mysterious, vulnerable heart at the center of that incoherent life within us, longings that had to do with the need to live a life of meaning. These longings haunted the Communists, arising as they did out of one of the great human hungers, a hunger that finally had a life of its own; so that while at first the Communists fed the hunger, at last the hunger fed off them. That hunger became, in short, a passion, a passion that was in its very essence both compellingly humanizing and then compellingly dehumanizing. For the law of passion is such that it is *all*; and when a thing becomes all, people do terrible things to themselves and to one another.

Thus, among the Communists, men and women who gained the courage to plunge after freedom were in the end not free. Men and women who had great intelligence were in the end in no position to use that intelligence. Men and women who were eminently reasonable and clung to the beauty and decency of reason were in the end a caricature of reason. Men and women who sought to control the cruelties of social relations through the justice of scientific analysis in the end used scientific analysis to impose new cruelties.

And surrounding the whole of things was the longing; *responsible* for the whole of things was the longing, the longing aroused by the vision of loveliness that was Marxism and could not be let go of even when the vision became a trap, a prison, a shriveling of the soul rather than the exultant enlarging of the soul it had been in its beginnings.

Richard Wright captures perfectly the beauty, pain, and irony of the Communist experience when—in his segment of "The God That Failed," an extract of his book *American Hunger*—he describes the trial of Ross, a black comrade who has been brought up on charges by the Communist Party in Chicago in the Forties:

> The trial began in a quiet, informal manner. The comrades acted like a group of neighbors sitting in judgement upon one of their own kind who had stolen a chicken. Anybody could ask for and get the floor. There was absolute freedom of speech. Yet the meeting had an amazingly formal structure of its own, a structure that went as deep as the desire of men to live together.

A member of the Central Committee of the Communist Party rose and gave a description of the world situation. He spoke without emotion and piled up hard facts. He painted a horrible but masterful picture of Fascism's aggression in Germany, Italy and Japan.

I accepted the reason why the trial began in this manner. It was imperative that here be postulated against what or whom Ross' crimes had been committed. Therefore there had to be established in the minds of all present a vivid picture of mankind under oppression. And it was a true picture. Perhaps no organization on earth, save the Communist Party, possessed so detailed a knowledge of how workers lived, for its source of information stemmed directly from the workers themselves.

The next speaker discussed the role of the Soviet Union as the world's lone workers' state—how the Soviet Union was hemmed in by enemies, how the Soviet Union was trying to industrialize itself, what sacrifices it was making to help workers of the world to steer a path toward peace through the idea of collective security.

The facts presented so far were as true as any facts could be in this uncertain world. Yet not one word had been said of the accused, who sat listening like any other member. The time had not yet come to include him and his crimes in this picture of global struggle. An absolute had first to be established in the minds of the comrades so that they could measure the success or failure of their deeds by it.

Finally a speaker came forward and spoke of Chicago's South Side, its Negro population, their suffering and handicaps, linking all that also to the world struggle. Then still another speaker followed and described the tasks of the Communist Party of the South Side. At last, the world, the national, and the local pictures had been fused into one overwhelming drama of moral struggle in which everybody in the hall was participating. This presentation had lasted for more than three hours, but it had enthroned a new sense of reality in the hearts of those present, a sense of man on earth. With the exception of the church and its myths and legends, there was no agency in the world so capable of making men feel the earth and the people upon it as the Communist Party.

Toward evening the direct charges against Ross were made, not by the leaders of the Party, but by Ross' friends, those who knew him best! It was crushing. Ross wilted. His emotions could not withstand the weight of the moral pressure. No one was terrorized into giving information against him. They gave it willingly, citing dates, conversations, scenes. The black mass of Ross' wrongdoing emerged slowly and irrefutably.

The moment came for Ross to defend himself. I had been told

that he had arranged for friends to testify in his behalf, but he called upon no one. He stood, trembling; he tried to talk and his words would not come. The hall was as still as death. Guilt was written in every pore of his black skin. His hands shook. He held onto the edge of the table to keep on his feet. His personality, his sense of himself, had been obliterated. Yet he could not have been so humbled unless he had shared and accepted the vision that had crushed him, the common vision that bound us all together.

"Comrades," he said in a low, charged voice, "I'm guilty of all the charges, all of them."

His voice broke in a sob. No one prodded him. No one tortured him. No one threatened him. He was free to go out of the hall and never see another Communist. But he did not want to. He could not. The vision of a communal world had sunk down into his soul and it would never leave him until life left him.

There is horror in what Wright has described. But there is glory in it as well. Here is no tale of alien and robotized creatures enslaved by mindless authoritarianism, no image of foreign betrayal and subhuman "brainwashing." On the contrary: here is the portrait of a man who, in contact with a political vision, was made *more* human than he ever dreamed he could be, and it is the memory of that initial humanizing experience that fixes and holds him. What Ross cannot let go of is that moment when, through Marxism and the Party, the vision of a communal world endowed his life with moral meaning. For in that moment there quickened to conscious life in him the longing to give over his own isolation, to take the incomparable risk of shared existence. That moment touched naked need: an unconscious wound made suddenly conscious. Such a moment has visionary properties: it is one of profound self-recognition, and it is there in that self-recognition that the source of Ross' passion is fixed, that his exaltation and his dread are to be located.

For Ross the moment of self-recognition is inextricably bound up with Marxism and the Party; the two have become welded together in his emotions; to lose one is of necessity to lose the other. The irony of the experience, of course, is that the visionary discovery of the self through the revelations of Marxism has ended in a dogmatic purging of the self through the authoritarianism of the Party. Therein lies both the glory and the tragedy of the

Communist experience: it is the journey toward the vision that is brilliantly humanizing, it is the dogma at the end of the road that is soul-destroying.

For thirty years now people have been writing about the Communists with an oppressive distance between themselves and their subject, a distance that often masquerades as objectivity but in fact conveys only an emotional and intellectual atmosphere of "otherness"—as though something not quite recognizable, something vaguely nonhuman was being described. This distance sets those being described (i.e., the Communists) apart from those doing the describing in such a manner as to imply that the observers would never have been guilty of what the observed are guilty of: as though *they* were infantile while *we* are mature; as though *we* would have known better while *they* were incapable of knowing better; as though *we* would have seen the writing on the wall while *they* in their neediness were constitutionally blind to the writing on the wall. In short, as though the Communists were made of other, weaker, more inferior stuff, and what was in them is not in us.

Ironically, some of the worst instances of this emotional distance are to be found in books written by ex-Communists. Some small amount of this confessional literature is powerful and dimensional—such as the testimonials of Silone and Wright in *The God That Failed*—but most of it is either apologetic or self-castigating in tone; whichever, it throws up a smokescreen between the experience and the reader.

The self-accusation of the anti-Communist Communist is dismaying in the extreme. This is the kind of confessional written with a sarcastic defensiveness which so overwhelms the remembrance that what one is continually reading is what's written between the lines: "Amazing! To this day I don't know what on earth possessed me! This experience is as strange and exotic to me now as it must surely be to you. Look at what I was. Could you believe it. I can't."

Perhaps the most complicated example of this kind of writing is to be found in Arthur Koestler's autobiography, *Arrow in the*

Blue. In this book Koestler details his nine years in the Communist Party: discovery through conversion through disillusion. Although he does indeed tell all—the good feelings, the bad—and attempts an objective rendering of the experience, still the language is such, the *tone* is such that one feels of Koestler that, like Lady Macbeth, if he could scrape from his flesh, scald from his memory the entire experience he would do so; his skin crawls over having been a Communist. His syntax is surly, sarcastic, self-mocking, the words and phrases of one writing about the flowing past in the language of the self-censoring present. The language of one who, in effect, is saying to the reader: "I can taste the ashes but I cannot recall the flame." Dozens of books of this sort have been written, both in this country and in Europe.

But it is in the "disinterested" intellectual commentary of the past thirty years that that abstract and alienating distance from the Communists is felt most fully. It is in the way a Lionel Trilling's language freezes over when writing about Communists that one feels most the chill removal from the flesh-and-blood reality. Or a Richard Crossman who writes of The Convert to the Communist Party as though describing a creature who walks through one door a warm human individual and emerges through another a rubber-stamped robot. (What is one to make of sentences like: "Once the renunciation has been made, the mind, instead of operating freely, becomes the servant of a higher and unquestioned purpose. To deny the truth is an act of service. This, of course, is why it is useless to discuss any particular aspect of politics with a Communist"?)

Everything in me rises up in protest against such language. This is the language of men who have assumed an intellectual opposition to the human falsifications inherent in the Communist passion, and in the process are themselves committing human falsifications. Denouncing a monolithic political reality that is summed up in one armor-plated word (the word, of course, is "Stalinism"), they deny the teeming, contradictory life behind the word, and in so doing deny the experience its complex human source. No, I always feel myself frowning when I read their words, it was not like that, it was not like that at all. It was not the monolithic experience you are here describing; it was rather a vast, sprawling, fragmented, intensely various experience whose complexity of detail adds up to a truth at variance with the sum of its parts. Yes, what you say is true, yet it does not amount to the truth. Yes, the passion was a formidable leveler, but oh, how many were the combinations of response to the power of that loved-hated passion. Yes, the loss of self was the truly terrible thing about Communism, but oh, the hundreds and hundreds who fought daily, hourly to hold onto themselves and *still* remain Communists, and the wealth of human experience that is encompassed in that struggle.

I see before me a schoolteacher who laughs and says, "The Party was down on Freud, but in the Bronx we said, 'Yeah, yeah, but your mother's important, anyway.'" I see before me a labor organizer who walked a tightrope for nearly twenty years—years composed of daily decisions, daily arbitrations—in order not to betray his union members and still remain in the Party. I see before me a section organizer who also daily disobeyed the Party in order to serve his Depression-ridden neighborhood. I hear the laughter and grit and self-mockery of countless people who spent a lifetime on the high-tension wire between being a communist with a small c and a Communist: some of whom fell and were horribly broken, some of whom fell, picked themselves up, and went further, some of whom walked the wire successfully and remained whole and strong.

All of this—this mass of human detail, this bulky human history—is lost in words like The Convert to the Communist Party. Those words create an unbroken, floor-to-ceiling image, a wall on one side of which "we" stand, on the other side of which "they" stand. Between us and them there is no vital relation; what is in us could never be in them; what is in them bears no resemblance to what is in us. We hold the life of the individual dear, they hold it cheap. We raise babies, they eat babies. We glory in the life of the mind, they put ideologic electrodes into the life of the mind. We walk straight and free and clear, they hide, hunched and shadowy, at the ends of alleys. We learn, they brainwash. They are *all* always they, we are *all* always we.

Ironically, this dissociativeness cultivated by the intellectual anti-Communists is the very crime for which the Party itself is hated and reviled. Theodore Draper's description of the making of a Communist turns, ultimately, on human denial. Draper's superbly accumulating point about the Communists is that the emotional identification with the working class which made a man or a woman a communist slowly became transformed into a binding identification with the Party—which made a man or a woman a Communist. This Party identification reduced the ability of a Communist to see himself in all those around him; rather he came to see himself only in "the Party." Thus, if a friend—or even a relative—fell afoul of the Party, a Communist was all too often capable of separating himself completely from that friend or relative. The person being charged, tried, or expelled suddenly became strangely unreal to the Communist; not like the comrade he had, only yesterday, been; not recognizable; not like *himself*.

And indeed, indeed: it was, all too often, too desperately true. How many times have I heard a Communist say in reply to some question about this, that, or the other person he or she had known half a lifetime and who had been expelled from the Party: "I felt disconnected from him. I felt that I was and always would be a good comrade, and he somehow was not. Yes, even though all these years he had *seemed* like a good comrade. Secretly, I felt that what was happening to him could never happen to me." It was this dread dissociativeness that disintegrated innumerable Communists and isolated them in a disbelieving world. For this willed blindness is the diseased symptom of a vision become a dogma; it is the criminal part of passion.

What, then, is to be made of those who scorn the passion, who declare themselves clear-headed and humane, and yet dissociate in exactly the same way as did those in the grip of the passion? What undeclared passion do *they* serve? What self-deceived disconnectedness is at work in them? For the purpose of humane thought, surely, is to close the gap of separating experience, not widen it; to seek out those human elements which bind us to all experience, to make all that happens humanly understandable. If an intellectual humanist writes about the Communists in such a way as to make the J. Edgar Hoovers of this world nod with pleasure, then surely that intellectual deprives us of understanding, makes less rather than more available to us the human meaning of one of the great political movements of the century. In the name of a higher ideal—i.e., intellectual integrity—such a writer wipes out the special claims of discrete human experience, thus sacrificing to an abstraction the whole trembling mass of impulse, need, fear, doubt, and longing that determined the life of each and every man and woman who gave him or herself to the Marxist ideal. In short: he does what the Communists did at their worst. He can deal with the human excesses no better than they could; he falls into the same pit of mind-fear they fell into; he longs for the same polemical salvation they longed for, and can face the swamp of emotional contradiction no better than they could. Facing the Communists across a spiritual gulf, he declares loudly: "I am *nothing* like you," and in that act is never more like "them."

It seems to me the real point about the Communists is: they were like everybody else, only more so. What was in them is in all of us, only more so. In them, as in the artist, the proportions of response were writ large. In them, the major spiritual and intellectual currents of their time ran strong instead of weak. In them, the scattered need for a serious life cohered. There were as many different communists as there were Communists—it's only in the dark that they all look alike—but of most of them I think it can safely be said: They feared, hungered, and cared *more*. They were indifferent to nothing, they had opinions on everything, they responded with intensity. Their overriding impulse was toward the integration of life—human and elemental. This impulse was coupled with great emotional energy—it is the thing which still characterizes most of them, those who are yet alive to tell the tale: enormous life energy—an energy whose forward thrust had, sorrowfully, not sufficient distinguishing controls.

Certainly it is true that the inability—*ultimately*—to make reason dominate emotion is what the Communist experience was often about. Also, it is true that the characteristics of passion are the characteristics of arrested need. But is this truth not what *all* our lives are all about? Do we not live most of our lives in the grip of emotions that dominate our behaviors and around which most of our reason collects? Is not every construct—religious, philosophical, political—made in relation to this moving spectacle of the trapped, struggling intelligence locked in unequal battle with unconscious fears and helpless longings? Is not such a spectacle worthy of compassionate recognition rather than scornful, alienated anger?

The Communist experience was, both in its glory and in its

debasement, an awesome move toward humanness; an immense
and tormented effort of the heart, will, and brain that cried out,
"I must have justice or I will die." In this sense, the Communist
experience is of epic proportions, arousing to pity and terror. It
is a metaphor for fear and desire on the grand scale, always telling
us more—never less—of what it is to be human.

The affective life of the Communist Party USA was approximately forty years in length. More than a million Americans were
Communists at one time or another during these forty years. Of
these million, thousands were held for a lifetime by the passionate
ideal. Many of these people led double lives, endured social isolation, financial and professional deprivation, and finally imprisonment. They were a generation of Americans whose lives were
formed by political history as were no other American lives save
for those of the original American Revolutionists. Their experience embodies the relation between spiritual need and historical
context as does the experience of almost no other Americans. History is *in* them, they are in history.

Who, exactly, were these American Communists? From which
America did they spring, those who gave the better part of their
lives to serving the Marxist ideal through the Communist Party
USA? Where, precisely, did they come from? What sprawl, if
any, of continental lives do they represent? What specific conditions in American life spoke to those dormant hungers alive in all
human beings, ready to be tapped by the explosive meeting of
time, place, and thought, and galvanized into passionate being by
the conversion to Communism?

Why, exactly, did people join the Communist Party? Why did
they remain? Why did they leave? What were their lives like
while they were Communists? What were they like afterwards?
What did the experience do for them? What did it do *to* them?
In short: what was the emotional and spiritual content of the political vision that shaped thousands of American lives?

It has seemed to me that these questions speak to a piece of
American experience that has not been accurately described; that
a result of this deficiency is that American Communists have re-

mained an abstraction, and at least one generation of Americans has come of age thinking them a uniquely evil group of people, a terror "from across the sea."

It has further seemed to me a good to have such images dispelled from the American psyche, to allow the actual flesh-and-blood shape of individual American Communists to emerge, in its finite reality, from the shadows of ignorant imaginings about the unknown.

Throughout the whole of one recent year I traveled across America—from New York to Illinois to California, and up into Canada, down into Mexico, out to Puerto Rico—speaking to former Communists about their lives, the origins of their political attachment, their years in the Communist Party: seeking to reduce the abstractions. My criterion for selecting someone to talk to was only that he or she considered the years in the Communist Party to have been a shaping force in his or her life, and my questions turned on the emotional meaning of the political experience. (What did you feel then? What do you feel now? What did it mean to stay in? What did it mean to leave?) The men and women I interviewed were between the ages of forty-eight and seventy-five, and I found them living all sorts of lives. They were doctors, lawyers, academics; schoolteachers, housewives, builders; union officials, actors, pants-pressers; writers, psychologists, businessmen and women. They now occupied every position conceivable on the political spectrum, and the stories they told were, I felt, remarkable for the variety of social background, psychological motivation, and response to immediate experience they revealed.

It was for me, personally, a turbulent year, moving me steadily as it did into the mysterious heart of the familiar. I found much, of course, that I expected to find, but much more that came as a jarring surprise. On the one hand, I found—as I had expected to find—almost none among the ex-Communists who were now political activists of any sort, and none who deeply understood the America in which they were presently living. On the other hand, my sense memory of the Communists was such that I had expected to find a great many burnt-out souls, people who had wandered in a kind of post-passion purgatory these past twenty years. I found nothing of the sort. I found, for the most part, people who had remade their lives brilliantly; people who when they could no longer organize the revolution had organized themselves; people who made me think long and hard about the before-and-after of passion.

Then, I learned that something I had been taught all my young life but had never actually believed was, in fact, *true*: the Communists had come from everywhere. Secretly, I think I had always believed along with J. Edgar Hoover that the Communists were all New York Jews of Eastern European origin. In my year's journey I discovered that in fact—geographically, socially, psychologically—they really were every kind of American: white, black, rich, poor, Jew, Gentile, American-born, foreign-born; abandoned, adored, put up with; from the rural South, from the shopkeeper Midwest; from the bleakness of the Depression Dustbowl and the get-rich-quick hunger of California in the 1920s; from Marxism born of European thought and experience, from Marxism straight out of indigenous American populism; from the middle class, the working class, the drifting class; from those who could trace their ancestry back to the *Mayflower*, from those who had no ancestry beyond their grandparents—out of this vast human richness Americans had become Communists.

And just as they came from everywhere—and this, too, came as a surprise—so they have gone back into everywhere. As there was no monolithic Communist experience so there is no monolithic *ex*-Communist experience. They have become again every kind of American person. Politically, they are radical, liberal, conservative, indifferent. Some have become attentive capitalists, some have remained deliberately proletarian. Some began to study, some abandoned study. Some are in psychoanalysis, some are in the country. Almost all are alive in their thoughts and feelings, and almost all pay a remarkable amount of attention to their personal relations. (*"Now,"* as they all significantly add.)

Sometimes, the talk flowed nonstop for hours, sometimes it was like pulling teeth. Sometimes, I started asking questions and a subject leaned back into his or her own life as though I had touched a wellspring of imaginative release: then gold, pure emotional gold came pouring out. Sometimes, a stream of bitter argument over my "frivolous and reactionary point of view" took the place of an interview (the abuse I took from old Marxists in that one year should alone buy my way into heaven). Sometimes they lied through the ingenious method of "confessing all" and beating their breasts loudly; sometimes they lied, transparently, by falsifying and idealizing the past. Some talked for posterity (especially the famous Communists) and, infuriated, I would think: This is useless. Waste, waste, waste.

But I was wrong. Nothing was wasted, everything served a purpose—"telling the truth" as well as "not telling the truth." It was all part of the story. It was all a measure of how deeply felt the entire experience had been, how very much everyone had at stake in this particular piece of history, how painful and mainly impossible it was after all these years to come to terms with the past, and, indeed, what an extraordinary effort of the emotional will it takes to transcend one's own experience, to learn and grow from it.

Two things about the entire enterprise struck me forcibly: One, in twenty years much of what is now living history will be hearsay (and, indeed, in the relatively short time since, a number of the people I talked to have died). Two, most Communists seemed profoundly ready to speak, ready not only to unburden themselves of the complex stories of their lives but eager as well to leave a personal record of the extraordinary political experience that their lives both embrace and illuminate. For the most part, the stories the Communists told were quite marvelous, both in their detail and in the telling of it. Most people were immediately alive to what I was asking and responded as though I had retrieved in them an exiled being, thereby releasing in them the incomparable sweetness of "imagining" their lives, of making the mythic connections, of understanding their lives anew.

Despite the complexity and variety of the experience I was now privy to, it began to seem to me that a certain structure was imposing itself from within on the mass of detail I was absorbing. The life of each Communist was most gripping or most revealing either for the way he or she had come to Communism, or for the way he or she had lived out the years in the Party, or for the particular kind of ex-Communist he or she had become. Thus, when I came to order the stories of the lives it seemed most natural to group them in relation to beginnings, middles, and endings. And, indeed, it still seems so. For, taken as a whole, the tale of the

Communist experience resembles a drama of classical proportions: encounter, performance, and consequence.

This book, then, is about the lives of some American Communists —as those lives were told to me, and as I perceived them. It is an attempt to put flesh on the skeleton; to make concrete what has been abstract; to make real and recognizable what for most Americans has been unknown and, therefore, unreal. It is an attempt also on my part to sort out the past, my own past, to make sense of the world of my parents, to give shape and character and understanding to that which I understood in my nerve endings long before I could understand it in my mind; to clarify political emotions which had the power, in the twentieth century, to change the shape of human expectation.

CHAPTER TWO

They Came from Everywhere: All Kinds of Beginnings

To BEGIN WITH, there *were*, of course, the New York Jews.

Although the founders were indeed a mixed lot—Jewish, Gentile, immigrant, native-born—the beginnings of the American Communist Party are, beyond question, entangled with the European experience of Marxist revolution and the effect that revolution had on millions of Eastern European Jews. Jews were the quintessential outsiders in countries which, by the turn of the century, were themselves encrusted with the alienating miseries of class rigidity and dying monarchies. To be a Jew in Russia, Poland, or Hungary was to experience the social hopelessness of those countries in its most oppressive form. The Russian Revolution exploded that hopelessness with pressure-cooker force, and Jews in their thousands responded to the excitement and promise the vision of socialism brought into their closed-off lives. An American Communist of Russian-Jewish birth—a man now in his seventies, living in a pretty little house in southern California—who was fifteen years old when the Revolution occurred, told me in 1974: "When the Red Army marched into my village I felt welcome in the country for the first time in my life. I remember, the first thing they did was to open a library in the village. I stood in the doorway of the library. Two young soldiers in Red Army uniform smiled, and beckoned me to come in. When I crossed the threshold of that library I felt I was stepping into a new world."

Coupled with this profound sense of exclusion was another, equally profound sense of things, which made so many Jews respond to Marxism. One of the deepest strains in Jewish life is the moral injunction "to become." This strain runs with subterranean force through most Jewish lives regardless of what other aspects of experience and personality separate them. Thus, Jews "became" through an intensity of religious or intellectual or political life. In the highly political twentieth century they became, in overwhelming numbers, socialists, anarchists, Zionists—and Communists.

The idea of socialist revolution was a dominating strand woven through the rich tapestry of unassimilated Jewish life. When millions of Jews crossed the Atlantic Ocean in the first years of this century, packed in among the pots and pans and ragged clothes were the Talmud, Spinoza, Herzl, and Marx. Eventually, two million Jews settled in New York City. Of those two million, a significant number were European socialists. Their ideas, their attitudes, their sense of things mingled powerfully with all of New York Jewish life. They were as natural a part of the stream of being on the Lower East Side, and then later in Brooklyn and the Bronx, as were the Orthodox Jews and the Zionists and the intellectuals and those who simply wanted to get-rich-quick in America. If a Jew growing up in this world was not a Marxist he may have scorned the socialists or shrugged his shoulders at them or argued bitterly with them, but he did not in the deepest part of himself disown them, or find them strange or alienating creatures. They were there, they were recognizable, they were *us*. Such worldly/simple acceptance inside this small society within a society had far-reaching effects on all who grew within its boundaries; it produced a people richly receptive to the possibility of conversion in any direction.

Commingled with the catalytic sense of outsidedness and the hunger "to become" at work inside these immigrant Jews was, oddly enough, the agitating presence of America itself. The streets of America were *not* paved with gold. For the most part, the ghettos of Europe were exchanged for the ghettos of New York. Filth, cold, poverty, and early death were in New York as they had been in Odessa and Warsaw. Worse: in Russia and Poland they could speak the language, in America not a word. They huddled together in their same dark, anxious, intelligent crowdedness in the New World as they had in the Old World. But there was one vital difference here: the laws were not written expressly to subjugate them. In fact, the laws in America guaranteed them rights instead of spelling out limitations. This difference was all the world. This difference was "America." It meant hope, openness, possibility, and, ironically, in many people it released the courage for Marxism that Europe had shriveled in them. My maternal grandparents were perfect examples of this phenomenon in operation. In Russia, my grandfather had been religious—and my grandmother silent. From the day they landed on Ellis Island my grandfather experienced an anxiety of dislocation, a longing for Russia and that which he understood, which never left him. He retreated into the Talmud, grew a beard down to his belly, and remained otherworldly religious for the rest of his life. My grandmother, on the other hand, although the world above New York's Fourteenth Street remained alien territory to her for thirty years, adored America. "*Frei!*" she would exclaim. "*Wir sind hier frei!*" And in America she became a socialist.

The Jewish Marxists

WHEN the Communist Party USA emerged, in 1919, out of a welter of dense socialist struggles, there were among its founding members many men and women who had been formed politically by some or all of these experiences. Two of them were Sarah Gordon's parents. Amos and Jenny Gordon had been "1905ers" in Russia and, in the fearful aftermath of that abortive revolution, had fled the country. They were passionate, lifelong supporters of the Russian Revolution, and here in America they quickly became socialists and then Communists. Amos was dark, hot-tempered, and gregarious. Jenny was blue-eyed, very intelligent, and wrapped inside a wounded, angry pride that held her together. They settled in the Bronx. Amos earned a meager living as a button-maker—and went to meetings. Jenny had three children— and spent most of her waking hours scheming to put chicken instead of beans in her children's mouths, and reading Lenin and Marx. Sarah and her two brothers were born in the Bronx between 1922 and 1926 into poverty and the Communist Party. The children respected their mother and adored their father. Between them, the two parents were for the children the embodiment of the loving warmth and stern morality of "the movement."

Sarah Gordon joined the Young Communist League when she was fourteen years old and left the Communist Party in 1956, when she was thirty-four. Now, in 1974, Sarah is fifty-two years old. A highly skilled administrator employed by a public health association whose offices are located in midtown Manhattan, she is a slim woman with thick grey hair and bright blue eyes, possessed of a quiet easy elegance that mixes appealingly with the warm, down-to-earth Bronx Jewish humor that still characterizes her thought and speech. "They should only know at work," she says with an eloquent shrug of the shoulder, "that I'm as good as I am because of the Communist Party." (Sarah is the first of innumerable people who will observe with humor and irony that they are as good as they are at their current work because of the organizational and analytic skills they acquired in the Party.)

"You know," Sarah says, curling up on the couch in her Manhattan living room, "when I was a kid—that is, when I was in my twenties—I used to envy people who had come into the movement in adult life. I used to think: What a thrill it must be for people to *discover* Marxism, to discover the Party. Me, there'd never been a moment in my conscious life when the Party wasn't there. There was Mama, there was Papa, there was the Party. I couldn't tell where one left off and the other began. Especially, I couldn't tell where my father left off and the Party began . . . If my mother had ever wanted to sue for divorce she'd have had to name the Communist Party as corespondent.

"We were so damned poor, and my mother hated my father for not making a living, and sometimes she blamed the Party in her helplessness . . . And even I, the only time I would have dared, if I could, hate the Party was when my father gave two dollars to the Party that meant the difference between beans and chicken for us.

"But that was it. The Party came first. Always. And because it *did* come first we often forgot how poor we were. That was another thing I used to think about a lot. Imagine being as poor as we were, and *not* having the Party. Imagine being that poor with *nothing* to explain your poverty to you, nothing to give it some meaning, to help you get through the days and years because you could believe that it wouldn't always be this way.

"That's what our politics was to us. It literally negated our deprivation. It was rich, warm, energetic, an exciting thickness in which our lives were wrapped. It nourished us when nothing else nourished us. It not only kept us alive, it made us powerful inside ourselves. During the Depression my father couldn't even get work as a button-maker. He made syrups—vanilla and chocolate, I'll never forget—on the kitchen stove, and he poured them into huge milk cans, and he lugged them around the neighborhood selling them door-to-door. From the time I could schlepp the milk can I went with him. . . .

"But every Sunday for thirty years, rain or shine, in blizzards, in heat, sick, starving or otherwise, he sold the *Daily Worker* down at the railroad yards. And when he sold the *Daily Worker* he seemed suddenly whole and strong, and then I loved him desperately.

"That's the way I grew up. In a tight little world where every day of my life I felt myself both as someone living in a small, coherent community and as part of something global. In the Bronx I knew that wherever I went in the world I would find 'my' people, the people who spoke my language, the people who 'understood.' In a word: my comrades. I was tremendously excited, al-

ways, by the thought of taking part daily in something historical.
You've got to remember, this was the Thirties. Me, my adored
father, all our friends and neighbors, we were turning as the world
turned, we were the wave of the future, in us and in all like us lay
the exciting, changing world. . . . Imagine the power this politics
had! Who were we? We were nothing! And look how we felt
about ourselves." Sarah's head tilts back just an edge. "Because we
were Communists," she says. "We felt like that about ourselves
because we were Communists."

Ben Saltzman, who had Sarah's longed-for pleasure of discovering
Marxism and the Party in adulthood, would nevertheless nod his
head vigorously at Sarah's last words about being and nothingness
and Communism. He knows *exactly* what she means.

Saltzman is a sixty-five-year-old cutter of men's clothing in
New York's garment district. He lives in Brooklyn and has traveled into and out of lower Manhattan by subway twice a day
every working day of his life. Right now, this spring, the Amalgamated Clothing Workers of America is on strike, and still Saltzman travels into the city each day: now to march on a picket line.

"You want to talk about the old days?" he says to me on the
phone. "What do you want to talk about the old days for? Who
cares anymore about those days? Tell me, is there one person in
America who cares about those days anymore?"

I assure him there is one person in America who cares about
those days.

"To tell you the truth," he says, "my wife doesn't want me
to meet with you. No, no, it's not that she's afraid. It's that my
health is not so good anymore, I'm a nervous man, she's afraid I
shouldn't get sick again. And it's true. When I talk about those
days I get nervous, I cry. Would you believe an old man like me,
I cry? Ah, it's no good, it's no good."

I remain silent, letting my silence do its guilt-producing work.

"Alright, alright," he says. "I'll meet you. But you'll tell the
truth? You promise you'll put down the truth just like I tell you?"

We meet at noon in a Greek restaurant in Greenwich Village.

The restaurant is pretentious and overpriced, the waiters languid and snobbish. Ben Saltzman is sitting at a table in a far corner of the half-empty room. When he spots me walking toward him he jumps up suddenly, nearly overturning his chair. He is a trembling, watery-eyed, blotchy-skinned, bald-headed little man, carefully dressed in a "good" blue jacket and immaculately pressed grey pants; he looks years older than he is. He presses my hand in damp haste and holds my chair for me. As I sit down a waiter saunters toward us. Saltzman immediately snatches up his menu and says to me: "He's coming! Quick. What do you want?"

His fear of the waiter pains me. I put my hand on his arm and say: "Listen, at these prices we'll order when *we* want to, not when he wants us to."

Saltzman stares at me; suddenly his anxiety dissipates. "You're right," he sighs, "you're right. I told you, I'm a nervous man."

Saltzman tells me he was born in 1909 on New York's Lower East Side into a very poor, very Orthodox Jewish family. Religion, as imposed by his father, dominated his young life: "My father was a rabbi. We had nothing, we ate dirt, but my father had the Lord, the Lord made him ferocious. Me, I hated the Lord. All I knew was the Lord wouldn't let me play baseball, the Lord wouldn't let me go out with girls, the Lord wouldn't let me *live*. But I was afraid of my father and the family, you know, the family among Jews was everything. I would never have dared say no to my father. So we lived. The life was bitter. I felt myself alone in the family, but I obeyed my father, I went to the synagogue, and inside myself I hated it, and hoped somehow I could escape someday."

He went to night school, and even started college. Then came the Depression. The family was literally starving. Young Ben had to go to work. The family influence was still so powerful for him that he had to seek employment where he wouldn't be forced to work on Saturday. He ended up in a men's clothing factory, since the New York clothing industry was dominated by Jews and no one worked on Saturday.

Ben was put to work at the cutting table; he was young, fast, and smart, and in no time at all he was an excellent cutter. And in no time after that he realized he was being exploited. The cut-

ters' union was then a father-son union, and he couldn't get into
it. So while cutters were making $30 a week even during the De-
pression, Ben was making $14 a week.

Saltzman stops for a moment. His watery eyes suddenly crys-
tallize into a hard, beautiful blue. He leans back in his chair. "I
worked in that shop twelve years," he says. "I hated every minute of it. I hated that boss with a passion. That boss," he raises a
finger in the air between us. "That boss. He made me a
Communist."

There was a union official in Rabbi Saltzman's congregation.
One day Saltzman's father and his uncle took him up to see the
official. The two old men with their long beards and their black
clothes, each with a hand on one of Ben's arms, walked into the
union official's office and presented Ben's case; they asked him to
please do something, as the boy was being worked to death for
half the wage he should be getting and this, clearly, was not just.

The union official nodded his head and said: "You're right,
you're right. But not just now. The time isn't right. But soon, I
promise, very soon."

The two old men and Ben made eight or ten trips back to the
union official's office. Each time the official said: "The time is not
right, but soon, very soon."

"So," says Saltzman, "I got to hate the unions, too. I saw they
would do nothing for the working man, they were going hand in
hand with the bosses."

The waiter is back at our table. Saltzman laughs and says: "Can
we order now? I'm hungry." We order, and he goes back to his
story.

After a time he joined the shipping clerks' union. In spite of his
distrust he was at heart (and has remained to this day) an ardent
trade unionist, and a union—any union—was better than no union.
At the shipping clerks' union meetings he never talked, shy and
frightened even then. But sometimes another worker would get
up and say something "right," something Saltzman would now call
"progressive," and then afterwards when the meeting was breaking up and everyone was leaving the hall he would manage to find
his way to the man's side and say to him: "You know, that was a
good thing you said."

One night—this was 1935—three of these workers who were always saying something "right" came up to him after the meeting and said: "We want to introduce you to some people. We think you'll like them and they'll like you. Next week, after the union meeting, you'll come with us to our friends."

Saltzman was mystified but at the same time proud that these men whose courage he admired wanted him to meet their friends. The next week after the union meeting he left the hall with them. It was midnight. They walked together through the deserted darkness of lower Manhattan until they came to a narrow doorway in a loft-crowded street in the West Twenties. They pushed open the iron building door and began walking up the metal staircase.

Saltzman grew frightened. Who, after all, *were* these men? Just workers in the shop. What did he know about them? Nothing. God knew where they were taking him, what they might do with him. But he continued climbing the stairs. At last, they stopped and pushed open a door. Inside a large, bare, badly lit room a group of men sat on hard chairs in a circle. The men from the shop pushed Saltzman forward. One of the men in the circle rose and came forward, his hand outstretched.

"We are members of the Communist Party," he said. "We'd like you to join us."

Saltzman stared at the man. Then he began to tremble.

"I was *fearful!*" he says. "To become a Communist! Who could I tell this to? Not my father! Not even my wife. I was scared. To join the Communist Party! This seemed a very great thing to do. But I knew they were saying the right thing. I knew that what they were talking about was just and good, and nobody else was saying what they were saying.

"So," he smiles, "I joined them. I put my fear in my pocket and I joined them. And you know what happened? After a while I wasn't afraid anymore. I had the Party and I had my comrades, and they made me strong, strong on my feet. Oh, in those days! In those days I had an answer for everything. Everything! I became outspoken, I could hardly believe it was me talking. In the family, in the shop, among my comrades. I talked! I had opinions. And yes, *I knew what I was talking about*. The Party sent me to school, I learned. The Party taught me how to demonstrate, in a crowd I didn't lose myself. Everything in my life became one. Everywhere, I was the same person."

Saltzman's face has altered remarkably while he has been speaking. It has lost its blotched, wavering uncertainty, his eyes have grown clear and expressive, the buried youthful shape of his face has begun to emerge. Now, abruptly, he stops speaking, and suddenly his face begins to crumple again. His mouth trembles, and in a single horrifying instant two coarse tears gather at the inner corners of his eyes, threatening disaster. The tears fall of their own weight and stream down on either side of his nose. "Now," he says softly, "I'm like I was before. Afraid. Afraid of everything. Everything seems always to be falling apart. Nothing seems together anymore. . . . I'm alone again in the family. . . . And in the shop. *Oy*, that lousy shop."

He wipes his face, takes a deep breath, expels it in a heavy sigh, and smiles. "But would you believe it, there was a time when I loved going to the shop. It was exciting. My life in the Party and my life in the shop were one. How many of us do you think there were in the shop? Six. Seven. We'd sit together at union meetings and we'd push each other to speak. '*You* get up. *You* say that.' Then they started yelling 'Sit down, you goddamn Commies!' So then we began to fan out. We sat all over the hall. Then, after the meeting, some worker would come up to one of us and say 'You know, you said the right thing.' " Saltzman laughs with the pleasure of triumph.

"There was a time in my life," Saltzman begins again with great dignity, "when the Party was everything. If I died I would have willed everything I had to the Party. I would have left my wife if necessary. I thought to myself, she can always get another husband but there's only one Party. Times, I was at demonstrations and the police came charging at us on horses, I was with a guy, another cutter like myself but a brilliant speaker, a man could organize his own grandmother, I thought better he should live than I should live, the Party needs him more than it does me, I'd push *him* to the wall."

Saltzman stops again, and again falls silent. He stares out before him, as though staring into some impenetrable distance. Then he bursts out: "Do you know how strong we were in 1946? We had the country in the palm of our hands! We could have taken over. Yes! We could have taken over. Only we didn't know it." His eyes grow fearfully bright. "Those May Day parades. Thousands marched! We were thousands! We could have had the country."

I sit quietly, looking directly into his face. Does he really believe what he's saying? After everything we have lived through, does he really believe this? This is the first but not the last time I will hear a Communist speak thus and find myself thinking: Does he really—still—believe this?

Saltzman looks at his watch. "I've got to go," he says. "You know, my union is striking. I've got to go relieve someone on the picket line."

He shakes his head in wonder. "It's not for myself that I picket anymore. I make good money now, I'm a privileged old man in the shop. It's for *them*. It's for these know-nothings who have come after me that I picket. You want an education in America? Come down to my shop building at seven o'clock in the morning. You'll see them fighting like animals to get up to the shop to get at their machines. And then stand in the bank on Friday and look at their paychecks. A man with a family takes home seventy-seven dollars."

Now Saltzman weeps in earnest. "For what?" he cries, forgetful of the fancy restaurant and the snobbish waiters. "All those years! For what? What have we accomplished here?"

Once again he wipes his face and pulls himself together. We rise and walk out of the restaurant. We shake hands on the corner, and I watch him moving away down the street. I stare after him, and I find myself thinking: As high as he went during his prime years, from fearful, sheepish worker to proud Party member, that's how low he has now fallen, bereft of what had sustained him.

But as I continue to stand there on the corner, staring after Saltzman, I begin to shake my head. No, I think, that is not completely true, not completely true at all. As Saltzman marches purposefully down the street in his "good" blue jacket and neat grey pants, every inch of his bowed, retreating back is saying to me: "I'm going now to take my place in a war to reduce the worldly humiliation of men and women like myself. After fifty years of fighting, I know that this war will never be won, but I go anyway. I take my place. I stand on the line. I do this because I was a Communist."

"Those May Day parades. We were thousands! Thousands marched!" Ben Saltzman had exclaimed. And now on a hot night in midsummer, in a gloomy housing-project apartment in the Bronx, after hours of talk with a woman very unlike Ben Saltzman, I hear those phrases reverberating in my head. They are, finally, the essence of what has passed between this woman and myself.

Selma Gardinsky is fifty-six years old. She is today a graduate student in psychology at Columbia University. A large, dark woman with a soft, spreading body and the downward curving nose and mouth of a sorrowing Jew, seriousness in her is expressed through a severe and permanent frown. Her voice—soft, hesitant, unbelligerent—is at odds with the somewhat fierce look of her face. Yet, altogether the face, the body, the voice form a wholeness of soft, dark, strangely shy intensity: an urgency of unhappy, inwardly turned concentration that seems to pervade this woman's being.

She gathers all the life in the atmosphere into her large body and frowning face; there is none left over for the rooms that surround her. The apartment in which we sit is bleak and utilitarian as a ten-dollar-a-night motel room: clean, neat, unobtrusive, without the slightest bit of decorative relief or personal choice to distinguish it. From the moment I walk into it and see that dark intensity in Selma Gardinsky surrounded by this vacancy of background, I feel I have walked into the melancholy pages of Dos Passos. All those Dos Passos radicals, framed in luminous obscurity, standing alone inside their clothes, their books, their intelligence, moving restlessly across a continent of furnished rooms, perched on the edge of a landscape into which they will never settle—they are all here tonight in this housing-project apartment in the Bronx in a midsummer fifty years after Dos Passos wrote.

Selma Gardinsky was born in 1918 into bleak Brooklyn poverty. She had two brothers and two sisters, and she was the smartest of them all. Her mother was a timid, uneducated, religious woman whose only instruction to her intelligent daughter was: Get married. Her father, on the other hand, was a laundryman who worked fifteen hours a day, had become inflamed by the Russian Revolution, and imparted to his adoring daughter a sense of the largeness of their condition that transformed their burdened existence into something great and stirring.

The mother and the father fought each other for the soul of this daughter: the mother in bitter vengefulness, hating the father for their wretched lives, the father in bitter helplessness, hating the mother for the spiritual isolation into which her ignorance had plunged him. Between them, they made and unmade the girl a thousand times over before she "escaped."

Of those dreadful years Selma has two clear memories: One, she is twelve years old and she is walking with her father. He is holding her hand tightly and saying to her: "Don't let them get to you. Believe nothing they say. *Nothing*." She knows that "they" are not only the capitalist world but all those—like her mother—who are frightened and seek refuge in religion or convention or a money-getting existence. Two, she is sixteen years old and her mother is forcing her to sit at night with her not-too-bright brother and tutor him so that *he* will get into college.

She married at seventeen to run away from all that Brooklyn despair. She did not love her husband, she hardly knew him; he simply appeared, was much taken by her darkness and her misery, and when he offered, she gasped "Yes!"

Her husband wanted her, that gave her a sense of power, that power became an instrument of self-discovery. She found herself—in Boston, where her husband's work had taken them—in sudden possession of courage and yearning. And what she yearned for was a political life. Her father's love had taken deep root in her; she realized then that from the time she could remember an unpolitical life had been inconceivable. From this moment on life without politics was literally unthinkable. And what was meant by politics—in no uncertain terms—was the Communist Party.

"So," Selma laughs now, "at eighteen, I called the Communist Party and told them I was ready to join. The slightly alarmed CP said to me: Don't call us we'll call you.

"I was temporarily at a loss. I say temporarily because, you see, from that moment on it became a burning, all-consuming need to join the Party, and I knew that *nothing*, not even the Party itself, could stop me. I figured: Okay, they want to test me, they want to see if I'm really a sincere and worthy comrade. . . . I must have had some vague image of the Party as a kind of mysterious, all-seeing Being, everywhere at once, watching and knowing what I was doing. I had only to do, and I would be called. Come to think of it," she laughs, "considering that this was 1936, I wasn't so far off.

"I went to work in an office that I knew was unionized. I didn't give a damn what kind of work I did, I only wanted to get active in something that would draw me to the attention of the Party. I immediately joined the union and became active in it. I learned —and they learned—that I was a natural. I had the gift of organizing people. I worked in that office for two years. In 1938 the union asked me if I would go to New York for them. I said yes, left my husband without so much as a backward glance, went to New York, and within months I was recruited into the Party. That was it. I worked as a union organizer for the Party for ten years. They were the best ten years of my life. I'll never have years like that again, that's for sure.

"Deep inside me I was a wounded, homeless person. The Party healed me, gave me the kind of home I could never have made with my husband . . . no, or even with the one who came after him. It gave me a home inside myself. *Inside*. Do you know what I'm talking about? Yes, you do, I can see you do. Ah, you're all so smart these days, you all know so much more than we did. I knew nothing of these things then, I understood nothing of what was happening inside me.

"Of course, I could never again find a 'home inside myself' through anything like the Communist Party, and certainly I feel the understanding I have now about myself is more genuine, better grounded. . . . But there is such a *loneliness* to this under-standing! A loneliness that was entirely absent from my life while I was a Communist. I know that's a cliché, but you cannot imagine the reality of it. Whatever else we were or were not as Communists, we were not lonely. This disease that's slowly killing off everybody today, that's killing *me*, this disease was unknown to us as Communists.

"For ten solid years I worked sixty hours a week for the Communist Party. I organized, I wrote leaflets, I worked on committees, I demonstrated, and I went to meetings. *Oy,* those meetings! You know why most Communists aren't politically active today? Because they can't stand the thought of ever going to another meeting!

"A lot of it was just sheer grinding shitwork. You think making a revolution is all agony and ecstasy? It's not, it's mostly drudgery. Hard, disciplined, repetitive work that's boring and necessary. But what keeps you going is that twenty times a week something would happen—out there in that lousy capitalist world or inside among your comrades—and you'd *remember*. You'd remember why you were here, and what you were doing it all for, and it was like a shot of adrenalin coursing through your veins. The world was all around you *all the time*. That was the tremendous thing about those times. The sense of *history* that you lived with daily. The sense of remaking the world. Every time I wrote a leaflet or marched on a picket line or went to a meeting I was remaking the world. . . . My father's bitter, forgotten life. I felt myself vindicating that life, and the millions of lives like his, pulling my father back inside the circle of the world, pulling him back off the edge of the map, because I was doing what I was doing. Because I was a Communist.

"My father's presence was a tremendous reality that I lived with daily. And all the people like my father. I saw them always in my mind's eye, becoming strong beneath the Communist banner."

Selma was expelled from the Party in 1948 when the Communist Party threw the entire weight of its support behind the presidential campaign of Henry Wallace, and many who opposed this action either left the Party or were expelled. The decision to support Wallace was—like so many other decisions in the history of the American CP—a traumatizing one. Thousands of Communists felt it was an act of accommodation to American capitalism that constituted nothing less than a betrayal of the revolution. A terrible rift was created within the Party. Those on one side of the rift—the ones who opposed the Wallace support— were castigated as being "left-sectarian"; those on the other side were denounced as "right-opportunists." Selma Gardinsky was on the side of the losing "left-sectarians."

An amazing change comes over Selma as she begins to discuss this old political quarrel. The reflective, somewhat philosophical manner that has accompanied her remarks until now suddenly evaporates. Her voice is now as though edged in hard light. The sentences come rushing out in a passion of certitude, obviously driving toward some waiting center. It becomes clear, what is happening here (oh, that kitchen table!). She will—and nothing will stop her—speak exactly enough sentences to make the unalterable, unopposable "rightness" of her position so apparent that there will be not another thing left to say when she is done speaking. The distance with which she has been talking about her life is, in an instant, annihilated. Twenty-five years disappear before my eyes. It is 1948 again, the wound is red, purple, and alive, and Selma's very life depends on her ability to argue well, in fundamentalist Marxist-Leninist terms, the case against Wallace support. She rushes on and on, ending finally with:

"I believed then, and yes, I believe now—yes, I know how this will sound to you, but still it is true—that if the Party had stuck to the correct revolutionary line it would *not* have been destroyed, and you and I would be sitting here today in quite another world."

I remain silent, deeply silent . . . "the correct revolutionary line" . . . When she has spoken the last sentence she too falls—terribly!—silent. We do not speak for a very long while. Selma frowns fiercely at the couch on which she is sitting, picking listlessly at its cheap tweed covering. Then she says in a low, defeated voice: "Ah, what am I getting so excited for. This is all ancient history."

She lifts her head very slowly. Her eyes meet mine. Her puzzled frown is wonderfully expressive. Very quietly she says: "And yet, I have, still, the vision of thousands of people, strong and united, made whole, marching beneath the Communist banner, toward a better world, toward their lives."

For hard-boiled Joe Preisen, Selma Gardinsky's last words are sentimental nonsense. Corny, soppy words that hide a multitude of Party sins. . . .

Joe Preisen is fifty-three years old: short, dark, bald, very heavy, with a black goatee beard shot through with grey and clever, cynical eyes behind black-framed glasses. Within five minutes after he has begun speaking, Preisen reveals himself as streetsmart, shrewd, intensely political, sensual, philistine. The articulate flow of words that issues from his expressive mouth is alive with crude energy, intellectual ignorance, and the force of sheer animal intelligence.

Preisen is a union local manager in one of the largest, most notoriously corrupt of American labor unions. As I settle into a seat facing him across the desk in his office in Pittsburgh on a beautiful spring morning, he leans back into a broken-down swivel chair, puts his feet up on the desk, lights an aromatic pipe, shrugs his shoulder, and says to me: "What can I tell you? I used to be a Jewish Communist, now I'm a Jewish gangster."

Preisen's brash defensiveness reminds me instantly of how difficult it has been to arrange this meeting: the endless phone calls, the broken appointments, the curt, repeated "Ah, you people, you're always wanting to write about the Commies, but you none of you ever tell it like it was. You'll only mash it around inside your intellectual little birdbrains and it'll come out shit, so why should I talk to you?" Now it's clear: the struggle to "tell it like it was" is inside Preisen, the fear that it'll come out like shit has been the fear that he'll make it come out like shit. But what the hell, he has apprehensively decided, now that I am actually sitting opposite him—he'll take the plunge. The responsibility, his brashness says, will now be mine, not his.

Joe Preisen was born directly into a *Jews Without Money* life. In Joe Preisen's Brooklyn, Jews either were gangsters or they fought gangsters, Jews either were trade-unionists or they were scabs, Jews either were respectable folk or they were pimps and whores. These were the givens of "the street." Whichever side you were on, you knew how to deal with the other side.

His mother, Preisen says with a curl of the lip indicative of much to come, was "a mouth-talking socialist," but his father, he says with obvious and immediate respect, who didn't know much about "theory," was a gentle-speaking, two-fisted housepainter embroiled in union battles from the time Joe can remember: fighting the scabs, fighting the mob, *fighting*. When he was eight years old his father was shot in the hallway of their apartment house. His mother became permanently hysterical from that time on, but Preisen and his two brothers were proud, excited, and permanently awed: because his father *survived*. What he means by survive, Preisen is quick to clarify, is that the shooting didn't unnerve him. He didn't grow meek and frightened; on the contrary, he fought harder than ever.

One vivid memory Preisen has of those years is an early Thirties strike during which two scabs took a job in the neighborhood. His father took Joe and his older brother to the building where the painters were working. As soon as the painters saw his father, one began racing for the staircase. His brother shot his foot out and the painter flew headlong down the stairs, landing on his face in a dead crumple without even a moan. The other one was on the ladder. His father pulled the ladder out from under him and he went down, too. Then his father grabbed the scab, stripped him, painted the scab with his own brush from head to foot, and shoved the brush up his ass. Then he grabbed the two boys, raced across the street, waited until the cops came, went up to a cop, tapped him on the shoulder, and said, all meek, shrugging Jew: "Officer. Excuse me, but what happened here?"

When Joe was thirteen years old they moved to the Bronx "so that my mother wouldn't lose her marbles altogether, she had become such a wreck over my father's activities in the neighborhood." The Bronx was different: all the trade unionists were also Communists. The street life that Joe joined there was also tough and Jewish but much more political than it had been in Brooklyn. At fourteen Joe joined the Young Communist League because clearly it was the center of all social life in the neighborhood (this was 1935). For him, the YCL became—and it is a permanent memory—Leninist-Marxist theory all mixed up with baseball, screwing, dancing, selling the *Daily Worker*, bullshitting, and living the American-Jewish street life.

He was a wild kid, hot with life and street excitement, quick to feel the emotional joy of Left-wing politics as it worked itself out in the courage and moxie of men like his father, but resistant to and resentful of all "that goddamned theory." In 1938, at the age of seventeen, he ran away from home: to fight in Spain. He joined the Abraham Lincoln Brigade, had the experience of his life, and returned to New York, at nineteen, "a changed man."

"In Spain something clarified for me. I discovered *why* I hated all that goddamn theory. The men in the Brigade were of an altogether other breed than I was. To me, socialism was the street mix I'd come out of. To them, it was all dense, celibate theory. Suddenly, I saw that these guys didn't know *anything* about the American working class. Me, I didn't know that I knew, but I knew in my *bones* what it was to be a worker, and here I saw how out of touch with the working class these guys were. And one thing I *knew*: the only way to socialism was to remain in touch with the working class at all costs and through all times and changes. That my father taught me when I was a little baby on his knee, and nothing I've learned has yet put the lie to that lesson.

"So I came home from Spain angry, bitter, confused. I didn't know which way to turn, what the hell to do with my life. Well, I thought, the hell with the Party, the hell with the revolution, I'll go be a simple worker. That I still know how to be."

He went to work in a steel mill. And, of course, within minutes he became a union organizer in the mill. And, of course, within minutes after that, he joined the Communist Party. "You see, there was no way out," Preisen laughs now. "In those days, no matter which way you turned, the best, the most exciting, the most *serious* guys in the labor movement were in the Party. If you wanted to do anything at all, you found yourself working with these guys. And, they were beautiful people. And, it was a tough, exciting time. History was all around you. You could touch it, smell it, see it. And when a labor organizer who was also a Communist got up to talk you could taste it in your mouth. How could a guy like me resist it? I couldn't then . . . and not for a long time afterward.

"But I started chafing at the bit almost from the beginning. I was always—from day one—in a state of conflict with the Party, always wanting in and wanting out at the same time. You see, for me the Party was an instrument of revolution, not a church to be worshiped in. I couldn't stand the hierarchy, the authoritarianism, the goddamn directives, the smugness and ignorance at the top, that fucking Marxist-Leninist jargon that poured out like a river of shit that never stopped flowing. I never screwed a dame in the Party, I never had a real friend in the Party. Something

in all those real Party types just left me cold. That smothering
sense of worship was something I always gagged on. I was an
American labor organizer first, and a Party member second. And
I thought it shoulda been that way with everybody in the Party.
After all, we were supposed to be an *American* Communist Party,
right?

"God, the things the Party did to these college boys, these intellectuals, these professional revolutionaries they tried to make
into organizers they could never become. They sent people into
industry who didn't have the foggiest notion of what it was all
about—the bones, the experience, the *years* of being a worker.
They were the kind of men who would have to live and work and
marry and go bowling among workers . . . and they could never
do it. They were the kind of men who spent fifteen or twenty
years among workers . . . always alienated, always confused,
always on the edge of things. Times changed, values changed,
history changed, their lives were destroyed. The Party never
understood what it was doing. I'd talk to a guy (intelligent, full
of theory). I'd say, 'This local is controlled by the mob. Understand?' He'd look at me, he didn't know what the hell I was
talking about.

"I was expelled from the Party twice. The first time was in
1946, when the Party as such was dissolved, and the Communist
Party Association was formed. It's funny how it was with the
trade unionists in the Party. I guess most of us have always been
mavericks in the Party. The first time we all walked out because
the Party was accommodating America, the second time we
walked out because the Party *wasn't* accommodating America.
That first time, I'll never forget, they gathered together hundreds
of trade unionists in a building on Fourteenth Street in New York,
and a Party functionary got up and told us of the creation of the
CPA. We hooted the guy out of the hall. Then they sent in Elizabeth Gurley Flynn. She couldn't get anywhere either. Finally,
they sent in William Z. He spoke as gently as he could, said we
shouldn't act rashly, if we didn't think we could live with this,
well, then, he said, times change, stick with it, it seems the best
thing to do now.

" 'Bullshit,' I said, and I kept on saying it. I was brought up
before the National Committee and expelled.

"Then, after the Party was reconstituted I joined again, and again I was expelled. This time was when I and other trade unionists—like Quill and Bridges—opposed the Party position against the Marshall Plan. As you know, if we'd supported the Party in this matter we would all have been thrown out of the CIO. And this, we'd be goddamned if we'd do. So I was thrown out again."

Preisen relights his pipe very thoughtfully, swings his legs down to the floor, and says with supreme irony: "As you also know, as things turned out, it didn't matter a tinker's damn *what* we did. The Party threw us to the wolves, McCarthy threw us to the wolves, American labor threw us to the wolves. . . . And here we are. Let's go to lunch."

Over "the best roast beef sandwich in Pittsburgh," I watch Preisen dig into his sandwich with enormous relish, and I find myself thinking: The juices of life as they run in this man could never have been at home in the Party, his spirit requires altogether other kinds of feeding than those the Party could give him. . . . Why then?

"Why did you join the Party the second time?" I ask.

Preisen looks up from his food, somewhat startled by my question. Then his eyes smile shrewdly at me, he puts his sandwich delicately back on the plate before him (his gestures, like those of many heavy people, are surprisingly graceful), wipes his mouth carefully, and leans back against the red leather banquette on which he is sitting.

"Well," he says, with a surprising softness in his voice, "socialism was a dream I guess I couldn't let go of. For a long time it kept pulling me. Even when I didn't know it was pulling me it was pulling me. And the CP? Well, in spite of everything it was damned exciting, and for a damned long time.

"Look." Preisen spreads his hand palm upward over the table. "Life is shit. People are shit. But," he leans forward intently, "sometimes life is great, and people are great. And when that happens it's hard to walk away from, no matter what else is happening. Well, that's the way the CP was for me. Sure, there was a lot of shit in the CP, and a lot of shitty people. But the only times I ever felt life was great and people were great were in the CP. Despite everything, the life had meaning. It redeemed itself.

Over and over again, it redeemed itself. Because it had real mean-ing. And while I was part of it I had real meaning.

"Now what have I got?" he asks dryly. "Just shit. Shit with no redeeming features. If an old comrade walked into my office and said, 'Preisen, this local is controlled by the mob. You know what I mean?' I'd know what he means."

Preisen grins and says to me, "You know what I mean?" But his eyes aren't grinning, and the wisecrack falls flat. We return awkwardly to our sandwiches, and finish our meal in silence. For a moment I wonder: Is *this* what he wants me to take the re-sponsibility for?

In another part of the country, another union official who was also a Communist bangs her fist hard on a kitchen table and, her voice metallic with anger, says, "Bullshit! These guys who think the whole world is as corrupt as they are, and weep in their beer, and take refuge in the fact that they were once Red. They make me sick! Nothing's changed. There are still a helluva lot of good people alive and kicking in the labor movement, and yes, *still* Red, and when things change, those people will be there, ready to do what's necessary."

Belle Rothman is fifty-eight years old. Her eyes spark when she talks, her salt and pepper hair springs up from her forehead in vigorous abundance, she hacks her way through four packs of cigarettes a day, and although we are sitting in a formica kitchen in suburban Cleveland the atmosphere around her is pure Bronx Jewish Communist.

I have known people like Belle all my life. She is one of those in whom one feels the power of the "clarifying experience." In Belle it becomes apparent that the radical is, indeed, often like the artist in that the radical, too, is made differently, with the parts somehow out of proportion. Just as in a poet like Dylan Thomas, for instance, the narrow power of adolescence burned intensely, allowing for no other kind of growth, so in Belle Roth-man there burns the political emotion that makes of her a poet in radicalism and a primitive in every other respect. If Belle is asked to think "differently," her face hardens before your eyes, and if she is asked to ponder an emotional relation between human beings instead of an economic one between social forces, she grows as uneasy as a Victorian at a pornographic movie. But talk to her about what it was like to be poor and Jewish and a Communist forty years ago and her talk grows rich and expansive, full of love and laughter and wisdom, alive with the kind of toughness that will always fill me with excited admiration. For Belle, Joe Preisen's cynicism is unimaginable. She will be hot, angry, and earnest until the last cigarette gasp.

Belle was the daughter of Max Rothman: cigar-maker and Communist. (Oh, these Communist women and their fathers!) Max looked like Trotsky, only better. Max thought like Lenin, only not quite so good. The passion of Max's life was Communism. The passion of Belle's life was Max. Max had an obedient Communist wife and three docile Communist children—but only Belle answered fire with fire. From the very beginning they both knew it was she who would pick up the torch when it fell from his hands. When she was five years old Max took her to union meetings, and when the Right-wing in the union voted against a strike, Max pressed his daughter's hand and said: "Listen. Listen and remember. All those who vote against strikes are your enemies."

The Rothmans were, like everyone around them, dead poor and dead political. Thus, Belle thought all Jews were poor and all Jews were socialists. (In fact, for years Belle thought everyone in the Soviet Union was Jewish.) She also thought the way they were growing up was America.

"When I think of the way we grew up," she marvels. "I didn't know from 'Mary Had a Little Lamb' and 'America the Beautiful' until I was thirty years old. When Max put us to bed he sang lullabies to us, all right, but they were Yiddish lullabies and they went . . . well, this one is typical." Belle throws back her head and in a strong, untrained voice sings a song that translates roughly as follows:

> Come here, my child
> I want to tell you something
> Before I leave this world
> A Jew, a Jew you were born

> Remain a Jew good and true
> And even the poor gypsy
> You should also help in his need
> He, too, is a brother of yours
> Give him water, give him bread

"And then, in summer. . . . You know, we didn't go to the beach. Who had the carfare? Like all other Depression children we took a jar of ice water and a blanket up to the roof. There Max would turn the pages of a book to entertain the children. The book was a book of world revolution, and the pictures in the book were pictures of all the famous revolutionaries all over the world."

In 1933, when Belle was seventeen years old, she fell in love with David Herbman. David was already famous in Belle's section of the YCL as a factory worker involved in some of the most terrible of the Thirties' labor union battles. When Belle met David he'd just been beaten up on the picket line and someone had tacked a poem he'd written up on the club bulletin board.

"Imagine!" says Belle. "Beaten up by company goons *and* a poem on the wall. What more could I want?" She smiles fondly at David, who's facing her across the kitchen table, a gentle but weary-looking man of sixty-four who smiles gamely back at her but doesn't talk much. Around Belle, who could?

Belle describes their courtship as follows: "Well, I'll tell you, it was like this. . . . Came a beautiful Sunday. And you were young and in love. What did you do? You joined a picket line!"

They married, and moved into Max Rothman's spare bedroom. Belle joined the Party, went to work in a factory, and remained her father's tough, explosive, ramrodding daughter. She was known far and wide, throughout the Bronx, for her stirring Depression speeches delivered on street corners, in clubs, at work, in the living room, in the bedroom. "What a *pisk* on that one," the women in the neighborhood would sigh longingly after her. "Who could listen to her and not become a Communist?"

In 1939 David quarreled bitterly with his section organizer over union policy and the Stalin Pact, and he was expelled from the Communist Party. Belle threw him out of the house and went immediately to the National Committee. "I've left my husband," she announced. The Party men shook their heads gently, and said this wasn't necessary.

Belle tells this story with much bravado. But somehow it doesn't come out all flushed triumph faintly tinged with self-mockery as Belle's voice clearly indicates it's meant to. David sits silently at the kitchen table, staring at his hands. I am obviously shocked. Belle turns uncomfortably from one to the other of us. Then she looks hard at me, and she says: "You don't understand. We had no choice. It's not like today, where the kids think they have the choice to be political or not be political, or be any other damn thing they want to be. *We had no choice.* We did not choose, we were chosen. Life came in on us, and we were bashed over the head, and we struggled to our knees and to our feet, and when we were standing there was the Communist Party. That was the time, and that's the kind of people we were."

I stare at her, thinking: She hardly knows what she's saying. She hardly knows that the "we" of her speech is not her husband and herself but her father and herself. Max and the Communist Party: that piercing, glowing rapture from which she would never recover and whose sources she would never uncover. Like Teresa penetrated by her angel's arrow, Belle penetrated by Papa's revolution.

Of course, it is precisely Papa's revolution alive inside her—whole, untouched by time and self-discovery—that makes her the embattled union fighter she is to this very day. Belle is as well known among Cleveland workers as she was in the Bronx during the Depression. Her sense of class war has not altered one iota in forty years. She sees the contemporary social revolutions being waged by women, blacks, homosexuals, and students as deliberate, conspiratorial, "diversionary" tactics fomented by the ruling class. This mentality makes her both appalling and powerful, both ignorant and savvy. In the world in which she operates —Belle's union is dominated by semiskilled and immigrant labor —worker exploitation is still the central ingredient, and the surging rage that Max Rothman's daughter feels over this unchanged condition makes her potent.

The very last thing Belle tells me as she puts me on the plane for New York is a story about her father:

"One night when he was seventy years old there was a rally in Madison Square Garden. It was a bitter night, a terrible snow-storm night. He was seventy years old. Tired, tired. He stood in the doorway and I said to him, '*Must* you go? It's such an awful night and you're so tired. Is it really so necessary to go?' He put on his old woollen overcoat and he stood there and he looked at me and he said, 'If I don't go, who will be there?' "

Again, Belle looks hard at me for a moment. Then she shrugs her shoulder slightly and she says to me: "That's the way it was with us."

They were a culture, these New York Jewish Communists, a nation without a country, but for a brief moment, a generation, they did have land of their own: two square blocks in the Bronx.

There are a few thousand people wandering around America today who became Communists because they were raised in the Co-Operative Houses on Allerton Avenue in the Bronx: better known to all who knew of their existence as "The Coops." The Coops were (are, they still stand) a set of houses built between 1923 and 1927—at a time when cooperative movements flour-ished all over this country—by an organization known as the United Workers Co-Operative Association. The UWCA was composed of men and women who were New York garment workers mainly, Jewish mainly, Communists all.

The Coops were two five-story buildings, each a block square, built around a system of inner courtyards and open gardens. In the vast basement space of these buildings there were clubrooms, meeting halls, a library, a nursery school, a community center, an auditorium. Within these rooms and courtyards a dense, self-contained life was conducted in which reading, talking, meeting, ball-playing, dancing, flirting, growing-up mingled continuously with Marxist-Leninist discussion, Communist Party meetings, and the revolution around the corner.

Up the street from The Coops, another group of houses also went up during the Twenties; these houses—The Farband Houses —were built by people like the people in The Coops, except that they were Left-wing Zionists. Then, still further up in the North

Bronx, another group of houses—The Amalgamated Houses—were built by working-class Jews who were Social Democrats.

Throughout the Nineteen-Twenties, Thirties, and Forties the love-hate conflicts acted out by these three groups of intensely political people were a thousand times more real to them than anything going on in the larger world. For them, The Coops, The Amalgamated, and The Farband Houses *were* the world: the real world, the true world. In this world, the Communists were Left, the Social Democrats were Right, everything else was somewhere in between—and the Democratic and Republican parties? What the hell was *that* all about? What did they have to do with the revolution? They didn't even know what game was being played, much less which ballpark to show up at.

The Coops, by the time people my age were growing up, was already something of a misnomer. The UWCA failed in 1929 when the stock market crashed, and although it was bailed out within the year, it failed again sometime in the Thirties and the houses were never again, properly speaking, a cooperative. (Many people now laugh and say they went bankrupt because the management kept turning the money over to the Party. Others shrug and say, "What did they know about business? They were *Kommunistische Idealisten*. Did they know how to run a business?") Nevertheless, although the three thousand people living in the Allerton Avenue Co-Operative Houses were now renters instead of owners, the homogeneous character of the houses remained intact until well into the 1950s, and in every real sense the houses were The Coops, and all those growing up in those houses experienced the place as a thriving world whose wholeness of values and activities dominated their sense of being.

Paul Levinson was raised in The Coops. An advertising copywriter now in his late forties, a prosperous suburban householder who wears a full brown beard and natty, Ivy League conservative clothes, Levinson was a member of the Communist Party between the ages of fifteen and thirty. Today, he is entirely apolitical. He reads, writes, goes skiing and canoeing, works in his garden, and is undergoing psychoanalysis. But once upon a time. . . .

Levinson's parents were "progressives," not active Left-wingers. His father was a gentle carpenter whose anxiety got carved daily into cabinets and bookcases. His mother kept their four-room apartment spotless, and she worried. The Levinsons were both more frightened of the world than not, but not so frightened that they chose not to live in The Coops—and because they lived in The Coops their son became a Communist. They never pushed him, they never stood in his way. They simply exposed him, and the exposure took.

In The Coops all social activities led to the Party. When he was ten years old Paul joined the Young Pioneers—the CP version of the Boy Scouts—because that's what all the kids in The Coops joined. That's where his schoolfriends were going, that's where he went. Levinson still remembers the blue and red uniform vividly, especially the red neckerchief. He loved wearing that red neckerchief. And he still remembers the Pioneers leader: "He was a wonderful guy. He loved the kids. He *listened* to us. And when there were 'events' in The Coops and the Pioneers went to those events, we saw that our leader was beloved by the adults, too, and that made us love him more."

When he graduated from grade school it was the most natural thing in the world to join a Coops community center where mainly teenagers hung out. "You've got to remember," Levinson says, pausing to take a swig of the drink before him in the Lexington Avenue bar where we are sitting this late September night. "The Coops was alive with clubrooms and meeting halls and auditoriums, every one of them in use day and night. Everyone—from the littlest kid to the oldest grandfather—belonged to *something*. There was literally not a person in The Coops who wasn't active in an organization of some sort. That was the life, the only life. From the time I can remember until the time I was thirty years old, I never really experienced myself, nor did anyone else I knew, outside of a political, organizational context."

The community center that Levinson joined in The Coops was led by a social worker who was a Party member, and when Levinson was fifteen years old this social worker invited him to join the Party. ("I was intellectually precocious," Levinson says wryly.) From that time on until the Khrushchev Report in 1956, Levinson was a dedicated Communist. He went to meetings, planned actions, sold the *Daily Worker*, read and discussed Marx and Lenin endlessly, got involved in local union struggles, marched in May Day parades—and waited for the revolution.

"Was the life good? Was it bad? How should I know? It was life, the only life I ever knew, and it was *alive*. Intense, absorbing, filled with a kind of comradeship I never again expect to know. In those basement clubrooms in The Coops, talking late into the night, every night for *years*, we literally felt we were making history. Do you know what I mean when I say that? We felt that what we thought and spoke and decided upon in those basement rooms in the Bronx was going to have an important effect on the entire world out there. Now, a sensation like that is beyond good or bad. It's sweeping, powerful. More important," he smiles cynically, "than good or bad. And," soberly, "infinitely more compelling than anything in that other, bourgeois world could ever be. The idea when I was twenty of having a profession? making money? becoming a middle-class American? I literally would rather have been dead than have ended up like that. I remember I sat through City College like a zombie, only waiting each day to get back to the neighborhood and the meetings and the important, righteous, just, *real* world."

"What *kind* of a Communist was I? Dogmatic," he says matter-of-factly. "Ah-h-h, I don't know. . . . I've always thought I was kinder, sweeter, more compassionate than others were, but I've known so many people who were such sons of bitches in the Party and who don't remember themselves that way at all, that how the hell do I know *what* I was like then? One thing I *do* know, though, and that's for sure. I was a madman on the subject of sex. You know, male chauvinism was a big thing with us. You were never supposed to take advantage of a woman, and of course, going to bed with her was taking advantage of her. I was most stern and puritan regarding this matter, ready to expel *anybody* on a charge of male chauvinism. But underneath," his voice grows thoughtful, "underneath I was *grateful* for the doctrine. After all," he looks up at me, eyes widening, hands spread out palms upwards on the table between us. "Who the hell knew how to go to bed with a woman?" Levinson's face darkens suddenly, the plastic mixer stick he's been playing with breaks in his strong, well-shaped hands. "I was a miserable, bottled-up kid. Somebody there should have said something to me. *Somebody*."

When Paul was twenty he met his wife, Laura. She was nineteen and she, too, was growing up in The Coops. Somehow, as children their paths had never crossed but now, working together to plan some demonstration or other, they met and "fell in love." The quotes are Levinson's, and he sets out to explain them:

"How can I really explain to you what it was like to fall in love in the Communist Party? I can't. It's impossible to capture the full flavor, to make you experience as we did emotions and circumstances that streamed together and were so strong you literally could not sort them out. Our love affairs blossomed, entirely entwined with the Party and Party affairs and our identities as Party members. We felt tremendous surges of comradeship, political excitement, the pity and beauty of human suffering, the mad wild joy of revolutionary expectation. We lived with these emotions *daily*. We shared them with each other. That was our intimacy. And, often, when a man and a woman shared these emotions things got all mixed up, and they took these feelings for romantic love.

"Mostly," Levinson says, looking down at his glass, "it was not love. Mostly, it was essentially platonic friendship mixed up with indiscriminate sexual urges. . . . God! The people who've lived together twenty, twenty-five years, without knowing they didn't love each other, their lives filled up with politics, and then suddenly the Party fell apart, and they're left sitting there staring at each other, strangers, not even friends anymore." Levinson, who has begun to stare into his glass, shakes himself now, almost as though he's pulling himself out of a revery.

"Well," he grins weakly, "I guess in a way it was like that with me and Laura, too. We met, we liked each other, we worked together, we were involved night and day in political activity, we started going together, we were 'in love.' And everybody loved us for being in love, and everybody said how could the revolution fail to come if revolutionary activity had produced such a beautiful pair of revolutionary lovebirds like me and Laura. So, after a while, it was as though if we broke up we were betraying the revolution.

"When we began to realize, both of us, that underneath this smooth surface, we were filled with confusion and conflict, and then with real apprehension—we had no place to go with it. We knew so little about ourselves, we only knew we felt disturbed and terribly guilty about our doubts. And this we couldn't tell to anyone. Certainly not our comrades. As close as we all were, living together as we did for years, we never discussed anything remotely connected to our emotional lives. We would have been mortified to reveal our sexual or emotional confusions to each other, we all pretended we didn't have any. All personal doubts or pains got submerged beneath Party language. If you stopped talking that language you felt guilty, confused, trivial.

"Well, things got so bad with Laura and me, every time we set a wedding date somehow or other we'd fall into a week of non-stop fighting, or she'd burst into violent tears when I touched her, or I would suddenly get so depressed I felt suicidal. Instead of breaking up, we clung to each other like frightened children, and decided no matter what anyone thought, we needed help. So," Levinson says with an expression of tender cynicism in his eyes, "we went to see a Party psychoanalyst. The Party analyst explained to us that since we were only *working* toward the ideal state the contradictions within society were such that they lived inside us now. Under socialism we would not be feeling what we were now feeling, and since socialism was right around the corner. . . .

"After that everything seemed clear, and a few months later Laura and I got married."

I know that Paul and Laura Levinson are still husband and wife. I look quizzically at Levinson. He laughs, his laugh a bit hollow. For one awful moment pain and confusion tear across his face. Then his eyes clear and he says: "We're all right now. We've been through a lot, I can tell you that. But we're all right. We're still friends."

Paul Levinson is the first Communist—and one of the very few —who will say to me: The Party stole my life. Levinson says openly, and without qualification, the Party fed off his adolescent sexual fears. Behind the language of theory and doctrine and the dense comradeship of Party days and nights Paul's bewildered sexual desires fluttered, and were damped down. A trade-off occurred in which his sexual and emotional fears of life, of genuine human contact, were made use of, and his years in the Party prevented him from early discovering the "world of reality": that is, learning about his own emotions and how they worked in the world outside.

Levinson lights a cigarette and leans back into the inner corner of the booth. (I am struck again by how many ex-Communists are still nonstop smokers. Almost as though: After what we've been through we should be afraid of lung cancer, too?) He falls silent, as though he is thinking about something, trying to find the right way to express his thoughts. I remain silent, to let him find his words in any way he can. When at last he speaks, the words come as a surprise. They are the last words in the world I would expect him to speak. Levinson says:

"You know, it's funny. In the old days, in the Party, I never had 'personal relationships.' Now, I have personal relationships. Everybody's in analysis, everybody's confessing their lives to each other day and night, and there are a lot of people about whom I just *know* an awful lot of personal stuff. And they know an awful lot about me. And yet, it really is odd. I don't feel intimate with any of these people. And I know I never will. And with the people from the Party, I felt intimate. I couldn't tell them anything about what we call my 'personal life,' but I felt an intimacy with them I also know I'll never feel again with anyone else."

The Dos Passos Immigrants

A WORLD away from the Eastern European working-class Jews who became American Communists—although they often lived side by side—were the Eastern European working-class Gentiles, many of whom came to the Communist Party out of an unimaginable isolation whose origin lay, at least partly, in peasant cultures untouched by the idea of Ideas. For thousands of working-class Czechs, Poles, and Hungarians Marxism came out of an intellectual darkness unknown to the most ignorant Jew, and it struck them with the force of blind need. A vast interior silence—the legacy of wordlessness—dissolved suddenly into the sounds of life; an unimagined self was found to exist; a human being declared himself with the wonder of original consciousness.

Dick Nikowsski is seventy years old. A lifelong Communist Party functionary, Nikowsski—a tall, handsome, blue-eyed man—is something of a romantic figure in the American Left. He spent years among auto workers, carpenters, electrical workers, and miners, and became known as a legendary organizer. In 1937 he went to Spain as a political commissar for the American CP: to "explain" the war to the International Brigade troops. He was wounded in Spain and returned to the United States a war hero. He went back to organizing for the Party, was arrested in 1949 under the Smith Act Laws of Sedition, sentenced to twenty-five years in prison, fought desperately—as, indeed, the government *was* framing him—and finally managed to have his sentence reversed: after having spent two really dreadful years in prison under detention and a full year in court. "God!" Nikowsski says, wiping his broad, beautiful forehead with a handkerchief, "I say it all so quickly, but God! It was just awful. Every day for a year in court. It dragged me down to the ground."

Nikowsski and I are talking on the porch of his sturdy little house in a Cape Cod village. As we sit in the blaze of an August afternoon, surrounded by the dense, sandy woods of the cape, all kinds of people troop by the house and wave hello or stop to chat. I look at Dick in puzzled amusement as much as to say: Do they know who you are? He understands the look and nods, wearily, laughingly: Yes, they do. The irony of the situation is inescapable.

Nikowsski bought the land on which this house stands twenty years ago when he left the Communist Party, and he spent the next few years building the house, working from morning to night, dropping into bed half-dead with physical exhaustion each night so that he wouldn't have to think, wouldn't be *able* to think. He also built the house because he honestly believed that he would never again be able to work in America except perhaps as an obscure carpenter in some remote village like this one, and he had to have a place for his family to live.

In the twenty years that have passed, this village has become a summer haven for middle-class, "radical" academics from New York—and Nikowsski has become the romantic Old Left resident. A man in Bermuda shorts and a sunhat passes by, waves, and yells at Dick, "Put it all down for posterity, man!" Another— younger, more deferential—pauses at the porch railing and tells Dick he understands he's going into New York next week to speak about the Spanish Vets, he's welcome to use his Brooklyn Heights house "anytime." "Anytime," he repeats with quiet intensity, looking deeply into Nikowsski's heavily lined face; as though to let Dick know he may not be a Resistance worker himself, but he's certainly ready to lend aid and support—yes, even if it means taking certain risks, making certain sacrifices— to a man like Dick Nikowsski. "Anytime."

There is something slightly ridiculous in all this, some slight contempt in the affection extended this old warhorse now looked upon as a harmless folk hero. This contempt hurts me. The entire history of the Communist Party USA is alive in this simple man. From the obscure, semilegal status of the Twenties to the vibrant Thirties to the prison days of the Forties to the terror and disillusion of the Fifties to the obscurity of the Sixties, Nikowsski has reflected the deepest currents of perception and feeling as those currents ruled the life of the Communist Party. For forty years Nikowsski has been the living embodiment of the true believer who swallows blind force, spits out assimilated wisdom, and keeps history moving. There is grandeur of a certain sort in this, deserving not for a second of anyone's patronage.

Dick Nikowsski was born a Polish Catholic in a tiny town a hundred miles from Warsaw. His father was a bootmaker and a drunk. His mother was a peasant woman who lived in terror of her husband's drunken rages, and tried with kind-hearted ignorance to shield her many children from the inescapable brutalities of the life into which they had been born. Nikowsski's sketch of life in the village, and life in his home, is so crude that

I feel impelled to ask: "Didn't your father love you at *all*?" Nikowsski looks reflective and says: "Actually, he wasn't unkind to me. He was a reasonable fellow. But he *drank*, you see."

"And your mother?" I ask. "Did she love you?"

Very hesitantly, Nikowsski says: "She did the best she could." Then he turns full in his wicker seat to face me. "You see, the life was so *hard*. It broke them so. They were silent drudges. It was all work, work, work. Just to stay alive. Their faces were bent, from morning to night, to the earth. There was nothing, nothing in their lives that brought relief or joy, nothing that made them take pleasure in each other. Now, you know, in such circumstances love is a luxury, the value of human relations is an unknown."

Dick's mother had a brother who had emigrated to the United States. He came back on a visit to the village when Dick was fifteen years old, and the sight of his sister's condition broke his heart. He begged her to leave her Old-Man-Karamazov husband, take the children, and come to America; nothing could be worse than what they were living through now. It took Mrs. Nikowsski two years to gather the courage to leave her husband and the village, and cross the Atlantic Ocean. When at last she did, the only children left for her to take were Dick and his two younger sisters; the rest of the children, unfortunately, had already grown up—and become their mother and their father. Mrs. Nikowsski arrived at her brother's house in Philadelphia in an even worse state of terror than the one she normally lived in. Dick was seventeen, the girls were fifteen and fourteen, the year was 1919.

Theirs was the immigrant experience at its worst. Isolated in a vast unknowable land, living inside an illiterate peasant-émigré community marked by fear, silence, and withdrawal, the Nikowsskis grew dumb inside themselves with unarticulated anxiety. Life had always been a mysterious set of commands: Thou Shalt Drudge. Thou Shalt Suffer. Thou Shalt Not Ask Why. Now, those commands seemed harsher than ever, and compounded even further by humiliations they had not known in Poland. They lived in the unremitting dirt, cold, and heat of the city, deprived of the air, light, and space of the village. Not only could they not communicate with most of the people around them, but they were yelled at and insulted as well for not speaking English. The poverty of the city was infinitely more grinding than that of the village, and the lack of education infinitely more degrading in America than in Poland.

Dick worked sixty hours a week for eight dollars, was grateful to be allowed to work, and dreaded the loss of the eight dollars. He moved forward, day by day, a drudge on a drudge path, surrounded by a vast darkness, a terrible silence, without mind or hope, so utterly void of even the barest notions of what power in the world was that he didn't know he was entirely without it. He only knew that this life was suicidal and it stretched endlessly before him with no hope of change.

In 1922 the Nikowsskis moved to the Polish section of Chicago, and Dick went to work in a slaughterhouse where he worked six days a week, freezing in winter, sweltering in summer, making just enough to exist on, never enough to save anything. Nikowsski's description of this slaughterhouse in 1922 evokes for me an image of men in hell, condemned to shovel coal onto their own doom-fires.

One of the men who worked in the slaughterhouse was a socialist, a thin, burning-eyed man in his thirties. Dick Nikowsski was twenty years old. This socialist worked beside Dick, and became his friend. He talked endlessly, obsessively about "the bosses" and "the working stiffs." Half the time Dick couldn't follow the socialist, didn't know what the hell he was talking about, thought only that he was going to get them all in trouble. But he liked the socialist because behind the rage he sensed something wild and wounded in the man, and besides, whenever there was a dispute between the foreman and a worker, the socialist was the only one who stuck his neck out for the worker.

Then, one day in summer when it was so blistering hot in the slaughterhouse the sweat was pouring down into the men's eyes, blinding them, the socialist suddenly turned to Dick and said to him: "Do you know where the owners are now? Right now while you and I are here sweating like pigs?" "No," Dick replied, "where?" The socialist took a folded page of newspaper from his pocket. "There!" he thundered. "At the coast!" Dick stared blindly at the picture of a group of men and women lying languidly by the sea. The blue eyes of the seventy-year-old Nikowsski stare at me, fifty years disappearing in their wide gaze. "I didn't even know what the coast *was*," he says in wonder as fresh as that of the twenty-year-old still alive inside him.

"Something happened to me then. I just stared and stared at that picture. Suddenly it was as if everything that socialist had been saying all those months clicked into place somewhere in my head, and I saw *me* behind that picture, I saw *me* knee-deep in blood and shit all my life so that that picture could be taken. I don't know how to describe it to you, I don't think I even knew what it was that was happening, I certainly couldn't have put it into words, but something came rising up in me, so swift and so strong it nearly took the breath out of my body. I can still feel it, the way I felt it then. As if it was coming right out of the center of me, as if it had been waiting there all that time, all my life, and now it had—just that fast!—run out of time.

"Everything happened so quick then. I *understood* everything the socialist had been saying. Everything! I saw it all at once. And all at once, I saw, and I could hardly believe this, *there was a way out for me.* Now, you gotta understand what this means. I didn't even know that I was thinking there's no way out of this life for me until suddenly I was thinking there *is* a way out. It's complicated, but you get what I mean? I saw that being a worker was literally slavery, and that the slavery came from being like a dumb animal hitched forever to the machine, and this *idea* of us as a class relieved the slavery, gave you a way to fight, gave you a way to become a human being.

"It's funny." Dick Nikowsski pauses, leans back on the railing of the porch. "I saw something else, too. And to this day it amazes me that I could see this. You can't imagine how ignorant I was. No, believe me, you can't! But I saw that if I was much smarter than I was, or if I had some particular talent, or maybe if I was sensitive about things, it was just possible I, as an individual, could have burrowed my way out of this working-class hell. But if you were *just* as smart as me, and just as talentless, and just as insensitive, you were condemned to life." The expression on Nikowsski's face is uncanny: wry, cynical, amused, tender—

and excited. Beneath it all, excited still by the meaning of this original, powerful insight.

"So," he relaxes, "that's how I became a socialist. The man in the slaughterhouse—Eddie was his name—and I became inseparable. Although I continued to support my mother and my sisters, I moved out of the apartment and went to live with Eddie, who shared a roach-ridden cold-water flat with three other guys who were also socialists. But—and I suppose you've heard this fifty times by now—we really didn't feel the cold, the dirt, the misery of that place. We were on fire with politics. We talked Marxism day and night, every minute we weren't working, shitting, or eating. No, I take that back, we talked it while we were eating, too. It was air, bread, light, and warmth to us. For me, it was so exciting it was almost physical pain. I was high all the time. I was discovering I had a mind, I could think, and I was doing it! Not only that, the sheer intellectual joy of reading Marx. . . . You know, that's one thing almost all Communists share, the memory of what it was first like to read Marx, like fireworks exploding in your head, and the love you felt for the human intelligence. . . . God, I have never felt so free in my life as I did in those first days when I discovered Marx and the existence of my own mind at the same time—in that cold, filthy apartment in Chicago.

"And then, too, it was like I was discovering the world for the first time. It was like I'd never seen anything before, and now all of a sudden I was seeing everything. The shapes of the buildings, the way the streets looked after a rain, the expressions on people's faces, the length of the women's dresses, the way Lake Michigan looked different at six in the morning, and then again at noon, and then again at twilight. . . . As though the world had been a blurred photograph and now suddenly I was seeing a clear print. And I loved everybody! God, how I loved those guys I was living with. When we were in the middle of some intense analysis of the Russian Revolution at three in the morning and we all had to be up on our feet and at work at seven, I'd look around the room at these guys, and they were my comrades, and I loved them so hard I thought I'd burst with it.

"You know," Nikowsski laughs, "they say Communists love

mankind but hate people, but I'm here to tell you here's one Communist who if it wasn't for Communism would never have loved *anybody* in this life."

The American Populists

I CAN see Will Barnes right now, leaning back in his rocking chair in the book-lined room in San Francisco, nodding his head at Dick Nikowsski's last words and saying in that light Western twang of his, "Know what you mean, comrade. Know exactly what you mean."

Will Barnes likes to say he is as old as the century. During the month I spoke with him he had just celebrated his seventy-fourth birthday. He is a tall, muscular man in magnificent physical shape who wears glasses only to read and looks like an intelligent John Wayne. He lives with his third wife in a neat, pretty, four-room apartment in San Francisco. A self-taught man, he has a large, indiscriminate library in which he reads many hours each evening. He also gets up at dawn to run four to six miles each morning down on the Pacific Ocean beaches, and four days out of five he puts in a full day's work. Barnes was a member of the Communist Party for thirty years, and for many of those years he was a high-powered organizer in the National Maritime Union. In the 1950s, when the Party and the union fell apart for him, hard times fell permanently on him. Now he makes a living as a day laborer. He will never stop working, he says. He'd rather drop in his tracks.

"And it looks like I'm gonna go out the way I came in," Barnes laughs, "a working stiff, if not still a bindlebum."

"Tell me about the way you came in," I urge him, facing him across the little study in which he spends so much of his time reading.

"Well," says Barnes, crossing his long legs and leaning back in his rocker, "you want to know what I come out of? There's a book I read recently, tells all about my life. My wife brought it to me, she's a real hot feminist now, and she got this book from a little press called the Feminist Press, it's a reprint of Agnes Smedley's *Daughter of Earth*. It's funny, that book. It's an exact reproduction of my life, only told from the point of view of a woman, and Christ, it taught me a lot about my own life. I never did see things quite the way Smedley did. That book was an eye-opener. Made me see my own mother in a whole different light."

Agnes Smedley's book is a classic American biography. Smedley was born into the harsh primitivism of Western frontier life in the last decade of the 19th century: the life of day laborers and itinerant workers, of mining camps, logging camps, lumber mills and river bums; a life of raw poverty and isolation, of drinking, violence, and brutal appetites. In short, the life of the drifting, declassed American frontierspeople whose sweated labor built the railroads and highways of this country, settled its lands, mined its minerals, turned its trees into lumber, its iron into steel, its raw material into textiles. The tale Smedley tells in *Daughter of Earth* is that of a person born into dumb primitivism who, through an amazing force of will, brains, and hungriness of spirit, made herself into a human being. And what a human being. Before she died, Agnes Smedley was a world-famous independent American radical whose name was linked with the Indian movement for independence as well as the Chinese Communist revolution.

"I was born," says Will Barnes, "in a mining camp in Idaho, the second oldest of five children, each one of us with a different father. My mother smoked cigars, had five husbands, shot three of them. All her husbands slammed her around, beat her kids, stole her money, drank themselves blind, and in the end either deserted her or ran down the road with my mother shooting in the doorway after them. The only solvent member of my mother's huge clan was her younger sister, Annabel. Annabel ran a whorehouse in Seattle, and from time to time Ma used to take us kids there to get us out of the way while she settled things with her latest husband. My Ma was a fierce lady. She lived in mining camps, lumber camps, tenements, and log cabins. She took in washing, she slung hash, she ran gambling parlors, and once she even went down in the mines. She was real pretty when she was young, but by the time she was forty she didn't have a tooth in her head. She was one of that great herd of people who roamed all over the West for five or six generations, belonging to no place and no one. She dragged us kids all over Idaho, Washington, Wyoming, Montana, always looking for the one place where she could finally 'settle.' She never found it. It's funny, I don't think she really loved us, any of us, but we were *hers*, we were all in the world that ever was hers, and while *she* could slam us around, she'd be damned if anybody else could.

"When I was fourteen years old I ran away from home, and that was it. Never went back, and never took another cent from Ma as long as she lived. Of course, that doesn't mean I never saw her again. No such thing. Ended up bringing her and my sister and youngest brother out here to California, where she finally got 'settled' in a house with indoor plumbing and food regular on the table. She grumbled and bitched, of course, about how tame and silly California was, but I think she enjoyed it. She died twenty years ago, when I was in the middle of all my Party troubles. She never did know why I was a Communist, or what the hell Communism was all about, but by then it didn't matter. She defended me as ferociously as she had from all those drunks she married who used to like to beat my head against the barn door on Saturday night. I was *hers*. It was that simple. And if I was a Communist, whatever the hell that meant, then being a Communist was an all right thing to be.

"When I left home I started drifting. I thumbed a ride out of the logging camp in Washington that was then home, climbed into a boxcar first town on the railroad I came to, walked five or six miles after I climbed off the boxcar, washed dishes for a meal, and slept that night in someone's empty barn somewhere in the middle of Idaho. I didn't exactly know it then, but I had entered the great world of hobo America. I lived on and off in that world for the next fourteen years, leaving it permanently only when I joined the Communist Party in 1928.

"Those were terrible years, between 1914 and 1928, not just for me but for a whole lot of Americans. That famous 1920s prosperity, it somehow just passed us by. 'We heerd tell of it,' " Will grins, " 'but none of us could rightly say we done *seen* it.'

When the Depression hit and everyone started yelling Depression! Depression! I thought: Hell, my whole goddamn *life* has been a Depression.

"I hitchhiked, and walked, and rode the rails. I must have crossed this country twenty times in those years, from Montana to Virginia, out to Arkansas, down to Pennsylvania, up to Maine, out West again. Always, out West again. I did everything you could think of to keep body and soul together. I was a hod carrier, a powder monkey, a logger, a teamster, a dishwasher; I went down into the mines, worked in a steel mill, cleaned out cesspools (man! I still dream about that one sometimes). And just kept on drifting. Something in me, something restless, lonely, wouldn't let me come to rest. I always felt removed, at a distance from things. I had an image of myself, and it was always of me standing on the edge of the horizon, never settled in the middle of the landscape. I never felt at home. Nowhere. Ever. America was like something closed off from me, something I couldn't get at. It wasn't mine, I couldn't make it mine. I used to look at these pretty houses in every town and city I passed through and for the life of me I just couldn't imagine what it was like to live in one of them.

"And then there were times, no work. No work at all. That was a nightmare. Going hungry for days at a time. Getting so tired from being hungry you couldn't work even if it was offered you. And, it never failed, when you were at your lowest, you'd get arrested for vagrancy and find yourself locked up in some goddamn pokey, spending the night dodging rats and being beaten up by some red-neck jail guard. More nights like that than I really care to remember. And always this loneliness, feeling cut off from everyone around me, not knowing why exactly, not knowing how to do anything about it.

"One day when I was about seventeen I was walking up and down in front of a restaurant in some small town in Montana. I had a sandwich board strapped to my chest and back, advertising the restaurant, and I'd been promised a meal if I walked that beat for six hours. So I'm walking up and down there, and some guy comes up to me and he's about forty, fifty years old, and he's got cold, angry blue eyes and a big beard like prospectors wore up in the hills, and he says to me: 'You an Amurrican?'

'Sure,' I says back. He points his finger, really angry, at the sandwich board, and he says to me, 'You're an Amurrican and a human being. It don't seem right that you should have to do *that* just to eat a meal.' And he made me take the sandwich board off, right there in the middle of the street, and told me to come with him. I was thunderstruck. No one in my whole life had ever said anything like what he'd just said to me. There was nothing for it but to do as he said, and go with him.

"He took me on out to the edge of town and there, on an embankment near a small river, was a campfire and a bunch of guys sitting around it. I thought they were hoboes, but they weren't. They were Wobblies. They sat me down, gave me some food to eat, explained themselves to me, and within twelve hours they brought politics into my life. I listened openmouthed to them. I didn't know what the hell they were talking about, and I thought sure as hell whatever it was it's gotta be illegal, and if that red-neck sheriff up in the town knew what these guys were saying! Solidarity? The working class? Fight for their rights? They built America, why were they living like beggars? Man, oh man!

"Of course, I took to the Wobblies right away. It wasn't just that they were kind to me, and that their talk hypnotized me, and that somehow I knew they were saying something important and they had a lot of guts to be saying it. No, it wasn't just that. I don't know how to explain it to you, but all that talk about solidarity and the working class, I didn't know what the words meant, but somehow, they were touching that loneliness in me. Something flickered up in me, it was warming, I didn't feel lonely listening to the Wobblies.

"I spent the night in their camp, and in the morning they gave me a green card and said I was now one of them. I touched my cap to them and went on my way. That green card. Do you know, there were times, riding the rails, in the middle of the night in some godforsaken town in the middle of nowhere, all of a sudden the railroad men would yank you off the cars and start beating the shit out of you, and I'd show them my green card, and they'd stop beating us, and let us get back onto the car. That happened quite often in those days.

"I was nineteen years old on Armistice Day, 1919, and I just happened to be in Centralia, Washington. Remember Centralia? A bunch of legionnaires decided to bust up the Wobblies' hall just to show how patriotic they were. The Wobblies defended themselves and those legionnaires—they have got to be the worst bastards who ever walked this earth—why, they just couldn't believe their eyes. These Wobblies, these fuckin' Reds, *defending* themselves? As though they had *rights*? That drove them into a frenzy. There was a shootout, and when it was over there were more dead Wobblies than legionnaires lying around Centralia, and the leader of the Wobblies, a World War I vet, he had his balls cut off and was hanging from the bridge at the end of town.

"I stood across the street from the Wobbly hall and I watched the whole damn thing happen. And something cold and hard and sick began forming in me, from that day on, about this country. I was only a kid, but even so, I knew that the Wobblies had no power, that they were no threat to anyone in this country, and that the year before the government had gone in and busted up every Wobbly camp and headquarters in the whole damn country, just like they did with the Panthers in the Sixties. The Wobblies were finished, and yet here were the legionnaires and the whole damn town killing them, just killing them. This country, I thought, oh this lousy country!

"But there's another part to this country, and I found that out, too, in Centralia. I hung around the town all that day and night, too sick and scared and dumb to do anything else. And do you know what happened? At dawn a thousand people marched into Centralia. They walked, they rode horses, they came in carts and Tin Lizzies, they came from every direction. And they camped all around the town, in absolute silence. They sat there a whole day and night without talking. You could feel the weight of their sorrow, and the power of their silence. It was like some really great tragedy had occurred. And the legionnaires and the town were more scared of them, and of their silence, than they had been by what had happened. I never forgot it. Those people, that town, the shootout, the lynching, and then that silence. I can still see it all like it was yesterday.

"In 1927, in San Francisco, I ran into a hobo I'd known. He told me he was shipping out, and suggested I do the same. I didn't know how to go about it, but he showed me how to get seaman's papers and within a couple of months I went to sea for the first time. From the first minute I loved it. I loved the sea, I loved the ship, I loved the life. I was a natural sailor.

"But that ship, it was like something out of *Two Years Before the Mast*. It was filthy, disease-ridden, the men were overworked and brutalized, cheated of their pay, unfairly punished for the slightest infringement. Sometimes, it really got frightening.

"There was a guy on board that ship, a sailor like the rest of us. One night, he started talking to a bunch of us, late, up on deck. After he'd been talking fifteen minutes I knew this was the voice I'd been waiting for all my life. Oh sure, he talked like the Wobblies about solidarity and the working class, but by God, he made me *feel* it like the Wobblies somehow never had. He didn't hit one false note. There wasn't a single point he made that he didn't link up with some aspect of our life on the ship, so that after a while everything that was happening to us on the ship became interchangeable with this larger picture he was drawing of what was happening in the world. His voice was full of a kind of painful excitement, and his words were so persuasive that every man in that group was captured and held long enough so that by the time he stopped talking each man listening knew he wasn't just a sailor, he was a proletarian.

"It was the moment of my life, that night on deck, listening to this guy talk. I suddenly saw the world politically, and I knew I was never again going to see it differently. That lonely misery inside me always had a kind of leaky feeling to it. Well, that night it suddenly cleared up, my whole insides got dry and light. I was burning up with excitement. You might say," Will's face splits in a big grin, "all those soggy branches inside me suddenly became kindling wood.

"The man was, of course, an organizer for the Communist Party. I followed him around like a little dog for the rest of the voyage, wouldn't let him out of my sight, all the time talking, talking, talking. It was as if I'd just found speech. When we hit San Francisco again, I made him take me with him, and that night I joined the Party. Within a month I was at sea again, only this time, like my mentor, a seagoing organizer for the Communist Party. For the next ten years I went to sea and I organized. They were the best years of my life. It was the Thirties. There was so much ignorance and misery everywhere, and among the people I knew swollen-belly starvation. The ships were no bargain, either. Some of these ships I lived on during those years: floating hellholes. But no matter how poor or filthy things were, for me they were good. I was organizing for the CP. Inside, I felt dry and light and clear. You see, I *understood* things. I knew what was happening. That saved me. Not only that, I was working for the revolution. I could take anything, knowing I was working for the revolution. Anything.

"You know, forty-six years have gone by since that time. That's a lot of years. I spent thirty of them in the Party, and now sixteen out of the Party. If I live long enough the years out of the Party will be equal in number to the years *in* the Party. But you know? They can never equal each other. Those years in the Party, *they* made me a human being. Nothing else ever did, nothing else ever could. The Communist Party did a lot of terrible things, but one thing I gotta give it: it took raw American clay and made a thinking human being out of it."

It is not at all impossible that one day between 1914 and 1928, when he was drifting endlessly across the country, Will Barnes knocked at the door of Blossom Sheed's house in Los Angeles and asked the lady of the house if she could spare something to eat. If he did, the lady who answered the door certainly gave him something to eat and, along with the sandwich or slice of pie, she probably handed him a short stern lecture on how he should quit being a bum, get married, start going to church, and settle down on the land. The lady would have been Blossom Sheed's mother.

When we settle down to talk in a friend's apartment in Los Angeles, Blossom Sheed is sixty-five years old, and bears the most extraordinary resemblance to Jane Darwell playing Ma Joad in *The Grapes of Wrath*. A large, ungainly woman with iron-grey hair gathered together in a bun at the nape of her neck, small fine features in the midst of a large fleshy face, and the shrewdest, tenderest blue eyes I have ever looked into, Blossom eases herself onto a fifteen-year-old Danish modern couch in this lower-middle-class living room in North Hollywood and says, "This is a mighty fine place you got here." Blossom is employed by the city of Los Angeles as a welfare department projects director. I know she knows this is not a "mighty fine place." But Blossom is proletarian to the bone; until the day she dies any set of rooms above a working-class tenement will feel like a mighty fine place to her.

Blossom Sheed was born in 1909 in Memphis, Tennessee to a father whose parents had been abolitionists and a mother who came out of democratic agrarian Nebraska. They were literally the salt of the American earth, the kind of people who had fought cheerfully in the Revolution, bravely in the Civil War, and then, in the incredible Panics and Depressions brought on by the rise of the robber barons, had formed themselves into Worker and Farmer Alliances and become the American populists. They were land-bound, family-bound Americans who really believed that the American democracy was meant to serve them not exploit them, and time and time again were shocked to discover that the democracy was not theirs by right, that they would have to fight over and over again simply to survive in it.

Blossom's father was a surveyor who was out of work most of the time, and her mother hated Memphis. So, when Blossom was two years old they moved to Los Angeles and Blossom and her sisters grew up among the families of the surveyors, engineers, and contractors who were building the new Los Angeles in the Nineteen-Tens and Twenties; it was a world of dam sites, aqueducts, dirty brown mountains, grit, dust, hard work, and respectable near-poverty.

There was a subtle kind of war going on between the parents. The father was witty and possessed of a rich love of life; the mother was stern, proper, and God-fearing. The father had wanted sons, but when he had only daughters he determined to raise them to believe they were as good as men and better. The mother was scandalized by everything the father taught the girls; she pursed her lips and shoved the girls before her into church every Sunday morning, hoping on that day to undo in the House of the Lord what the father did six days a week in the World of Man. Blossom adored her father and fought her mother. She didn't want to go to church. When she was eleven years old she stole into her father's office. She found and read *The Appeal to Reason*. She knew then: she was right not to want to go to church. With the book under her arm she felt powerful. The book was her weapon, stronger' than anything her mother could threaten her with.

Reading *The Appeal to Reason* at the age of eleven was probably the beginning of Blossom Sheed's political life. Some secret, separate intelligence began forming inside the little girl who had inherited her father's grit and her mother's stubbornness and, like a genetic characteristic that skips a generation, the political tendencies of those honest American rebels who had been her forebears.

At seventeen, Blossom married her cousin and set up housekeeping in an outlying district of Los Angeles. Why she married him she doesn't to this day know. What he meant to her she doesn't know. What their married life set out to be she doesn't know. The only thing she does know is that very quickly she realized he was not and never could be the companion of her thoughts or of this peculiar "sense of things" growing in her, and those thoughts and that sense of things began to take immediate and urgent hold of her.

"Our first married quarrel was the result of an argument over the causes of the First World War," Blossom says, laughing grimly even all these years later. "He never knew what hit him. Neither did I, for that matter. I couldn't figure out why it all meant so much to me. But all around me everyone was poor. I mean *suffering* poor. No matter how hard they saved, no one could get ahead. I couldn't stop asking why. That drove my husband crazy. And my whole family, for that matter. They'd say to me, 'People are poor because they're lazy or stupid.' But that didn't sit right with me. I just *knew* that wasn't true, I just knew too many poor people who weren't either lazy or stupid for that to be true. I said no, and I kept on saying it. 'No, that isn't why these people are poor. There's got to be another reason.' My husband wasn't interested in asking why. My asking made him terribly uncomfortable. He wanted to know why I couldn't just help him work, and let things be.

"Well, inside of me things kept getting worse. Some awful angriness was there all the time, and it made me real lonely. My husband and I, working for this or that, to buy a little house, go visit the folks on Sunday, sit around and talk about nothing, it all just got on my nerves. I wanted to talk about what was going on all around me. Only, you see, I wasn't quite sure what *was* going on, and I had no one to find out from, no one to talk it over with, figure out my own thoughts with.

"My son was born the day Sacco and Vanzetti were killed. I heard about it in the hospital while I was being wheeled into the labor room. I got so agitated the doctors feared I would make myself seriously ill, feared something would happen to both me and the baby. What's wrong? they kept asking me. What's wrong?

"I didn't know myself what was wrong. What could I tell them? 'I feel ill because two Italian anarchists are dying in Boston'? It sounded crazy even to me. But it was true. Something terrible was happening inside me. Something tearing at my insides worse than the pains of childbirth.

"When I got out of the hospital I knew I had to do something. My family was outraged. My husband was miserable and confused. But I didn't give a damn, anymore. I knew I had to go my own way now. If my husband had said 'I'll leave you,' I would have said 'Go.'" Blossom stares thoughtfully at me for a moment. Then she says: "You see, I didn't respect his opinion. And I knew this was important. All around me people were suffering. It was Nineteen Twenty-Nine, Thirty, Thirty-One. They were terrible years in California. People were eating dust. I couldn't ignore that for a man whose opinions I didn't respect.

"Didn't I feel I had to stay home and care for the child? No, I guess I didn't. I was on fire to go, and nothing was as real to me as that fire burning inside me. So I left my kid with his father, with my mother, with neighbors, anybody. But you know, I look around at all these kids who grew up with their mothers there when they needed her, and they're no better than my son is now. No better, no worse. Somehow, they all grew up. If I'd stayed home to take care of a child I'd have ended up hating him, and he'd have had to grow up with *that*, too. Like a lot of these kids who had their mother's devotion *and* her secret hatred."

Those were great left-wing years in California; the natural flamboyant radicalism of the 19th-century American populists was abroad. Everywhere, the Co-Operative Movement was forming and, Blossom recalls, the spirit of all these public meetings seemed to be: "We'll remake our lives. The shoemaker will make shoes, the doctor will treat the ill, the artist will make beautiful things, and we will share among ourselves." "Once," Blossom says, "a man stood up on a wooden platform on a streetcorner in Los Angeles and said: 'Just as the river wears away the sands so will the Co-Operative Movement wear away the injustices of capitalism.' And," she adds, "I thrilled to the sound of this man's voice."

She joined the Co-Operative Movement. This, she thought, was it. Here, she was at last among her own people, people who understood, people who cared, people who made clear to her why in a country as rich and open as America millions of people were doomed to poverty. Here, for the first time, she learned about The System, and those two words became the source of a magical piece of understanding for her. To those words she could address her "whys" satisfactorily.

There were Communists in the Co-Operative Movement, and they shook their heads at everything. No matter what the Co-Operators did the Communists said, "It won't work." Blossom said to them: "Why are you people so gloomy? Why are you always undermining us?" All they would say was the Co-Operators were on the wrong track. Another thing about the Communists that got on Blossom's nerves: "They were always making *connections*." Connections where Blossom thought there were none.

"But the Communists were right," Blossom sighs. "No matter what the Co-Op did it came up against the dead end of capitalist power and production ownership: Salinas Valley strikes, lettuce a penny a head, worker violations, the lot. There was no end to it, and the Co-Op couldn't make a dent."

Finally, the Communists said to Blossom: "If you think we're on the wrong track, join us and make your opinions known." She did think they were on the wrong track, she thought despite its failures the Co-Operative Movement was right and that it would be stronger if the Communists would join it wholeheartedly, and maybe the thing to do *was* to join the Communists and make them see that. She joined the Communist Party in 1932 "to change them," and remained in the Party for twenty-five years taking, as she says, The Red Veil.

When Blossom joined the CP she was placed in a club in which she was the only American-born person and the only woman. A natural radical, she thought: Where are the Americans? A natural feminist, she thought: Where are these men's wives? Why are they sitting home while their husbands are here planning the revolution? Oh well, she concluded, tomorrow. The women and the Americans will come tomorrow. Everything was tomorrow . . . especially the revolution. But meanwhile, there was today, and there was work to be done.

By the time she joined the Party, Blossom was already a worker in the International Legal Defense Fund, a Party-run organization that raised money, committees, lawyers, petitions, and bail bonds in those despairing-exciting California years of the great farm labor strikes. Under the skill and impetus of the Party, Blossom rose to become secretary-general of the Fund, battling daily in the midst of that extraordinary time of American radical battle. She was involved in every major and minor California strike of the Thirties, every legal defense concerning workers, the evicted, Mexicans, corrupt police, the Scottsboro case, political arrests. She ran for congress on the CP slate innumerable times. She went down to the strikes in the Imperial Valley, where "they'd as soon string up a Communist as look at him," where workers were jailed, beaten, and shot daily, and when they were shot Blossom read funeral orations from the Bible. She was alive to the pain and beauty of the time, she soared with the sense of political moment. Once, a complicated Thirties struggle between police and workers in a small town near Los Angeles resulted in the police commissioner being replaced. The commissioner called her and said, "Well, Blossom, you did it. You dumped me." Blossom replied exultantly: "Why, you dumb bastard, I didn't dump you, you dumped yourself. You're on the wrong side of history."

She spent twenty-five years of her life submerged in the dailiness of radical battle. Only when she went to New York did she see the power struggles of the Party. . . . and came home sick and confused. But she shook her head, shrugged her shoulders, and plunged in again. If she had been expelled from the Party at any time during those years she would have been shattered; her life, her work, her friends, her people, all were the Party. Yet, in 1957 she looked around at a roomful of these same people, and they were suddenly useless and dead to her. "Dry rot had set in," she says briskly. "Sclerosis of the mind." And she walked away from that which you couldn't have dragged her kicking and screaming from twenty years earlier.

When Blossom's mother was eighty-nine years old she broke her hip. There was no money, and the old woman had to be sent to a city hospital. The hospital was dreadful, and a nurse said to Blossom, "If you want your mother to live take her home."

Blossom sighs and eases her large bulk back against the foam-rubber couch, looking more than ever like the enduring Ma Joad. She stares sightlessly at the coffee table for a moment and then says: "Those were hard days and nights, I can tell you. You see, my mother and I had never made peace. We'd continued to fight all these years. She was close to my sisters who did, I guess, what she thought it was right to do. But when she got sick, suddenly there was no one to take care of her but me. So I swallowed hard and did as the nurse had advised me to do. I took her home and I nursed her day and night for weeks that felt like years. Then, when she recovered, one day as I was turning away from her bedside she took my hand in hers and she said to me, 'You know, I got to tell you. You were always right. There is nothing but the world of man.'" Tears well up in this old fighter's eyes as she repeats her mother's words, but her voice remains steady as ever, and she continues talking over her falling tears.

I can't help asking, "Do you have any regrets, Blossom? If you had to do it all over again . . . ?" Her answer comes back quick as a shot: "None!" A wide grin splits her tough, magnificently enduring face. "Like all good Americans," she says, "I put a premium on my life. I wouldn't trade a minute of it for ten million dollars."

At first glance the man sitting opposite me in a deserted corner of a student lounge at the University of Chicago on this wet, snowy December afternoon seems to bear little or no resemblance to Blossom Sheed; until I look directly into his eyes; then I see the mixture of irony and tenderness permeating that pure American blue, and the stream of common ancestry between

Blossom Sheed and Jim Holbrook flows sharply toward me, over-riding the difference between Blossom's Dustbowl-frontier look and Holbrook's Ivy League Midwestern look, putting that shared native rebel I-want-to-know-why look squarely in possession of the human territory before me; explaining more than any other single aspect of his appearance why Jim Holbrook was an organizer for the Communist Party for twenty years.

Holbrook is a tall, rangy man who looks ten years younger than his fifty-five years. His face is a cross between Thomas Wolfe and Scott Fitzgerald: narrow nose and mouth, deep-set blue eyes, lank yellow-brown hair lying lightly on a high clear fore-head. His voice comes as a surprise; it is soft, oddly old and with a strong country-people accent: the accent of the American itin-erant, old at twelve.

But the speech that goes with the voice seems exactly right: it is larded with bits of poetry, country-people wisdom, literary fragments, a self-taught self-consciousness that is slightly em-barrassed, slightly self-important, continually tinged with a need to "make sense of it all," to put things into an order in which the man speaking can place himself. When I look around the room in which we are sitting, silently asking with my look: What the hell are you doing here? (Holbrook is an unemployment inter-viewer in Chicago and an amateur historian using the university library now while he is writing a Marxist history of the Midwest), Holbrook laughs and drawls at me: "You mean if they knew what I've been, what I still *am*? Fuck 'em. They've never liked me, I've never liked them." Then he shrugs and says: "I guess it's like Huckleberry Finn. Huck was told—of all the things he did, being a runaway, helping a slave—you'll go to hell. 'Why, then,' says Huck, 'I guess I'm going to hell.' "

Jim Holbrook was born in 1919 in Nebraska to a family of tenant farmers who were natural Jeffersonian democrats. Amer-ican to the core, Holbrook's mother used to say of anything she disliked or rejected, "It isn't worth a Continental." The parents were very unhappy together ("They were misyoked," sighs Hol-brook), but their unhappiness contributed oddly to an atmosphere not of isolation within the family but of fierce individualism in the family. No one seemed to go under emotionally; rather, the mother, the father, Jim, and his brother, Bob, seemed to be left to explore the world, in silence and wonder, each for him or herself. Holbrook's memory of Nebraska is "a dream of childhood." He pushes his fingers through his lank, straight hair and recites: "Then, if ever, there were perfect days."

Economically, Holbrook remembers nothing but hard times. They were poor, poor, poor. His mother and father worked from dawn to dusk, and still they ate cornmush three nights out of five. Hard times didn't make his father bitter, though, they made him rebellious. The mother grew silent as the years wore on, but the father talked angrily, as though he knew that as long as he stayed angry and talking he was alive; if he retreated into silence or depression he'd be dead—and *they* would have won. So every night for years the father and his two sons sat down to cornmush and greens, and they talked, talked, talked. It was incumbent on them at the dinner table to talk about "weighty matters," subjects of substance. The thing was: whatever they turned their attention to became a subject of substance. They talked politics, religion, ideas, movies, music, local customs, village gossip, all with the same fervor. They all loved to argue, they all felt it was important to take positions, never to be indifferent to any subject up for discussion.

When Jim was twelve years old the farm burned down. The owner wouldn't rebuild, and the Holbrooks left Nebraska, Mr. Holbrook thinking he'd go someplace else, make some money, come back, buy the farm, and rebuild it himself. Of course, things didn't work out that way. It was 1931. There was no work or money to be had anywhere. They never did come back to Nebraska, they never again had a home or a place to which they belonged. For the next ten years the family wandered, drifting here and there in search of work that would simply keep body and soul together.

Between the ages of twelve and sixteen, Jim lived with his family in the mining towns of Kentucky, his father moving from place to place in wretched search of work. It was during these years that Jim began to take his first sustained—albeit unconscious—look at *his* America.

"In Kentucky I learned violence and drinking and hillbilly smarts. The men in these towns, on a Saturday night, they'd just tear each other up. I can still remember the streets in those towns, wooden boards mainly, and the sound of men's heads hitting those boards when they got bounced out of a saloon. They were a fierce people, frightening to a boy, yet beautiful to me in their pain. I can still feel my eyes narrowing as I searched their faces for the truth of their lives.

"They didn't know anything about politics, but they were political, all right. They talked about the mines—that is, before they got too drunk to talk about anything—they talked about the bosses, they talked about the De-pression . . . like it was some mysterious thing that had been invented back East. And something inside me began listening to them with another ear, one I didn't know was there before. I figured it was a mystery, too, the way we were all living, but I thought: There's got to be some explanation for it, it's not like it's fire or flood, it's people doing this to other people, and," Holbrook grins, "I wanted to know why. Just like the boy in Sherwood Anderson's story. I wanted to know *why*. Now, the funny thing was, I didn't know consciously I wanted to know. But bit by bit, like a beaver building a dam, this desire to know was building inside me. And then, finally, desire became necessity.

"We left Kentucky and drifted back to West Virginia, where my father got work in the mines. It was the same in West Virginia as in Kentucky, maybe a little worse. My brother and I began having these long conversations about the mines and so forth, and then we began talking to the people in the towns, people older than ourselves, we figured maybe they knew something we didn't. One day, a man in one of these towns said to me, 'You talk like a socialist.' I stared at him, and, I remember, I said real slow, 'Well, maybe I am one.'

"Mind you, I'd heard the word, I hardly knew what it meant, but after that I set out to find out what it did mean. I went to the library, read a book, slammed it shut, and said, 'By god, that's what I am, a socialist.' So then I set out to find some people I could talk socialism with. And that led me straight to the Communists. It was 1937, it was West Virginia. The only game in town was the Communist Party.

"So one fine day when I was eighteen, and my brother Bob was twenty, we joined up. And then all of a sudden, it was like the drifting stopped. I'd come to rest. I had a home again. And for the next twenty years, no matter where I was, I had that home. And in that home I discovered I could think, act, learn, be . . ." Holbrook stops talking abruptly. The blue of his eyes deepens, and for a moment he seems very far away. "It wasn't that way for my brother," he says. "Bob lasted only a year or two and then he dropped out." Holbrook drifts again, then blurts out again: "He always *was* more honest, more courageous, more morally self-sufficient than I was. . . . After a while he'd come to CP meetings and he'd listen to them, and then he'd say, 'Why, you fellers is just a bunch of liars, like all the rest of them out there.' And then he said it once too often.

"But from the first I felt connected up to the world, being in the CP, and I loved and needed that feeling. Why, there I was in West Virginia, for Chrissake. You'd get the *Daily Worker*, you'd get other CP literature, you'd get all fired up at meetings, why, you felt yourself piped into Joe Stalin! You were at the end of a long line, but you were at the end of a line. I knew what was going on in New York, Moscow, Hungary. I was part of the world. I felt sustained, supported."

The Party sent Holbrook back to school, made him a teacher and an organizer. He married a miner's daughter—of his first wife Holbrook says sadly: "She was born with coal dust in her hair"—and he went down into the mines to organize. In the early Forties, the Party yanked him out of the mines and sent him East. He left his wife because she wouldn't leave West Virginia ("She could always get another husband," Ben Saltzman had said, "but there was only one Party"), and then he took another. In time he left her, too. He worked hard in the Party, but he brooded, he brooded on life. Some poetic uneasiness in him never left him, deepened his sense of socialism but made him a maverick Communist. In his forties, Holbrook read *Moby Dick*. Instantly, he says, he knew what the whale was, he knew it was death and, he says, "I'm no hero. I guess I can't throw a harpoon into a whale and leap upon that spear and go down with the whale. But I have a sense of it, I have a sense of it." And, somehow, in his mind, that "sense of it" is all mixed up with the inner search for his life his years in the Communist Party took him on, and with this brooding on life that is his most striking characteristic, this brooding that led him ultimately to his deepest insight about the Party, made him struggle for years with it, and forced him finally to leave.

"As time went on, I began to see that something was wrong in the Party. Just as I had seen that something was wrong with capitalism back in Kentucky when I was a boy. And, just as it had happened before, so now I wanted to know why. And, once again, that desire to know why became necessity. Finally, of course, I knew, and then there was no way not to know, and I had to go. The Party's understanding of Marx and of the revolution that we were working for involved—deeply—the tension between the individual and the collective. The Party never understood how vital this tension was, never paid attention to it. Over and over again, insistently, bullheadedly, deludedly, it sacrificed the individual to a false notion of the collective and its needs. The aberration of the individual advances the life of the collective. If that aberration is consistently destroyed the collective becomes arid, dead, dries up the life within it. And that is precisely what happened to us, what we did to ourselves. . . . But all that took a long time in the knowing, a much longer time than it had taken me to realize I was a socialist."

It took such a long time, Holbrook muses, because of the pull of connectedness. As he speaks now of the largeness of things, the connectedness of things, his face clouds over with a pain rich with memory. And he takes that search, that promise, that longing for connectedness right back to his American roots, to the Protestant-Puritan ethic and its teachings: "Why, when we were kids we learned 'There's only two on that road to Jericho, you and Jesus.' And there you had it, the problem of man and God, not just man alone rutting along in his isolated little place in this world. There were *two* of you, and those two together were the problem of making sense of it all, making it larger, richer, something to place yourselves in. . . . Well, in my adult life, nothing has spoken to that problem as much as the Communist Party did. And nothing, I don't think, ever will. And I think most of us feel that way, I think it's true for most of us. Let me tell you something, whenever you come across an old Communist you find something different, someone special, no matter how small that specialness is. Someone who is a little better able—or believes himself a little better able—to make sense of a tale told by an idiot.

"The Party gave me Marxism. For that I'll always be grateful. Why, hell yes, I'm still a Red. Redder than ever. I joined SDS. I've still got young comrades. I'm involved, I'm connected, I'm *there*. Capitalists?" Holbrook grins deeply. "I hate the motherfuckers. Imagine a country about to celebrate the fact of two hundred years without a revolution. Why, that's nothing to celebrate. That's something to put on mourning for. It isn't as if everything's been getting better and better. What the hell is there to celebrate?"

Those of the Middle Kingdom

WHILE it was indisputably true that thousands of people joined the Communist Party because they themselves were actually members of the disenfranchised working or subworking class, it was even truer that many more thousands joined because they felt themselves to be the spiritual and intellectual heirs of the disenfranchised. These people always reminded me of what the Chinese called "those of the Middle Kingdom"—meaning those who were motivated by conditions of the spirit rather than of class history. They were often the people who led the revolution wherever in the world it actually occurred, and who most often came to brilliant, deadly power in every Communist Party in the world: including the Communist Party USA. Mainly, they came from the educated middle class and were sensitized in individual and emotionally mysterious ways to Marxism and the Party. Many of them were intellectually or artistically gifted, and often the fate of their gifts is directly related to what Communism and the Communist Party meant in their lives.

In a large, plant-filled room in a wooden house on a small island in Puget Sound that faces directly across the water toward Seattle, a lanky, young-faced man with expressive humorous eyes comes walking toward me, one hand buried in the pocket of his olive-drab cotton trousers, the other outstretched in welcome. His face, his body, his gait have the unmistakable, irrevocable bearing of those born into the upper middle class; his handshake is strong and confident, his speech calm and educated. He motions me towards a daybed covered with a gaily colored Mexican blanket that reflects the comfortable, bohemian seediness of the entire room; he drops himself gracefully into a painted wicker chair opposite me; we begin to talk.

Mason Goode is sixty-two years old on this wet September day, and he is a long way from "home"; although, he says, in the last few years he has finally begun to feel that home is wherever he is. Goode, a man of physical grace and spiritual delicacy, was born with artistic gifts of his own into a talented, wealthy segment of American life. He could, he was told, become "anything." He became a Marxist and a professional revolutionary. He was a functionary of the Communist Party for eighteen years. In the McCarthy period his life was smashed to bits. He never really recovered from that terrible time, and for the past twenty years has lived in a strange kind of limbo here on Puget Sound with his wife, Dorothy, operating a commercial fishing boat.

From the beginning, Mason Goode is something special to me. As the man begins to speak, carefully, conscientiously, trying hard to reconstruct his childhood for me, I feel as though we are caught in a movie "dissolve," fading back into a re-creation of popular American history, a dream of glamor and the ironic juxtaposition of fabled Twenties wealth and equally fabled Thirties socialism. For Mason Goode is the son of a famous man, and the child of a famous time and place, and there is in the story of his childhood, young manhood, and political conversion a melancholy radiance, a compelling, ingathered sense of some very special moment in American life, somehow green and still, and at its center the golden children who were called to Marxism when a fullness of history filled the European and American continents exactly at the moment that entire history went smash.

Mason was born in 1912 to a father who had a talent for writing and a mother who was a great beauty; both parents were the children of cultivated, well-to-do, intensely assimilated German

Jewish families. By the time Mason was ten years old his father was rich, famous, and drunk. When he was twelve his father left home. When he was twenty his father was dead of suicidal alcoholism.

Mason's childhood is, in some senses, that of the poor little rich boy. There they were—the mother, Mason, the two younger sisters—rattling around in a twenty-room mansion in a wealthy New York suburb with the father coming home drunk, or two days late, or finally not at all. There were three cars in the circular driveway—one of them a Rolls—but often no money for gasoline. There were servants whose pay was often weeks late, buying groceries on credit, and holding the children tight while they wept secretly in the kitchen. The mother was absolutely childlike, absolutely self-absorbed. She withdrew into a chronic depression and became for the rest of her life a neurasthenic burden, weighing down the lives of her relatives.

Once the father had, rather brutally, established his permanent absence, he began to visit, and a curious thing happened inside the boy. Feeling desperate with abandonment, he became very nearly speechless, and his nights were riven with dreams so bad he would sit bolt upright in bed at three in the morning, sweating and terrified; he experienced such powerlessness he could not imagine his being had any affect on others at all. Yet, at the same time, he was drawn to his visiting father, and perceived with a kind of child-wisdom that he, too, was desperate. Living as he did on the confused edge of his father's sophisticated, literate world, Mason was nevertheless given glimpses of that world at times, and when he was it would come upon him that—despite the brilliance and the nonstop gaiety—there was a dreadful emptiness at the center of his father's life. Years later, of course, Mason realized that his father drank and made love as much as he did to appease the panic and hunger that emptiness induced in him, but at the time it was all happening he only knew that his father was confused and driven, and the boy was awash with love and pity for this glamorous man who *wanted* to be kind to his children, but was not.

One spring morning in 1927, when he was fifteen years old, Mason and his father were standing at their suburban station waiting for the train to New York. It was a beautiful morning, very clear and bright. Mason's father had had a good night's sleep and was feeling good. He was, as always, carefully and beautifully dressed. He whistled as he brushed some barely perceptible lint from his blue jacket and straightened the creases of his white flannel trousers. His shoes, he decided, needed polishing. He walked over to the shoeshine stand beside the station's waiting room. The man shining shoes was an Italian immigrant who was just about Mason's father's age. He wore a shirt rolled up at the sleeves and a pair of shiny black pants. His arms were strong and brown, his hands work-blackened. He worked quickly and well, and as he did a sudden sadness spread itself across the father's face. He turned to Mason and said softly: "Poor devil. I wonder what kind of a life he must lead." Before he could think, Mason said to himself: "*I* know what kind of a life he leads."

His father was always saying things like that, as though in anxious, mysterious wonderment that he himself had escaped, and how could anyone who hadn't *live*. Suddenly, Mason saw the great disparity between his father's discomforted liberalism and the reality of the suffering world made up of the small, the powerless, the disenfranchised. He realized with a shock that he felt wounded, deeply wounded for that other world. Mason knew in that moment that the Italian immigrant was more real to him than his father and, sensing the import of what was happening, he felt intense sorrow both for his father and for the Italian. He knew also that the quality of his sorrow was different for each of them.

In 1928 when it was time for Mason to go to college, he chose to attend Alexander Micklejohn's experimental college at the University of Wisconsin. Worried, confused, unhappy, knowing his father was drinking himself to death, the sixteen-year-old Mason went off to school, not really certain why he was going at all. The speechless boy had by now become an attractive, poised, but oddly detached young man. Not much seemed to touch him, or to matter very much. At the same time, he did not consider himself without feeling or desire or curiosity. Rather than inhibition it was as though some powerful confusion of life had produced a fatal hesitation in his soul, an unknowingness that made engagement prohibitive. He seemed always, in those days, to be listening, for what, exactly, he did not know; but it was as though he were listening for the sounds of his life: poised on the brink, waiting to begin. And all around him, he recalls, in that rich, ripe September of 1928, the world seemed to echo his own internal state of being: as though it, too, were listening, gathering itself together for some supreme effort, some transforming moment of clarity.

Micklejohn's school—which only lasted a few years—was an American experiment in the English university tradition: great books, Athenian humanism, seminars, tutorials. From the first, the atmosphere was heady and altogether wonderful to Mason. Young men of intellectual talent and erudite opinion seemed to converge in droves on Micklejohn's school. Mason began to read voraciously, with a sudden exploded need that took him by surprise. And to talk. To talk as though there were no tomorrow and everything must get said today, right now, this very minute. The talk at Micklejohn's was rich, constant, overflowing. Philosophy, religion, history, art, aesthetics, politics filled the talk of the intelligent, beautiful young men as they sat in seminar rooms, dining halls, bars, and lounges, walked across lawns, played tennis and swam, lit pipes, changed from white ducks to Harris tweeds. Ideas swam in Mason's head, but even more important than ideas themselves, the idea of ideas soaked through him. The idea of a large frame of reference—a context within which one placed one's own experience—that was what most amazed and gripped him. The "men of context" were people with theories, theories of art, of history, and above all, of politics. Here, for the first time Mason met men of varying political ideologies. He met libertarians, anarchists, socialists, syndicalists. And he met Communists.

At the very same time, Mason discovered that he was a talented painter. He had been drawing all his life, mainly in secret and to comfort himself during his lonely childhood. Now, at Micklejohn's, he put oil to canvas for the first time and experienced revelation. The world of space, color, and composition opened up to him and he began to move, like a child following a string into the labyrinth, toward this new world. But, as time went on he saw that painting did not claim his whole soul. He perceived—and it was a crucial perception—that painting did not make him feel less lonely; only the exciting talk of ideas made him feel less lonely, and at that, most particularly, talk of political ideas. He would not, he thought, give up painting. Only for now. . . .

In the spring of 1929 Jeremy Lewiton came to Micklejohn's,

and set Mason Goode on the course he was to follow for the next twenty-five years. Lewiton was a large-hearted, full-minded young man of richly expressive temperament. Lewiton was a Communist.

From the moment they met, the two young men cleaved to each other, becoming very quickly inseparable companions. Without question, Lewiton, the elder by six or seven years, was the teacher and Mason the pupil, but the power of stimulus and response that flowed between them like electric current produced a dynamic of self-discovery equally shared. For Mason, the beauty of being he felt in Jeremy Lewiton became inextricably bound up with Lewiton's Communism, and the emotional impact it made on him was formidable, alive and rich with promise. Even now, forty-five years later, as Mason Goode tells the story of his friendship with Lewiton, that impact can be felt. As Mason speaks, a picture forms itself in my mind. I see the two young men in late spring, standing on a lawn of intense and vivid green, dressed in white flannels, holding pipes whose fire is long dead and forgotten, talking swiftly, intently, oblivious to the afternoon's fading light, and at the center of the excited talk a stillness is gathering—Mason is listening, listening with an inner ear, and hearing, for the first time, the sounds of his life—a stillness like that in the eye of the storm, a clarifying stillness gathering in Mason and Lewiton, in the town, in the country, in the Western world (within the year there will be Depression, within the decade fascism and world war and the reactive explosion of socialism that will mark millions of lives forever). This image of white flannels, green lawns, that powerful rich young stillness, a moment in American life when a certain spiritual-political clarity could sink into a man like Mason Goode fills my mind. For it was here that Mason Goode began to *feel* socialism and his conviction, grown full then, that capitalism was immoral and socialism moral, would last a lifetime.

Seven years later Jeremy Lewiton would be dead in Spain and Mason Goode would be a branch organizer in New York for the Communist Party. The years that followed were, for Mason, often filled with irresolution and conflict but the memory of Lewiton as the prototypic, idealistic Communist held sway over him, and the largeness of promise, the beauty of being that had been Lewiton's Communism, would not run its course for another twenty years.

There were many like Mason Goode who, in the Twenties and Thirties, seemed to stir as though in a spirit-dream toward Marxism. Possessed of talent, education, economic freedom, they nevertheless experienced profound spiritual disconnection. Marxism touched—and healed—that wound in the soul, and made them Communists. Arthur Chessler was one of these people.

Arthur Chessler is sixty-nine years old. A man of slender build with an impressive, leonine head covered with a thick mat of iron-grey hair and the face and mien of an intellectual, Chessler leans back in his book-lined Greenwich Village living room on a hot July evening, knocks the ashes from his pipe into a brass spittoon beside his chair, and says quietly: "It wasn't Depression or starvation that made me a Communist. It was the excitement of the times. A new world was coming—and I wanted to be part of it." This statement will prove to be remarkable before the evening is over in a number of ways, not the least of which is its emotional directness.

Arthur Chessler was state chairman of the Communist Party in one of the New England states for twenty-three years. A thoughtful, amiable, intelligent man, he is renowned in Party circles for his long years of gentle rule, the often discomforted decency with which he attempted on innumerable occasions to intervene between a Party member's "transgression" and swift Central Committee retribution. Nevertheless, a number of years after he had left the Party, Chessler wrote a book about his life in the CP which, while it stopped short of renunciation, put him in the camp of the anti-Communist Communists. The tone of the book was more-in-sorrow-than-in-anger (a tone that perfectly matches the gentleness of Chessler's personality) but, essentially, the book said, "How could we have done these things?" rather than "This is why we did these things."

When I read Chessler's book I was struck by its failure to come alive emotionally, and I remember saying to myself: "Well, the man is not a writer, he doesn't have the ability to transfer to the page the living sense of what took place." But, now as I sit talking with Chessler, urging emotional remembrance upon him with my questions, I see how difficult it is for him, in the flesh, to communicate the sense of his life. It's not that he doesn't want to, he *does* want to. It's almost as though he can't. He demonstrates remarkable difficulty in speaking "personally"; right here before my eyes he seems to be trying to retrain the process of emotional response, as though this kind of reflectiveness has been foreign to him almost all of his sixty-nine years. Clearly, he *wants* to speak (or, significantly, as he puts it, he wants to be "helpful" to me), but he seems literally unable to do so. Every now and then he delivers what he considers a really "personal" piece of information to me and then beams in triumph at me. In actuality, what he has given me is the kind of sentence that appears in the biography on a book jacket.

Arthur Chessler is neither the first nor the last Communist I will meet who, ask him a political question and he comes to instant, vibrant life, ask him a question having to do with his own feelings or emotional experience and he draws a painful, quizzical blank. Sad, ironic. Men like Chessler came of age in a time when his kind of wraparound political response was the mark of a serious person; as Communists, particularly, they sneered at any other kind of response to human experience, calling all else "bohemian." Now, they are bewilderedly beaten about the head by their wives, their children, their younger associates who are being formed and reformed by the social conviction that human relations, knowledge of "self-realization," and psychoanalytic savvy are the hallmark of a serious person. So many old Communists like Chessler have that hunted, confused look about them as they open their old, animated, Marxist mouths to speak and their words are greeted with impatient glares or embarrassed silence. They look anxiously about them, mutely asking: "What'd I say? What'd I say?" But to such a question there is no answer forthcoming: at least none that can be "heard."

Thus, every *real* answer Chessler gives me, as opposed to his automatic Marxist answers, is the result of much prodding on my part, many many question-statements, carefully framed, patiently reiterated. With all that, however, Chessler offers up one of the most interesting "details" about how men like him became Communists in the Nineteen-Thirties.

Arthur Chessler was born in 1905 in New York City into a family of shopkeepers. His father was an intellectual Orthodox Jew whose religious sense was large rather than narrow, encompassing with vigor the social and political world around him. To Isaac Chessler, Jewish Law was a thing of beauty, radiant, absorbent, containing within it the possibility of all questions and answers, the framework for a world view. If you studied the Law fully, deeply, over a lifetime, you would find in it an explanation for all things human.

The large Chessler family (there were six children) was close, happy, mutually supportive, taking its cue from the glowing spirit of the father. What was absorbed, almost unconsciously, was the osmotic sense that one lived a serious life by thinking and feeling in context. The Law, in the Chessler home, produced freedom through discipline, happiness through sacrifice, a sense of self through the civilizing loss of the anarchic, lonely self.

Arthur was that golden child, the adored firstborn. His responsive intelligence was a treasure to his family, something to be held in trust, nurtured and developed as part of the only real human wealth the Chesslers possessed. When there was money for nothing else there was money for Arthur's education. He responded to such loving care by doing very well. He was sent to Brown University, where he performed brilliantly, and then he entered Harvard Law School, at a time when it was almost unheard of that people of his background should attend Harvard.

By the time he got out of Harvard—in 1931—Arthur had already been long removed from the sphere of his family's influence. He had entered the larger world and begun to feel—with sharp reactiveness—the subterranean currents of that world moving through him. He responded to the Nineteen Twenties fully, recklessly; an abandoned semibohemian, semi-intellectual sense of life that would have horrified his father seized him; he drank, he experienced sexual promiscuity, he drove fast, read modern poetry, cut classes, and was exhilarated by the feeling soaking through him that there was nothing and no one in the world but himself, and there was no tomorrow, only an incandescent today.

The stock market crash of 1929 began, for him, as for count-less others, a stunning descent from this remarkable "high"; an uneasy sense of retribution began to permeate his being. He felt as though he, and the entire country, were living out a biblical parable. Slowly, the "hedonism" that had taken hold of him began to evaporate and in its place there appeared an arid, wasted sense of things.

He returned to New York and began to practice law, a law so unlike that other Law, a law he daily felt tempted to break him-self. It was 1931, all around him stun and misery, all around him the sounds of a new language beginning to push against the inter-nal silence he now lived intimately with. The language was Marx-ism. Bit by bit, the language overtook the waste, bit by bit the hun-gry mind and soul turned away from the passivity of depression and faced toward the activating renewal of fresh understanding. Arthur had a friend, Ralph Bernstein, a lawyer like himself, whose state of mind reflected his own. Together, they began to read Marx; together, they began to ponder the meaning of their lives.

In 1933, Arthur and Ralph left home to think things through. They gave up their law practices, left New York, and began an extraordinary *Wanderjahr* through America—to decide whether or not they should become Communists. Arthur's description of that year is the most compelling feature of his entire story. He doesn't know it, but what he's describing is a duplicate of the mystic-poetic-spiritual journey across China that Mao Tse-tung took in order to decide whether or not *he* should become a Com-munist; and as Arthur talks, visibly struggling—under the pressure of my nonstop "And then what?"—to recapture the felt memory of that crucial year, I experience with a thrill the loss and now momentary recapture of the imaginative faculty that once lived in Arthur Chessler and which forty years of Marxist jargon have effectively killed off. He describes the discovery of America by these two New York Jewish intellectual lawyers during an his-toric moment of wounded, open, vulnerable life, a moment when the Protestant guard against two such abberant Americans was profoundly down, and the sense of the country washed through them, binding them to the nation as no other experience ever had. Simultaneously, they felt purposeful self-discovery moving through themselves. They associated this newfound sense of self to the life of the nation, and the whole of it was filtered through the prism of Marxist thought, so that by the end of 1933, having reached the Western coast, they had become convinced that, out of love for America, they must join the Communist Party.

Arthur and Ralph returned to New York and in the spring of 1934 joined the CP. Within a year of their joining they had both become Party functionaries; from that moment until they both left the Party in 1958, they did not waver in their devotion to that set of spiritual-political decisions that had been made in the deepest part of themselves during their journey of discovery in 1933. For Arthur, the spiritual meaning of joining the CP was particularly acute: he had found once again the context he had lost on the day he left his father's house.

The Thirties. The Depression. The Great Depression. Reams have been written about that quintessential experience in American life. Nearly every American writer who lived through it has used the Depression, in one mythic sense or another, to say something important about what it is to be human and what it is to be American. Ordinary people have written, almost with religious awe, of the wondrous despair through which they lived in the 1930s. Other, not so ordinary people have written of the equally wondrous spiritual exhilaration they experienced during the Thirties. After the Second World War, a French resistance fighter wrote: "We were never so free as during the Occupation." Thirty years later an American intellectual paraphrased the Frenchman and said: "We were never so free as during the Depression." The time was all things to all men and women. Certainly, it was profoundly crucial to the making of many Communists. The Depression was for many of them the clarifying experience, imprinting upon them in lines of fire memories of comradeship that became the rooted source of their political passion.

For Marian Moran the experience of the Thirties was certainly such an influence—unforgettable and life-determining. What happened to Marian Moran in the Thirties in the United States is what happened to George Orwell in the Thirties in Spain. For a single moment socialism came to felt life, for a single moment they each felt themselves at one with all other men and women in the world; the living meaning of a classless society—void of privilege and unequal power, alive with genuine comradeship—sank into them and changed each of them, influencing thought and action for the rest of their lives. Ironically, the experience made of Orwell a passionate anti-Communist—in the name of that experience he could not forgive the Soviets their transgressions—while it made of Marian Moran a passionate Communist—in the name of that same experience she could forgive the Soviets anything.

Marian Moran at sixty-two is a beautiful woman; at thirty-two she must have been breathtaking. A goodly part of her beauty lies in the life and character that emanates from her physical person and surroundings. Slim and graceful, a cloud of grey-blonde hair atop her small head, deep-set grey-blue eyes, aristocratic nose and mouth, she smokes cigarillos, wears work shirts and corduroy trousers, drinks coffee from a cracked mug, speaks in a cigarette-husky voice rich with humor, intelligence, and suggestiveness, and lives in a bad neighborhood in Los Angeles in a two-room cottage whose floors are sagging from the weight of the 2,000 books that line its walls and doorways and overflow onto its Salvation Army furniture. (She waves her hand toward her books and says, "They're all I own in the world. It's either them or welfare.")

Marian Moran was for twenty-five years state chairman of the Communist Party in one of the large Western states. In the 1940s she was already a member of the Party leadership and was one of those who were under indictment for seven years (that is, she spent six months in prison, and lived for seven years believing she would spend five years more in prison). Although more than 2,000 Communists went underground in those years—as the entire Communist Party leadership believed that fascism was coming to America and they would all be killed, exiled, or imprisoned—for Marian, and those like her, there was no going underground. They *were* the Party; whatever was coming for the Communist Party USA would have to come to them.

In 1956, a week before the results of the Soviet 20th Congress were made public, a meeting was called in New York and Khrushchev's de-Stalinization speech was read to the Party leadership. Of that meeting Marian says: "He began to speak at seven o'clock. At eight I began to cry. I sat there, silently weeping, until eleven o'clock. Then I took a plane back to California to tell my people that we had made a great error in learning to depend upon anyone but ourselves."

Five years ago Marian left the Party over Czechoslovakia. As the American Communist Party was one of the very few in the world to remain blindly pro-Soviet on this—as it did on every other—issue, she felt at last that to struggle from within (as she had been trying to do since 1956) was entirely useless. She had come, she says, to the conclusion that "the Party is an obstruction to Communism."

The question to ask a woman like Marian Moran is not "Why did you leave?" but "Why did you stay so long?" Any honest answer to this question would, of necessity, have to include the sentences "I could not give up the power. I could not give up the structure. I could not walk away from the only identity I have ever had." But those sentences alone cannot explain Marian Moran and her overlong devotion to the CP. To see her, to listen to her, to know how beloved she is in radical Western circles, to feel the full weight of this woman's being, her remarkable internal balance, her strong sense of self is to feel oneself in the presence of a true religious struggling for visionary life in a rigid, frightened church. And when, after long hours of talk, you begin to get to the heart of that visionary life, that envisioned sense of being to which she has clung so fiercely through all these long, disintegrating years—against the judgment of intellect and conscience —you arrive at the Thirties and the great California farm labor strikes, which, in their surging intensity and noble hopelessness, resemble the Spanish Civil War probably more than any other single event in American radical life.

California farm labor: a national agony that seems to have been with us forever. There are young people in this country who have grown up never having eaten lettuce or grapes because Cesar Chavez's grape and lettuce pickers have been striking since they can remember. To many of their parents and grandparents, Chavez' strike is only the most recent effort in a fifty-year-old struggle to end the pain and humiliation of a segment of American labor that has, very nearly, assumed mythic proportions in the national consciousness.

"The history of California [farm] labor," wrote Carey

McWilliams in *Factories in the Field* in 1939, "is the history of industrialized agriculture. . . . Why the valleys are made up of large feudal empires, why farming has been replaced by industrial agriculture, the farm by the farm factory, to realize what is behind the terror and violence which breaks out periodically in the farm valleys [one must] know something of the social history of California."

And then McWilliams went on to explain: "Nearly seventy years of exploitation of minority, racial and other groups by a powerful clique of landowners whose power is based upon an anachronistic system of landownership dating from the creation, during Spanish rule, of feudalistic patterns of ownership and control. The most remarkable single circumstance pertaining to the entire record is the unbroken continuity of control. The exploitation of farm labor in California, which is one of the ugliest chapters in the history of American industry, is as old as the system of land ownership of which it is a part. Time has merely tightened the system of ownership and control and furthered the degradation of farm labor."

Between 1929 and 1935 a series of spectacular strikes broke out among laborers in the California farm valleys. As McWilliams wrote: "Never before had farm laborers organized on any such scale and never before had they conducted strikes of such magnitude and such far-reaching social consequence." In a time of common desperation the desperation of the farm laborers had reached an unbearable pitch. Repeatedly, rhythmically, explosively the strikes went on and on, gathering speed, force, and numbers. One was stifled and two broke out; fifty people were jailed and a hundred took their places; men were shot on the picket lines and wives and children were soon standing where the men had fallen. The farm laborers had become, seemingly overnight, what human beings become when they are ready to die rather than go on living as they have lived: a unified people, steel snaking down through their souls, dry-eyed fury filling their faces, a power of organized defiance. Thousands of that vast, ragged army of America's most disinherited workers surged onto the picket lines, transformed from enduring silents into striking workers, sustaining and urging each other on with the raw eloquence that comes to those whose social sense of self is sudden, direct, overwhelming. And sustain each other they surely needed to do, for the terror and violence that accompanied the farm valley strikes was almost unimaginable. Strike leaders were beaten, jailed, and killed. The towns, owned by the farm combines, were filled with armed vigilantes. The press, the clergy, and the courts were unified in their outrage against the farm workers. It was years and years of wholesale arrests, scares, beatings, and killings.

Journalists from all over the country came to observe the California strikes. Some of them were moved by what they saw and became partisans of the workers. One of them, Orrick Johns, wrote: "Looking over those halls of swarthy men and women, I saw faces that reminded me of the ruined faces of Michelangelo's Day of Judgement. . . . They were a desperate and courageous people, compelled to exist as primitively as the aboriginal Indians, and asking little. . . ."

How had it all happened? Who had put the iron in the souls of the isolated farm workers? Who had organized them? The A.F. of L. wouldn't go near them. An official of that conservative union said: "Only fanatics are willing to live in shacks or tents and get their heads broken in the interests of migratory labor."

Those fanatics were the Communists. It was the California Communists who, following the spontaneous outbreak of farm labor strikes, organized and sustained the workers throughout six bloody years of labor warfare. It was their skill, energy, and passion that infused the migratory workers with a nearly inexhaustible will to go on fighting. Hundreds of Communists were among those beaten, jailed, and killed. They organized under almost every conceivable condition, sometimes working in near isolation, but almost always to real effect; (in October of 1933 four CP organizers brought 18,000 cotton pickers out on strike up and down the 114-mile length of the San Joaquin Valley).

Many communists were made Communists during those eloquent times. Marian Moran was one of them. Although Marian had been born into the movement—her parents were intellectual California radicals—and had been in the YCL since the age of fourteen, it was the farm labor strikes of the Thirties that made her a Communist. In 1930 the fruit pickers of the Imperial Valley went out on strike, and the Party sent Marian down to join the strikers and help organize them. She was eighteen years old. She had gone down to the valley expecting to stay only a few months. She stayed for four years. When the Party wanted her to go to San Francisco and organize intellectuals she refused, she would not leave the fruit pickers.

What happened to her during those four years was what happened to thousands of people—in a dozen different places, under a dozen different but parallel kinds of circumstance—during the Thirties. She experienced "being and becoming" in a state of class-conscious classlessness. She experienced what Orwell and countless others had experienced in Spain, and it was as unforgettable for her as it was for them.

"The years with the fruit pickers became a world within the world," Marian says, "a microcosm of feelings that never left me, not even when I left them. I lived with the pickers, ate, slept, and got drunk with them. I helped bury their men and deliver their babies. We laughed, cried, and talked endlessly into the night together. And, slowly, some extraordinary interchange began to take place between us. I taught them how to read, and they taught me how to think. I taught them how to organize, and they taught me how to lead. I saw things happening to people I'd never seen before. I saw them *becoming* as they never dreamed they could become. Day by day people were developing, transforming, communicating inarticulate dreams, discovering a force of being in themselves. Desires, skills, capacities they didn't know they had blossomed under the pressure of active struggle. And the sweetness, the generosity, the pure comradeship that came flowing out of them as they began to feel themselves! They were—there's no other word for it—noble. Powerful in struggle, no longer sluggish with depression, they became inventive, alive, democratic, filled with an instinctive sense of responsibility for each other. And we were all like that, all of us, the spirit touched all of us. It was my dream of socialism come to life. I saw then what it could be like, what people could always be like, how good the earth and all the things upon it could be, how sweet to be alive and to feel yourself in everyone else.

"You know," Marian continues, taking a swig of coffee so that she can wet her throat so that she can take another drag of her cigarillo, "I'm enough of a woman so that I sit here sometimes, thinking it all over, sort of dreaming my life back into existence, saying to myself, 'Which were the best, the very best times?' I've had three husbands, slept with more men than I can count, borne children, had political power, and known the incomparable thrill of hearing ten thousand people cheer when I spoke. But I tell you, those years with the fruit pickers were the very best years of my life. Nothing since has even remotely touched them. No love affair, no Party power, nothing can compare with what I felt then among those people during that time of struggle. I don't know, in the end maybe that's what makes the difference between Communists and other people. Of all the emotions I've known in life, nothing compares with the emotion of total comradeship I knew among the fruit pickers in the Thirties, nothing else has ever made me feel as alive, as coherent. It was for that, for the memory of that time, that I hung on. For that I lived with the narrowness and the stupidity of the Party. For that I fought. It's what socialism was all about for me. The great sweep of Marxist revolution had that image-memory of the Thirties woven into its fabric; that fabric wrapped itself around the dailiness of political life, Party life; when the twists and turns of that daily life grew confusing you pulled that fabric closer around you, felt its warmth coursing through you, and you said to yourself: '*This* is what I am.' "

Abruptly, she stops talking. Neither of us speaks for a long moment. Then: "That's not exactly true, is it?" Marian says softly. "The dailiness is what you are, and there is always the danger that you will become what you are . . . isn't there?"

Being and becoming. At the heart of the Communist experience always the question of being and becoming. On the surface that question often seems posed against contradictory circumstances— so many different lives, so many apparently different notions of what it is to be, what it is to become—but beneath the surface there is no contradiction, things tend always toward an overriding likeness of inner circumstance.

Diana Michaels is a Philadelphia lawyer. An energetic, fast-moving, fast-responding woman of fifty-four, Diana seems as though she's been steeped in her profession all of her adult life. In fact, she's been practicing law only for the past nine years. Between the ages of eighteen and thirty-six she was a member of the Communist Party and, while she did many things during that period to earn a living, her profession was that of being a Communist.

Diana Michaels is a strikingly attractive woman who exudes an air of expensive glamor. The two major characteristics of her physical appearance are her thick, lustrous, dark hair worn in the helmet-like style affected by Marlene Dietrich in the Thirties, and her long, nylon-smooth legs. Her face is carefully made up and her clothes are elegant: classically chic with only an accessoried touch of current fashion. Her eyes are clever, humorous, observant; her mannerisms are vain, self-conscious, self-absorbed. I wait to hear the story that will illuminate these odd juxtapositions of character.

Diana moves out from behind her desk on this late June afternoon and, gracefully pushing her fingers through her hair, walks across a short stretch of grey carpeted floor toward a mahogany cabinet. She opens the doors that reveal a bar and small refrigerator and, reaching for a bottle of gin, says: "I need a drink for this. How about you?" I nod. Diana fixes herself a gin and lemon twist on ice and me a scotch on ice. She hands me my drink, takes her own, drops into the depths of the blue-grey velvet couch opposite her desk and motions me into the Eames chair beside the couch.

"Well," she sighs, "what can I tell you? The whole story is right here in my office. All this," she waves her hand through the air, clearly indicating the sleek, expensive look of the room and her own person as well. "If I hadn't been a Communist," she giggles suddenly, "it would all be worse, much worse."

Diana was born in 1920 in Philadelphia. Her father had graduated as an engineer from the University of Pennsylvania and her mother had been "the most beautiful girl in Philadelphia." The father had married the mother for her beauty and the mother had married the father because his education conferred status on her. Almost from the beginning, they realized they had made a terrible mistake, and they were bound together in a union that was not only loveless but without compatability of any kind. The father's life spread in waves of disappointment all about him: not only could he not get work as an engineer because he was a Jew but he was locked up with a stupid, insensitive woman as well. He retreated into bitter aloofness and became cruel and despotic towards his family. The mother, filled with confusion and self-pity, retreated into the only values she had ever known: social-climbing, pretentions of gentility and the patrician arrogance of "good taste."

"Good taste," Diana says grimly. "She was ignorant as hell and her life with my father was despicable, but she had good taste. Her good taste became a standard, surrounded by terror and longing, something like the Holy Grail: it was out there, we must search diligently for it, but we knew—my two sisters and I— that we could never reach it, never measure up to my mother's impeccable sense of it. But oh, how we longed for it! She made us allies in her war against my father by instilling in our un-formed little souls her pathetic values.

"When I was thirteen or fourteen I suddenly began to read books. I realized quickly how ridiculous my mother was, how dreadful her measuring rod for human worth. And the war inside me began. My mother would say to me, 'Diana, you're pretty, intelligent, you'll marry a rich boy. You won't make my mis-takes.' I hated my father, but her words made me freeze. She'd say to me, 'Diana, why don't you bring Lillian Bergstein home, she's such a nice girl.' 'She's dumb,' I'd say. 'Her father makes thirty thousand dollars a year, how dumb can she be?' she'd say. I'd turn away, lock myself in my room, and read for hours. Until my mother knocked on the door to tell me to stop reading, I'd develop a squint and ruin my looks. Miserable, confused, isolated, locked up inside myself. The thing was, I already *was* my mother to some extent, you see. Preoccupied with clothes, looks, money, good taste. Couldn't help responding when I felt the full weight of my mother's patrician approval or disapproval over the way I— or anybody else—looked. But I hated myself for it. I knew there were better things in the world to care about, I knew people's souls were more important than their clothes. But I could not pre-vent myself from responding anyway.

"When I was seventeen years old I discovered the YCL and a whole new world opened up for me. The people in the YCL were the opposite of everything my mother knew or wanted of the world. They were brilliant, idealistic, committed to a passionate view of revolution. They wore the foulest-looking clothes and they read constantly. They were balm to my divided young spirit. And don't forget, this was 1937. No sooner did I hear them talking than I knew they were the world, the *real* world. Everything in me came together. I joined them, and I fled the house." Diana tucks her long legs underneath her and laughs. "Some girls marry to get out of their stinking houses. I became a Communist to get out of mine.

"At eighteen I went off to school. The University of Wisconsin. I think practically the first thing I did in Madison after I checked into the dorm was to join the Communist Party. In 1938, on every college campus in America, it was easier to join the Party than it was to join a posh sorority, and at Wisconsin, well, the best and the brightest were in the CP.

"At Wisconsin the twin influences at work in me ran neck and neck for a long while. On the one hand, I was involved in being smartly dressed, madly flirtatious, collecting marriage proposals like shrunken heads. On the other hand, I was a serious political person, giving an enormous number of hours a week to Party work. (I was no good at what the Party called 'leadership,' but I was terrific at Jimmy Higgins work. The Party needed to organize a conference or a demonstration? I did it. They needed five thousand leaflets by morning? If I didn't do it myself, I could dig up the person who would do it. Fifty people were needed to applaud a certain speaker? I delivered the fifty people.) My education, needless to say, was something I attended to in my spare time.

"Bit by bit the Party gained ascendancy over my conflicted predilections. The Party people were the brightest, the most serious, the most moral people I knew and yes, they made me bright, serious, and moral. God! I remember once I worked in a department store. The people I worked with used to come in early and steal display materials or salesbooks or pens and pencils from each other's departments. I was scandalized. The Party had taught me the simplest of moralities. I was a moral human being as a Party member as these poor benighted laboring fools were not.

"None of us considered the work we did on the 'outside' important. Because, after all, we knew it didn't matter what you did out there. You were living in a bourgeois capitalist world where everything was shit, everything fed a single purpose, so what did it matter what you did? Your real life was with the Party, with your comrades, with the things you did at meetings and demonstrations. It never occurred to us that there was any reality to a particular field, or discipline, or the idea of 'making something of yourself,' or developing your special talents. . . . We lived in another world, a world in which you worked and waited for the revolution.

"There were sacrifices, though. At least for me. Often, I'd meet men on the 'outside,' and I'd be attracted to them. Attracted suddenly to that simple, comfortable world they seemed to come from. But I knew I could never go out with them. I knew I'd have to explain my life to them and I couldn't do that. I'd have to let them go. They'd say, 'Why can't you go out with me?' and I couldn't answer.

"In my senior year at Wisconsin I married a Party intellectual. We came back East together, and we worked for the Party for ten years. And then one day, oh, it must have been Nineteen-Fifty or Fifty-One, it was suddenly all over for me."

"How was that?" I ask lightly, trying to conceal my surprise.

"Oh," Diana says, and she stretches her arms and unwinds her legs, "I don't know." She gives me a level stare and says: "One day I read a piece in the *Daily Worker* denouncing psychoanalysis and I said to myself, 'This is foolish.' And suddenly," Diana's voice softens, "that was it.

"But I couldn't get out for another five or six years. McCarthy wouldn't let me go." She laughs. "You see, what happened here in the Fifties was incredible. It wasn't just the *Commentary* types who went berserk. It was everybody, everybody I'd ever known. You'd be at a dinner party and suddenly the person on your right was very carefully, and from out of left field, going to great lengths to let you know that he was an anti-Communist. It was unreal. People who five years before would have been either neutral or sympathizers were suddenly finding a new identity in anti-Communism. . . . I couldn't leave the Party under those circumstances. No, I just couldn't go then. It took the 20th Congress to blast me out, to tell me in no uncertain terms that times had changed, life had changed, I had changed, the Party, for me, had changed."

Diana rises from the couch and walks across the room to pour herself another drink. She stands in silence with her back to me. Then she turns around, leans against the mahogany bar, and says: "I was vain, shallow, pretty, and energetic. Mad for sexual success and popularity, and yes, secretly wanting bourgeois comfort and bourgeois success. But," her head goes back, the dark helmet-like hair swinging out in a graceful, defiant arc, "I was a Communist. And being a Communist made me better than I was. It was the great moral adventure of my life. I wouldn't—not then, not now—have traded it for anything. There's been nothing else in my life of which I can say that."

CHAPTER THREE

Living It Out:
From Vision to Dogma
and Halfway Back

To BECOME a Communist was one thing, to remain a Communist was quite another. What—both in its parts and in its wholeness—did that other, second thing consist of? How did American Communists who remained Communists "live it out"?

Mainly, it is the experience of *being* a Communist that has been written of in monolithic terms, terms that level and homogenize. The image that is created by these terms is one of a group of men and women sitting in a smoke-filled room, drugged with Marxist-Leninist jargon, supported by Moscow gold, obeying Kremlin directives, densely making anti-American, pro-Soviet policy.

For most Communists it was not even remotely that way, and

for all Communists being a Communist was as varied an experience as the initial conversion to Communism had been.

There were those who rose quickly in the ranks of the Party to become functionaries at middling and high levels and who were, indeed, some or all of the time privy to the major policy-making processes of the Party. There were those whose knowledge of policy-making never went higher than that of the branch (the lowest organizational unit of the Party) to which they belonged or the section (the next highest organizational unit) to which they belonged. There were those who experienced the Party as a neighborhood club, those who experienced it as an extension of their working day, those who saw themselves as foot soldiers in the army of the revolution, and those who felt themselves akin to heads of state, with the burdens of the world upon their shoulders.

Many Communists gave themselves instantly and completely to the structured authority of the Party; like Mason Goode's Illinois fundamentalist wife, Dorothy, who said: "I had been a devout Christian and now I was a devout Communist. I have always responded to structured authority in this way, once the idea behind the authority seemed absolutely right to me." Many others anguished over the structured authority of the Party; like Mason Goode himself, whose distaste for the authoritarianism of the Party plagued him throughout his life as a Communist.

For thousands of Communists, being a Communist remained as nourishing an experience as becoming a Communist had been. For thousands of others, it became a bitterness of vision evaporating into dogma: the growing self disintegrating into the stifled self. The former experienced the wholeness of the CP world as a transcendent source of personal integration, the latter experienced that same wholeness as a mental prison within which their own development languished, arrested.

What *was* true for all of them was that being a Communist defined them in a way that is almost impossible to understand today. It was *the* overriding element of identity, the one which subsumed all others.

Today, the question "Who are you?" is a euphemism for "What do you do?", and it is generally answered with "lawyer, academic, therapist, editor, electrician." These replies are considered defining answers: they tell people who you are, and what you are is then assumed. The Communists lived in a world in which the work they did on the "outside" was largely ignored, and "What kind of a Communist are you?" was the defining question.

This question, of course, produced a vicious tyranny of its own —a tyranny that fed all the abuses inherent in the system of "democratic centralism"—and there are many, many Communists who remember with fear and self-loathing the cruelties both inflicted and received in the name of "What kind of a Communist are you, comrade?"

Still, it is even truer that, for the most part, Communists remember the credo very much as Orwell remembers Spain: as characteristic of a time and a place when men and women experienced genuine comradeship, and were equalized by the deeper socialist definition of value and being; an experience closely parallel to that of the pioneer societies in which work loses the hierarchical value towards which all middle-class societies tend, and becomes subordinate to the fact that all work has the same value—i.e., that it is being done in the service of the new society, the one being built, the one to come. I think it is safe to say that for most Communists this sense of things dominated "living it out."

The Ordinariness of Daily Activity and the Revolution Around the Corner

"IDEALS," wrote Theodore Draper, "play little part in the day by day organizational drudgeries, political maneuvers, and struggles for power. Yet the eternally frustrated pursuit of the ideal gives revolutionary movements a special dimension. . . . Without it, much that is tragic would merely be sordid."

What is striking about the common experience of most Communists is the ordinariness of their daily Party activities coupled with what Draper calls the "eternally frustrated pursuit of the ideal." For thousands of Communists, being a Communist meant years of selling the *Daily Worker*, running off mimeographed leaflets, speaking on streetcorners, canvassing door-to-door for local and national votes, organizing neighborhood groups for tenants' rights or welfare rights or unemployment benefits, raising money for the Party or for legal defenses or bail bonds or union struggles. Only that and nothing more. They never set foot inside Communist Party headquarters, they never laid eyes on a Central Committee member, they were never present at a major Party meeting or convention. Yet, all of this grinding ordinariness was fed and nourished, offset and borne by the continually resuscitated vision of the Marxist ideal: the bonds of comradeship and the "revolution around the corner."

Sarah Gordon clutches her head and moans: "My God! How I hated selling the *Worker*! I used to stand in front of the neighborhood movie on a Saturday night with sickness and terror in my heart, thrusting the paper at people who'd turn away from me or push me or even spit in my face. I dreaded it. Every week of my life for years I dreaded Saturday night. And then canvassing! Another horror. A lady would shut the door in my face before I'd gotten three words out—and if she was a socialist she'd *slam* the door—and I'd stand there sick. I'd tell myself a thousand times: It's not *your* face she's shutting out. . . . God, I felt annihilated. But I did it, I did it. I did it because if I didn't do it, I couldn't face my comrades the next day. And we all did it for the same reason: we were accountable to each other. It was each other we'd be betraying if we didn't push down the gagging and go do it. You know, people never understand that. They say to us, 'The Communist Party held a whip over you.' They don't understand. The whip was inside each of us, we held it over ourselves, not over each other."

For countless people, ringing doorbells or handing out the *Worker* was an agony but, as Sarah says, the Party and all the people in it had become a source of moral accounting to each of them. Sarah, during her years in the Party, would have done anything that was demanded of her—up to and including going to jail—because not to have done so would have been to become a pariah in her own eyes. The same was true for Ben Saltzman and Selma Gardinsky and Diana Michaels, as well as Jim Holbrook and Paul Levinson and Mason Goode.

Beyond and connected up with the moral accounting lay the incredibly concrete vision of "the revolution around the corner" most Communists carried within themselves during the Thirties and Forties. Selma Gardinsky describes how when she first joined the Party in New York, the leader of her branch took her for a walk one day around New York's Central Park. "Do you see those fancy, beautiful houses?" he demanded, waving his hand in the direction of Central Park West. "Workers built them with their blood and bones," he railed, "but do workers live in them? No!" But, the branch organizer assured Selma, the revolution would correct all this. "When?" Selma asked. "In ten years," the organizer replied calmly. Years later, Selma adds, she met this same organizer in Washington at a demonstration to save the Rosenbergs. "It's been a long ten years," Selma said.

Blossom Sheed tells a similar story about a well-known Left lawyer who in a court case during the Thirties said nonchalantly in court: "Everyone knows the revolution is around the corner." During a recess someone from the Party said to the lawyer: "That was an error. We never say that." The lawyer went back into court and said: "Ladies and gentlemen, I was in error this morning. I said the revolution was just around the corner. The revolution probably won't come for another ten years."

But he didn't really believe that. He believed the revolution was around the corner. And most Communists did. The sense of political time was so urgent people could taste it in their mouths. Fascism abroad, the New Deal at home, socialism surging up all over the world, Edgar Snow coming back from China, announcing, "There, too!" Every twenty-four hours seemed to send the pulse of the world racing toward Marxist revolution. The worse things got in Europe, the better it seemed for imminent socialist explosion. . . .

And the wholeness of the CP world was so complete, so deeply felt, that it was impossible not to believe it capable of making the revolution not in some unforeseeable future but right now, today, tomorrow, certainly within one's own lifetime. That wholeness: its depth, its dimension, its utter circularity are almost impossible to describe. Very nearly, one had to have lived through it to understand its holding powers.

The Wholeness of the CP World

DINA Shapiro is a seventy-year-old dressmaker in the Los Angeles garment district. She lives in Hollywood in an aquamarine-colored apartment house with a tiled interior courtyard in which three sad palm trees are planted. The southern California sun glints off Dina's glasses and off the needle that flashes in her deformed fingers as she hems the skirt lying in her lap while we sit, drinking tea, at a small table covered with a plastic cloth made to look like lace and set before a window that looks out onto a parking lot.

"You think I sew because I want to?" Dina asks, and shrugs her shoulders in a Yiddish reply to her own question. "I sew because if I didn't the arthritis would cripple me altogether. I must keep my hands in motion, otherwise they become frozen. Then not only are they useless, but the pain is something terrible."

I look at her, thinking: Dina, you could substitute the words "loss of Communism" for "arthritis" and it would go a long way toward explaining your life.

Except for the arthritic fingers, Dina Shapiro looks fifteen years younger than her seventy years. Her body is slim and graceful, her short thick hair grey-black, her step strong, and her voice clear and lively. Dina is still an active member of her union, a vigorous community worker, and a member of the Communist Party. She marched against Vietnam, she attended Angela Davis' trial daily, she boycotts lettuce, she presses the *People's World* on "sympathetic" strangers, and she will "explain" Hungary and Czechoslovakia to you at the drop of a hat, as well as the "divisive" character of the social revolution being waged by blacks, students, and women. (Social revolution, of course, is a phrase that will never cross her lips. "Anarchy," she sneers. "Anarchy, pure and simple.")

Dina Shapiro has been a Communist for forty years. She was a militant unionist in the dress factories of Chicago and was recruited into the Communist Party in 1934 by Earl Browder's brother. Dina, like Belle Rothman, was dynamite on her feet. When Dina talked 2,000 people crowded the union hall, and when she laid her hands on the machine the whole shop walked out.

The Party wanted to train Dina in organizational work, but she refused. "I wanted to remain a worker," she says, holding her head a bit higher. "I did not want to become a functionary."

Nevertheless, she did indeed become a Communist. "The Party was to me the holy of holies. Until I joined the Party I was a communist. Now, I was a Communist. Suddenly, I didn't feel free to simply speak for myself. I was now responsible to the Party: a representative. I felt that *weight* of responsibility."

How, exactly, did you feel that weight, Dina? Where? When? Under what conditions?

"Everywhere. Always. Under all conditions. You see, it wasn't a matter of *conditions*. The world in which we lived was the condition. The Communist Party was a condition. Being a Communist was a condition. Your life as a Communist was everywhere: in the shop, at home, at meetings, in the neighborhood. You were always being a Communist. There was never a time when you weren't a Communist. You were a Communist when you went to the store to buy a bottle of milk, when you went to a movie, attended a party or a meeting, voted in the shop, sewed up the last two dresses of the day for the woman at the next machine whose kid was sick, returned a dollar to a clerk who had shortchanged himself, sent an ignorant neighbor to a tenants' council when the landlord wanted to evict her . . . as well as when you went to Party meetings, carried out Party assignments, and obeyed or handed down Party directives. It was all one. The life was of a piece. There was nowhere in my life that I turned that I didn't know who and what I was. . . . Ah yes! *That* was a life.

"But," Dina grins, "have no fear. It will come again, it will come again. And meanwhile I take Lenin's advice: patience and irony. I hold on because I know it will come again."

For Arthur Chessler, too, it was the wholeness of their lives as Communists that is the compelling memory. Again and again, the former functionary who has so much difficulty "speaking personally" reiterates the inextricable mesh that was the Utopian Vision and the dailiness of life, love, friendship, interests, activity, and all-in-allness of life in the CP.

Chessler says the best, the very best times for him, occurred during the meetings he held regularly with a handful of ILGWU (International Ladies Garment Workers Union) Communists with whom he met and organized for years. Those meetings with the workers were the most alive, immediate, and binding in the sense of oneness they created.

"Of course," Arthur adds dryly, "it was something of an illusion, that sameness. After all, *I* didn't have to get up at seven o'clock the next morning and go to the shop. Still, there it was: Marxism alive and working right there in that room. It went through me every time, like adrenalin coursing through my veins. And I took it with me, everywhere. I took it into every other situation in my life, my marriage, my Party decisions, my intellectual discussions, my good times. It was alive inside me all the time, glittering. It was stronger than the Nazi-Soviet Pact, stronger than the Duclos letter, very nearly it was stronger than the 20th Congress Report. It threaded through everything, bound everything together, made a wholeness where otherwise there was only bits and pieces, fragmentation, isolation.

"People speak of that wholeness with a sneer. Koestler, finally, sneered at it. As though this wholeness was the evil—the proof of the closed system of Marxism—that made people give up their powers of independent judgment. Did it ever occur to any of them that maybe it means that the need for integration is, at the very least, as compelling as the need for intellectual freedom, and when those two needs clash it is a sorrowful day in the soul of a man or a woman who has sighted wholeness and felt it as an *instrument* of intellectual insight?"

Norma Raymond—as different from the dressmaker and the functionary as it is possible to be—eyes filled with an ironic smile, lips drawn together in a slightly tight line, nods ruefully at Arthur Chessler's words when they are repeated to her.

Norma Raymond, still beautiful at fifty-seven—dark eyes, dark hair, a marvelous laugh—was known as the Perle Mesta of the CP. Married to Charles Raymond, a Party journalist, Norma and her husband were for many years Party "stars." Intellectual, privileged, with a far-ranging circle of acquaintances, they spent the war years in Washington where Charles was correspondent for the *Worker*, and then afterwards came out to San Francisco, where he continued writing for the *People's World* (the Western equivalent of the *Worker*). Norma entertained lavishly, and the Raymond home was for nearly twenty years a Party salon. Norma had the best of it, the most independent of it, and also some of the real harshness of it. In 1952 Charles Raymond became "unavailable" —that is, he went underground. For three years he and Norma lived apart, meeting twice a year in an atmosphere of fear and anxiety. Now, when Norma speaks of that time she shakes her head in amazement and says: "Honestly, I will never understand how the Party came to such a decision. To send its middle ranks underground. Afterwards, we used to say it was as if someone in the Central Committee got hold of a Bulgarian plan *circa* 1919 for what to do when the fascists come after you and said: 'We'll use this.' "

Norma Raymond is one of those Communists (and there are quite a large number of them) who now says: "All our lives we were told and we believed that Communists were people dipped in a special mold. It just isn't true. There were lots of fine people outside doing many things in American life we simply couldn't see or admit to. After all this, here I am, a social worker, and the people I work with—none of them Communists—are certainly as good as I am or ever was."

For all that, her loyalty to her years in the CP is tenacious, and for the same reason as binds Dina Shapiro and Arthur Chessler: the memory of the wholeness of world she experienced as a Communist.

"All my life," Norma says, "from the time I was fifteen years old, the Party was an enormous support system which came through in every crisis, political and personal, with love and comradeship. The Party was always there for me, always ready to come to my rescue. When Charlie went underground, people in the Party brought everything from chicken soup to apartments to clothes for the children to airplane tickets to . . . you name it, they brought it. And even beyond that, beyond crisis, it was a total world, from the schools to which I sent my children to family mores to social life to the quality of our friendships to the doctor, the dentist, and the cleaner. There was an underpinning to everything in our lives that affected the entire variety of daily decision, reference, observation, everything! No one who didn't live through it can understand what it was like or why it was so hard to give up. People now long for community, they're dying for lack of it. Community can't be legislated. It's an organic sense of things that comes up out of the social earth. It's a commonly shared ideal. That's what it is. Nothing else will ever create community. And we had it. We had it in every conscious as well as unconscious response to ourselves, to each other, to the world we were living in, and the world we were making. Right, wrong, errors, blind pro-Sovietism, democratic centralism, the lot notwithstanding. In our lives, as Communists, we had community. We had integration. We had that civilizing sense of connectedness, it's the heart and soul of all civilized life. It wasn't just good wine in our veins, that life, it was ambrosia."

Inevitably, if one wishes to illustrate what that Communist Party wholeness in its detailed dailiness was once like, one is drawn back to a man like Eric Lanzetti. Lanzetti walking the streets of *his* Lower East Side in New York in 1938, *that* was the wholeness of the CP.

Eric Lanzetti, sixty-two the summer I met him, is a whirlwind of a man. Slim, medium-sized, with young dark eyes, a beautiful bald head, and a white spade beard, Lanzetti—an intellectual of the Left (writer of endless books, articles, and pamphlets) with the life-regenerating air of a Picasso, surrounded by women, children, grandchildren, children the age of the grandchildren—is a man capable of speaking at a passionate, infuriated pitch alive with facts, anecdotes, analyses, war stories about the Left and America that fill him with force and youth and compellingness.

Lanzetti is also one of those Marxists to whom my thesis—the passion at the heart of the Communist experience—is anathema, smacking of reactionary frivolity. But rather than abuse or dismiss me, he has chosen to make me "understand." At nine in the evening on a steaming night in July, I sit down in his living room in lower Manhattan and Lanzetti starts talking; at four in the morning Lanzetti is still going strong and I am punchy. Punchy but hypnotized: the most startling thing about Lanzetti when he is off and running is that while he talks at a fast, authoritative clip and his language is a marvelous racy mixture of educated coarseness and his hands cut the air in continuous emphasis, the expression in his eyes is anxious, beseeching, very young (about twelve years old). It is an imploring expression, an I-must-have-justice-or-I-will-die expression. I feel frightened for Lanzetti when I concentrate on the look in his eyes.

Eric Lanzetti was born the son of an Italian socialist who emigrated to America in 1924 in flight from the fascism he saw coming to Italy. Although the father had been a civil servant in Rome in America he became a miner and Eric grew up in a coal-mining town in West Virginia. Two things happened to the boy in West Virginia: he was emotionally traumatized by the suddenness with which he became an outsider, and he was deeply marked by the life of the miners. Together, these twin influences made him keenly responsive to his father's socialism.

Eric was a very smart kid. The force of his personality, coupled with his brains and drive, destined him to live out the life he has indeed lived out, a life filled with event and focus, large and dramatic doings. He won a scholarship to Brown University at a time when it was unthinkable for someone like him to go to an Ivy League school. At Brown, he says, he was drawn to drama and literature. But even as he speaks the words, one feels the unreality behind them—literature like a luxurious dream, a wistful longing around the edges of a consciousness pulled even before it knew it was being pulled toward politics and an overriding sense of class struggle. He graduated from Brown in 1935 and won a scholarship to Oxford; on his way to Oxford in 1936 he thought he'd just stop off in Spain and see what that was all about.

Spain politicized him for life. He fought with the Anarchists, and when the Spanish War was over for him he determined to "learn about the world"—that is, to become a serious Marxist. He also decided to get married. Over and over again, Lanzetti stresses that he became a Communist in order to help avert the fascist war he saw coming, and he got married in order to reassert civilized human connection.

Lanzetti and his wife (who had both become members of the

Communist Party in England) returned to the United States and joined the American Communist Party in 1938. Within a very short time they both rose within the functionary ranks of the Party, and by year's end Lanzetti was section organizer of New York's Lower East Side.

In the fall of 1941 the Party asked Lanzetti to become the director of a popular front agency formed to fight fascism. Lanzetti agreed, and left the Party, as it was generally agreed that he would not serve two masters simultaneously. Six months after Pearl Harbor he offered his services to the US government. Shortly thereafter, William Donovan requested him for the OSS. In thinly veiled language Donovan told him that if he was a Communist he, Donovan, didn't want to know it, and that if there was ever to be trouble "afterwards" he, Lanzetti, was on his own. (This was common practice during the war. Every government agent in America knew that the Communists were the best organizers in the country and for this reason many were impressed into wartime intelligence work; when the war was over the lot of many of these Communists who had served America hard and well was that of the spy who came in from the cold.)

Lanzetti was one of the first casualties of the Cold War. He served throughout the war in Washington, rose to become a section chief in the OSS, and when the war was over he was the first man in America to be indicted as a leftist: for having "defrauded" the government with regard to his Communist past. Lanzetti served three years in prison. When he came out he was a Cold War hero to the left, pure poison to the right.

The very best years, Lanzetti says, were the years on the Lower East Side. They were the years of radical integration at its most intense, both within the Party itself and in the world around it. The Communist presence on the Lower East Side during the Thirties was a live, influential, working presence, as it is in Europe today and as it has not been again in the United States. The life streamed together, and the world of the CP as it was experienced then was a world that haunted the deepest dreams of American Communists for decades afterward.

In an unpublished autobiography Lanzetti has written of that time, he says:

The East Side . . . was a city within a city, the town of *Jews Without Money*: polyglot, teeming, colorful, its heart on its sleeve, where you breathed people like air, and you had better like the smells or move. . . . It was a sovereign state, working-class and radical to the core, bounded on the south by Chinatown, on the West by Greenwich Village, on the north by the Protestant World, and on the east by its river, moody cradling river. Our republic had its own newspapers (the *Jewish Daily Forward*, the *Day*, the *East Side News*, the *Freiheit*, the *Daily Worker*), its own bus . . . and Tomkins Square threw longer shadows in American folklore than Washington Square.

The System on the East Side was more than a phrase, it was a *gestalt*. It was capitalism in all its complex and tortured detail. The East Side was politically *sui generis* in America: there were practically no conservatives. The right-wingers were the New Dealers, and the political conjugation went on from there: Social Democrats, Socialists, Communists, Trotskyists, Anarchists. The majority party was the Democratic, then the ALP, then the Communist Party.

Lanzetti's section ran from Second Avenue to the East River, from Fourteenth Street to Delancy Street. Packed into this relatively small section of the city were 250,000 people. Three thousand of them were Communists. (That proportion is roughly comparable to the Italian or French Communist parties of today.) Never before or since have American Communists been more like the fish that swims in the sea of the people. Everyone on the Lower East Side knew the Communists, and the Communists knew everyone plus. At all times—even when they were hated as they were in the months between the Nazi-Soviet Pact and the German invasion of Russia—everyone wanted to know what the Communists thought; and at all times, the people of the Lower East Side (even if they were registered Democrats!) turned first to the Communists for help—as the Communists were better organized, more responsive, more actively engaged in the life of the neighborhood and the life of the Depression than were any of their political counterparts.

To hear Lanzetti tell it, the CP on the Lower East Side during the Thirties was like an enthusiastic Boy Scout troop: cheerful, hard-working, open, and honest. Of the politics behind the politics

—the wheeling and dealing, the back-room decisions, the infamous manipulation—not a word. But for sheer vivid detail of how the organization worked—the *density* of its involvement with the people in the community—his memory is invaluable: a remarkable gauge of the all-in-allness with which people like Lanzetti were Communists.

The organization of the CP was constructed at a national, district, section, and branch level. At each level there was an organizer, an educational director, an educational secretary, and a literature director. National was responsible for district, district for section, and section for branch. The section was responsible not only for the needs of all its neighborhood branches but also for all the Party-affiliated mass organizations and all the Party branches organized along industrial lines that were located within its boundaries. Beyond that, it was responsible for the creation of some active relationship with all the mass organizations beyond Party influence, all the neighborhood organizations, and all the local political clubs also within its borders.

There were thirty branches in Lanzetti's section (approximately fifteen people to a branch). Twenty-eight of the branches were open (that is, publicly known), two were secret (two teachers' branches). The neighborhood branches met every other week in private (in each other's homes), every other week in public (at CP headquarters, where anyone could walk in off the street and attend a meeting).

As for the individual Communist at the branch level, four-fifths of the time he followed Party directives, one-fifth of the time he was on his own; on his own, he was supposed to respond to whatever happened in the course of a day in the neighborhood. ("What exactly does that mean?" I ask Lanzetti. "Oh," he replies, "if there was a tenant conviction, or a sick comrade, or if he was needed to join a picket line, or canvas during an election. Or if the neighborhood needed a traffic light, or a shopkeeper was having trouble with the Fire Department. You know," he grins, "just like the neighborhood Democratic Party would have operated—only we always got there first.") The branch member's other duties consisted of contributing a week's wages to the Party once a year, selling the *Daily Worker*, and running off weekly leaflets.

Beyond the section's regular branches were the Party branches inside the factory unions located on the Lower East Side. These branches could come at all times to section headquarters for mimeographing, pickets, and leaflet distribution.

Then there were the Party-affiliated mass organizations. On the Lower East Side in the 1930s these were the International Workers Order (IWO), the National Negro Congress, the International Defense League, the Unemployment Councils, the Tenants Councils. It was the section's obligation to be responsive to the immediate, practical needs of these organizations as well as their long-range problems and needs.

Then there were the *non*-Party–affiliated organizations: the local industrial unions, the PTA, the teachers' unions, the—most important on the Lower East Side—settlement houses and thousands of immigrant "landsman" associations. To these the section supplied speakers, help with specific projects, and aid of a generalized but continual nature.

As for the local political clubs, the section's influence was greatest with the American Labor Party, next greatest with the Democrats and least important with the Republicans. The CP was powerful enough during the Thirties so that Lanzetti's section could veto the Democratic Party's candidates for any local office on the Lower East Side.

In addition to all this, the section started—through the YCL— forty or fifty Youth Clubs consisting of neighborhood kids who, on the Lower East Side, were often pretty tough. "The rules of these clubs," Lanzetti says, sounding like the Father Flanagan of the Left, "were no stealing, no mugging. You could drink beer but not whiskey, you could neck but not fuck, you could fight but no guns or knives, you could play cards but no gambling. In short: we were the first social workers on the Lower East Side. And it was terrific, how these kids responded. And then, of course," he laughs, "every now and then, one of them wandered down to CP headquarters, just to see what it was all about, all this Commie stuff that the YCL worker at the club seemed so hot on."

The two major tasks of the section were education within and organization without. Education consisted of attendance in the new members' club for initial Marxist-Leninist indoctrination, then attendance at the Party's Jefferson School and, afterwards, reading assignments in the Party's magazine, *Political Affairs*. Once a year every branch sent one member for attendance at advanced classes held by the section organizer; the idea, Lanzetti claims, was to send the person who would most be benefited by attendance at these seminars, not necessarily the one whose attendance would be of most use to the Party.

The task of organization was highly schematized. It consisted, first, of concentrated periods of work—from six to eight weeks —during national elections, fund-raising time, and recruiting drives; second, of an open forum held once a week at Party headquarters; third, of running a speakers' bureau and supplying every organization in the neighborhood with a speaker from the CP for every occasion imaginable; and fourth, of running off leaflets. At the branch level there was a runoff of perhaps 2,000 a week; at the section level, whenever a current issue warranted it, there was a runoff of 50,000–100,000. Needless to say, no one was better than the Communists at leaflet distribution.

Eric Lanzetti presided over this extraordinary array of activities from 1938 to 1941. What has remained with him—as vivid in him today as it must have been thirty-five years ago—is the sense of integration: how the Communists affected the life of the neighborhood, how the neighborhood affected the life of the section, how the section affected the lives of the Communists.

"No matter what happened politically in the Thirties, on the Lower East Side everyone always wanted to know what the Communists were doing and thinking, what *their* analysis was. Even when they hated us, we were still their own. After *Der Pakt*, overnight we became 'Communazis.' People practically spit in my face when I walked down the street. But even then, I'll never forget, one night I was handing out leaflets in front of the subway on Delancy Street. An old Jewish woman came up out of the subway—old, tired, her legs swollen, two shopping bags in her hands. When she saw me her face changed from tired to angry. She began to curse me in Yiddish. I didn't understand all the words, but I got the message. I just stood there, looking at her. I didn't say a word. She started to walk away. Then she turned back. It was a bitter night, cold and windy. All I had on was a thin jacket. The old woman came toward me, pulling a scarf from around her neck. 'Bubbela,' she said, 'what are you doing, dressed like that on a night like this? You'll get pneumonia.' And she wound the scarf around my neck.

"When the Germans invaded Russia, everyone went wild. Pure relief ran, like a fever, through the neighborhood. What a night that was! We must have run off two hundred thousand copies of the leaflet we wrote. And, believe me, we didn't have distribution problems that night. People were grabbing it from us as fast as it came off the machine. They didn't give a damn what *anybody* else said, not the Democrats, not the *Times*, not the radio, nothing. They only wanted to know what the Communists were saying."

Lanzetti leans back in his chair, lights a cigarette, refills his diminishing scotch-and-soda, and looks around his comfortable living room. "And of course," he says, "the impact of the neighborhood on *us* was tremendous, tremendous. Look," he leans forward, his hand out palm up, "there's decency in everybody. Also laziness, inertness. A night like this, I'm sitting here talking to you. What do I want to do? I want to go on talking to you. But there's a rally, or a leaflet to run off, or a campaign to fight. I go. The structure shames me, doesn't allow me to give in to my shallower desires, makes me act on the best in me. Now, that structure was the Communist Party, but if it wasn't for the *reality* of those streets and those people, believe me, that structure would have been operating at half-mast. It was the Lower East Side that made us such good Communists. We matched and raised each other.

"And what all this did for so many Communists, individually! Well, here's a typical example. There were many others, but this one sticks in my memory. We had a young woman in one of the branches, Lilly was her name. Lilly was one of the people who took my advanced classes. She wasn't the smartest person in the world, but she was a hard-working, conscientious Communist, with a powerful sense of class. She lived alone with her father on Rivington Street. The old man was an Orthodox Jew who paid absolutely no attention to her or to her politics or anything. She made his breakfast in the morning, went to work, came home, made his dinner, went to a meeting, came home, made him hot milk, and that was it. The old man sat reading the Talmud all day long. Lilly ran the house entirely. If it wasn't for her working, they would have both starved. But he was her father and she was scared shitless of him.

"One night after a meeting she asks me if she can talk to me. I nod sure, she sits down and starts to tell me, very hesitantly, that there's this man she's in love with. I think she's about to tell me she's afraid to sleep with him, and I start to tell her if you're in love there's nothing wrong with. . . . 'Oh no, no, no,' she interrupts me, 'it's nothing like that. Of course, we've been sleeping together. It's that he's Chinese. I'm terrified to tell my father we want to get married.'

"I stare at her. What the hell do I do with *this*? Finally, I say to her, 'Look, if you're afraid to tell him alone I'll go with you.' 'You'll go with me?' she says. 'Not only me,' I say, 'we'll take a delegation if that'll make you feel any better.' 'A *delegation*?' she says. 'Sure,' I say, getting into the swing of it, 'we'll take the whole damned Communist Party. Why not? You got a right.' 'I'll think it over,' she says, and she goes away.

"Well, of course, I forgot all about it, the work went on, and a month later, after another meeting, Lilly suddenly comes up to me again, and she's beaming from ear to ear. 'What happened?' I say. 'Well,' she says, 'it took me all this time to get up the nerve to say anything to my father, but last week I came home from work one night and I marched into his room and I stood in the doorway and I said: "I'm getting married." He looked up at me and he just stared at me for a long time. Then he said: "Is he Jewish?" "No, Pa," I said, "he's not, he's Chinese." My father stared at me in such a way I knew he was thinking one of us had lost his mind and he wasn't sure which one it was. But after a while he was sure. "I'll kill you," he said. My knees started to buckle. Then all of a sudden it was like you were there in the room with me. I saw you and my branch organizer and all the people I work with and I felt like the whole Communist Party was right there in the room with me. I looked at my father and I said to him: "If you kill me, who'll cook your eggs?" He hasn't said a word to me since. Li and I are getting married next week.'

"Years later I saw her one night at a rally while I was still fighting my indictment. She came up to me and grinned: 'If you kill me, who'll cook your eggs?' . . . and that whole world came crowding back in on me."

°

The Party Unionist

FOR thousands of people life as a Communist was inextricable from life as a trade unionist. Many of these people—like street-smart Joe Preisen—were brilliantly savvy about what they were doing, but many were simply devoted soldiers in the army of the revolution. Life in the shop, struggling in the name of Marxist revolution to organize American labor, that was *their* wholeness as Communists, their sense of Marxism intimately bound up with the dailiness of working-class life. For many of these people Communism and unionism was a confusion: at first useful, then fatal. Such a person was Maggie McConnell.

At fifty-seven Maggie McConnell is cheerful, boozy, over-weight, her eyes a rich, startling blue, her hair a prematurely white aureole that surrounds her bobbing head, her conversation alive with working-class humor and her face repeatedly trans-formed by her dazzling smile. Maggie can also of a sudden turn hard as nails, tight, stubborn, won't give an inch: the perfect Party functionary, the perfect shop steward.

When Maggie sits down on my living-room couch one cool evening in autumn I fill her glass with bourbon-and-water; that glass will not be empty for very long at any point in the hours we will spend together. Maggie will sip continuously as she talks, her voice growing honey-rich, whiskey-rich, her speech curving from animation to mellowness to sad drowsiness. . . . Maggie will also finger some portion of the great quantity of gold jewelry she wears—a brooch, an earring, a pendant—as she talks. At one point, when she catches me staring at all the jewelry, she says wistfully: "I have always loved beautiful and elegant things. I have had two pairs of jade earrings. I lost one of the first pair on a picket line. Last year I lost one of the other at a bar-lounge in my hometown. That pretty much tells you where *my* life has gone."

Maggie McConnell was born in a small factory town outside of Boston to working-class parents with a distinct desire to see their children rise in the world. Both of her parents worked in the factory and, while her father was marked by the boozy good cheer that Maggie has so abundantly inherited, it was her mother's stubborn insistence that she go to college and make something of herself, be a serious person, that shaped her deeper being.

In 1935 Maggie entered Boston College. (The tuition fee for Radcliffe was five-hundred dollars, for Boston College two-hundred-fifty. Boston won hands down.) It was the height of the Depression, and Maggie became, on the instant, a Depression college student: antifascist, Spanish Loyalist partisan, aware of the horrors of The System, etc. etc. Everyone around her who was of any interest at all was a Communist. She took a comparative religion course, and that sent her "over the wall" with regard to her Catholicism. She took an economics course with a brilliant teacher who was a Communist and that politicized her. In 1939 she joined the Citizens' Union. There she met two people who influenced the active course of her life: a woman who became her lifelong friend, a man who became her first lover. Both were devout Communists. Before the year was out Maggie joined the Communist Party.

The emotional recklessness of the Depression and the promise of Communism made Maggie entirely susceptible to the idea that a career was absurdly irrelevant; to work for the future was to be at the center of things. With this incentive, and the powerful notion that Communism had "opened a window on the world," she became, and remained for fifteen years, a Party organizer.

Also, there was the headiness of the Party coming after her full force. "You see, darling," Maggie says, her voice richly edged with laughter, "I was *Irish*. That was the key. That was always the key. They wanted me because I was Irish." And, in fact, the first thing the Party did was to get her into an Irish-dominated union in south Boston. That converted her to working with the working class forever.

After a year in Boston she was sent to New York to attend Workers' School classes, and was immediately plunged into work as an organizer in a white-collar union. Maggie spreads her hands out, palms upwards, and rolls her blue eyes to the ceiling. "What did I know about organizing? Nothing! It was a holding action. I was scared shitless, but the Party said go, and I went. It was always like that, from the very beginning. I believed in the discipline, I believed in the revolution, I believed I was at the center of the world. I've been scared always, but I pulled myself together always, and I worked for my Party. From the very beginning, the Party came first. I would have done whatever was necessary, gone wherever I was told to go, done whatever I was told to do. When I'd been married a few months and the Party said to go underground, I was prepared to go."

In 1943 Maggie was told to go into industry. That decision on the part of the Party provided her with the richness and the wholeness that were to become Maggie's life as a Communist. For the next fifteen years she could not tell where she left off and the Party began, and where the Party left off and the men and women in the shop began. She became an integrated Communist unionist. To her, every major and minor struggle on the floor of the factory was a preparatory battle for the revolution. As a result, she became an extraordinarily skilled negotiator who worked longer hours, performed harder tasks, took greater risks than any other member of the union staff. It was people like Maggie who had built the CIO.

Maggie became an electrical tester at a Westinghouse plant that was organized into the United Electrical Workers' Union, and was soon chairman of the grievance committee in her Communist-dominated local. When she went to work for Westinghouse her mother cried. She said: "I worked my hands off to keep you out of the shop. Why are you doing this?" "What could I tell her?" Maggie says. "How could I explain to her that it was *because* she worked, and made me what I am, that I was doing what I was doing?"

She remained at Westinghouse until 1950, when the Taft-Hartley Law was passed, the union was challenged by the right-wing International United Electrical, and overnight the UE was severely reduced in numbers and as a left union just about destroyed. Maggie immediately became a pariah, fired and banned from shops across the country.

When she was fired men she had worked with all those years said to her: "We know you people are the only real union people here, but what can we do? We need a true-blue union now or we're all finished." And, says Maggie, "I didn't blame them, I didn't blame them. People say to me: After all you sacrificed for them [meaning the UE], and look how they treated you. I sacrificed *nothing*. I was doing what I wanted to be doing. They were great years, the best of my life, they gave me meaning and focus, and nothing like that is ever gonna come my way again. What was I sacrificing?"

When she was thirty-three years old she married Bo Mason, an assembler at the Westinghouse plant. Bo was an ex-Marine, Irish to the core, a prize for the Party. "A true working-class intellectual," Maggie says proudly. Also a hard-drinking, undisciplined wild man, dead at forty-nine of alcoholism.

"I did a terrible thing to him, a terrible thing," Maggie mourns. "The Party came to me and asked me did I think Bo would be a good organizer, they wanted to make him an organizer. And I said no. No, I didn't think so. I didn't think he was disciplined enough. I did *that* to Bo. I did it for my union guys, and I did it for my Party. But I was wrong! Like the Party was so often wrong. They never understood the working class in America, and I forgot what I knew, also. Bo never knew what I had done to him. But I knew, and it ate at me."

Once unionism fell apart for Maggie confusion came crowding in on her. She had never really had anything to do with CP functionaries, she had lived her entire Party life among trade unionists, for her Communism *was* trade unionism. (To this day she thinks everyone in the Party was just fine, she never heard any of these awful stories you hear now about trials and expulsions. . . .) Deprived of the shop, her sense of herself as a Communist began to disintegrate rapidly, and her many deep confusions about the Party itself began to surface at a frightening rate of speed.

After the years at Westinghouse, Maggie went to work directly for the Party, training intellectuals to go into industry. She did not last very long at this work. The Party, she says, was falling apart, losing its way, going middle class. "They didn't know *what* the hell they were doing anymore!" she bursts out. "For Chrissake, they had a goddamn *foreman* as the educational director for this workers' project I was on. A foreman! How the hell could a foreman be a Communist? It was ridiculous!"

Brooding further into her bourbon-and-water on the bewildering complications of the Communist Party and the working class, Maggie says hotly: "The Party never understood the American working class. Never! For instance, take May Day. My mother was the true working class. She didn't know from shit about May Day. Labor Day. *That* was her holiday. The Party simply would not understand this. And kept insisting on May Day —while the American working class ignored it and celebrated Labor Day. Sure we marched in our thousands on May Day. But there were millions out there, and they never got the May Day message."

Maggie's own confusion about the origin and radical usage of May Day is painful to behold because it speaks not to ignorance so much as to a shattered sense of things, some voided wholeness into which shabby bewilderments fall. Inside that void bits and pieces of ideological mouthings thrash about inside her, at war with the now-fragmented reality. She speaks of Rockefeller referring to the unemployed as a statistic, and it drives her into a frenzy; in the next moment she turns the human abstraction on its head and speaks as Communists did thirty years ago, of the necessity of sacrificing artists and intellectuals to the revolution; in the third moment she weeps bitterly over what she and the Party did to her beloved Bo. On the one hand, it is possible to say "the closed system" of CP Marxism has created a creature desperate in the face of independent thought; on the other hand, it is equally possible to say the loss of wholeness has made a capable human being babble.

When I ask her if she feels she sacrificed her life to the Communist Party, Maggie's face loses its now-blurred appearance, the blue eyes clear and spark. She leans forward on the couch, one hand on her hip, her mouth breaking into her irrepressible smile, and she says: "Sacrificed my life! Of course not. Hon, we were in the world-changing business. You can't get much better than that. What's better? Money? Position? Are you kidding?"

Ambivalence: Beneath the "Wholeness" Disintegrating Conflict

SARAH Gordon, in describing how a directive came down from the office of the section organizer and how everyone in her club would discuss the directive, laughs richly and says: "Of course, we ended up agreeing with whatever the directive was. But *oy!* Did we *discuss* it!" But—and equally of course—Sarah's laughter is nonsense. It doesn't alter the fact that despite the easiness of her approach she would never, not in the remotest part of herself, have dared challenge the Party at any level on any issue.

This, too, was the "wholeness" of the CP. And there were many people for whom *this* wholeness was anathema. They did not laugh—not then, not now—over the directives; they writhed inside themselves. They lived as Communists in uneasy relation to inner divisions that were at one and the same time attracted to and repelled by CP wholeness, recognizing always, by virtue of original consultation, the irreconcilable nature of much in human experience that orthodox Communism not only made no room for but whose very existence it vehemently denied. One of these people was Esther Allen.

A woman of witty, mercurial ambivalence—small and anxious, birdlike, with a headful of curly grey hair, narrow darting eyes, and an acid tongue—Esther Allen is sixty years old, and she lives in a cottage on the Connecticut side of Long Island Sound. Her house is calm and sunny, filled with plants, oriental rugs, modern-design china and glassware, and a large music library. She is, she says, through with the world: finished, ended, has washed her hands of the whole damned thing; she will remain here in this house for the rest of her days, hopefully never having to talk to one more asshole as long as she lives, never having to go to another meeting or have another "discussion." She was a member of the Communist Party for twenty years.

Esther Allen was born the daughter of educated, assimilated German Jews who were, as she says, "comfortable." She grew up on New York's Upper West Side in an Ethical Culture, *New Republic*, nursery-and-nanny atmosphere: rich, cultivated, liberal and self-satisfied. She couldn't wait to grow up and sit at the table with the rich grown-ups—and when she did she was bored to death. This, at least partly, because by the time she got to the table she was already at a vital remove from her parents' world.

Two things separated Esther. One, she was a sickly child— rheumatic fever—often spending weeks and months of her childhood in bed in a darkened room. Two, it turned out she had been born with a remarkable amount of musical talent. The illness induced in her a sense of frailty and nervous remove. The music induced in her a growing inwardness. The two together made her feel set apart from the society around her. She played the piano almost continuously when she wasn't bedridden. Music became an extraordinary absorption, the single greatest source of mental and spiritual nourishment; it sensitized her to herself, made her glory in the act of living. It also made her sly and fearful, and exacerbated from earliest childhood the universal twin impulse to move both out of the self into the world and back into the self away from the world.

Esther was twenty-one years old in 1935. By now she was an accomplished musician living in a studio-loft on Lexington Avenue, playing long hours, absorbed in music. But when she left her studio and went out into the streets and apartments of New York the world engulfed her. Everywhere she saw the Depression, everywhere she found herself involved in trying to puzzle out "the meaning of it all." It nagged at her, demanded of her. Suddenly, everyone she knew was a Marxist. Suddenly, everywhere she went she felt she had to explain why she wasn't political. One day she joined the Communist Party.

Immediately, she entered into a state of conflict from which she never seemed to emerge: when she was playing the piano she felt guilty because of all the people starving to death in the world, and when she was at Party meetings she felt uneasy because she knew she wasn't really very good at being a Communist and longed to be back at her piano. She couldn't talk about Beethoven with anyone in the Party, and she couldn't put the Party out of her mind when she was listening to Beethoven. The split in her hovered on a scale of evenly balanced tension. Then the scale tipped: she gave up music.

The conflict, of course, did not resolve itself, it merely went underground. And whenever it rose up to swamp her, she dealt with it by becoming more dogmatic, more doctrinaire, more Marxist-Leninist self-assured than she had been before.

One night in 1937 at a party for Spain she met Roger Allen, a southern academic just arrived in New York from Texas. Allen was a kind of Marxist Tom Wolfe: lanky, good-looking, a hard drinker, talking a blue streak of wild, brilliant, imaginative rhetoric that pulled together literature, politics, history, the world. Esther fell instantly in love. Within six weeks they were married, and she had induced him to join the Party.

"From that moment on," Esther says, lifting a blue and white cup of tea to her lips, "my life as a Communist was signed, sealed, and delivered." She sips her tea and stares out the kitchen window at Long Island Sound. "What I didn't know, of course," she says dryly, "*couldn't* know, was that Roger was just like me: also full of conflict he was pushing down. We conned each other. I think for nearly twenty years we never spoke one fully honest word to each other, each of us outdoing the other at the game of being a *better* Marxist-Leninist, a *more* doctrinaire Communist, neither of us having a clue, not one fucking clue, about how to get at all that anxiety eating away at us.

"And, of course, you mustn't forget, the life was exciting, very exciting. We felt—he did, and I did, too—like we had our hands on 'the throttle of history,' as we used to say. That's an extraordinary feeling. When Hitler rose to power and all those lost, floundering liberals were wandering around saying 'How could it happen in cultured, civilized Germany?' we *knew*. That was a tremendous comfort. We were inside the circle of light, unlike those poor benighted others in the dark outside. They had to contend with the existential dilemma of a crumbling civilization. Not us. That, of course, was the other side of the coin. Not one of us knew what the hell was going on inside ourselves, but we *all* could explain the world.

"When I think back on it. The childishness! The arrogance! The days, nights, *years* of self-righteous talk. My husband—the big academic intellectual—talking every night for twenty years until three in the morning as if he really had the explanation for every goddamn thing in the world. . . ."

Esther breaks off suddenly and stares out the window. She sips her tea in silence for a moment. Then she blurts out: "He was a silly, self-deluded, infantile man who never had a grasp on reality. What he was, really, was a tremendously gifted organizer, he could talk people into joining the Party like *mad*. Because he himself was so lost in the magic of Marxist discussion and Marxist interpretation. In time which made a monkey of us all I came to see him as pathetic, truly pathetic. Which doesn't mean, of course, I had *compassion* for him. Oh no! Not me, my dear, not me. Scorn was more my style. Heaps and heaps of scorn.

"My God," she sighs, "there was so much of it I hated. Those endless, fucking meetings. Those masturbatory discussions. That heavy-handed intellectual Marxist authority that was always putting you in your place. The way the Party line controlled our lives, our thoughts. . . . Every now and then I'd remember my music. The thought of it would go tearing through me like pain. Sometimes like panic. Then I'd forget it, and go on. After all, my dear, the rev-o-*llew*-tion needed me.

"But in a sense I'm bullshitting myself even now. For instance, all those years our house was the central meeting place for our group. Every meeting, every party, every visiting CP fireman was put up at our place. I always hated it. At least, I always *said* I hated it. I'd have endless fights with Roger. Three nights out of the five when we weren't having a meeting or throwing a party he'd show up at eleven at night with a mob of people, and guess who had to feed them and keep trotting out the drinks? 'Who the hell does all the goddamn work?' I'd yell. 'While you sit on your ass making the revolution, *I'm* out there in the kitchen like a slavey. What we need is a revolution in this *house*.' But, of course, he simply ignored me, and of course I simply went on doing it. And every goddamn time we moved—and, of course, it was me who went hunting for the house—I'd always end up getting the *big* house with a living room just perfect for big gatherings. And it was like that to the very end. We always had a houseful of Party people, and organizers, and, finally, FBI agents."

Esther rubs a hand wearily across her forehead and says quietly: "Lord, what a mess it all ended in. One day in the Fifties we woke up to see our names smeared across the headlines of the small Jersey town we were living in. 'Allen and wife Reds,' the papers screamed. 'Secret Communist Party meetings held in house in woods.' It read like we were running a white slavery operation. It was insane, just insane. Our kids were humiliated, frightened, we had to yank them out of school, sell the house at a terrific loss, and flee to New York. Where we spent the next two years battling indictments."

She looks up and grins: "Busy, busy, busy. Nobody can say life in the Communist Party was dull."

She moves across the kitchen to the stove to boil some more water for fresh tea. She rinses out the teapot, places fresh tea in the bottom, and waits for the water to boil. When it does, she pours the water and waits for the tea to steep. After a while she returns to the table and pours out the fresh tea. Then she says:

"Ten years ago Roger ran off with another woman. A good comrade, naturally. A woman who'd been in my house a hundred times over the years. The whole thing was simply unbelievable. Screaming, yelling, crying. Him, her, me. Telephone calls in the middle of the night. Children being taken to neighbors. My father threatening to call in the police. Rage, revenge, and dementia. Finally, of course, he came back, sat in the kitchen weeping, said the world had gone up in smoke, he didn't know what to do anymore, what to do.

"Well, I thought about it. Thought about taking him back. And I found I was weary, weary of it all. I simply wanted out. Out of politics, out of my marriage, out of the world. So that was it. I told him to go. I packed up the remnants of my life and I came out here."

Esther moves to the window, stands for a long moment with her arms wrapped about her chest. When she turns back she says: "The thing is this: given the time and the place of our lives, given the kind of person I was, there was nothing else I could have done but be a Communist. But I associate my years in the Party with years of not knowing who or what the hell I was. I associate them with guilt, conflict, apprehension, divided feelings, a fatal kind of unknowingness.

"Now all I have is relief. Relief that it's over. Relief that I don't ever have to go to another goddamn meeting, have another goddamn discussion, nod my head at things I only half agree with or half understand.

"Nowadays I feel very little about anything, including music. I haven't played in years. It's all gone. The only satisfaction I have is that now I make up my mind very fast about everything. I don't discuss anything with anyone, including myself. I just *act*. The joke, of course, is the only things I have to act on are the stupid little things of daily life."

What Mason Goode shares with Esther Allen is the secret conviction that the loss of his creative talent is the price he paid for the festering conflict within which *he* lived out much of his life as a Communist. What he also shares with her is a deep-seated memory of the profound distaste he felt in his educated middle-class soul for the intellectual and emotional crudities of life in the Party.

When Mason Goode left Alexander Micklejohn's school in 1931, two large stirrings were at work in him: one had to do with the magical pull that painting exerted on him, the other with the yearning Jeremy Lewiton's Communism had set going in him. At the time, Mason did not worry about the polar opposites of these twin stirrings. Certainly he did not view them as potential sources of serious inner conflict. On the contrary, he saw them as enriching each other, multiplying experience, enlarging his relation to himself and to the world. He received a scholarship to an art institute in Pittsburgh and went off to study painting with the full conviction that he was a socialist and somewhere, somehow, in the world that lay before him the two parts of himself —the "private" and the "political"—would stream together fruitfully.

In 1933 Mason's father was dead of acute alcoholism, the family fortune was revealed to be nonexistent, the Depression was at full tilt, and Mason was soon lost to his art studies. He remembers he wandered the streets of Pittsburgh for days, nights, weeks feeling as grey-and-black inside himself as the city around him. He remembers Pittsburgh as a city of bridges under each one of which homeless men camped and slept. "The man under the bridge" became his lifelong image of the Depression.

He returned to New York and began to look for work: in the theater, in graphics, in advertising. None to be found. There was, in fact, a great deal of art and theater going on; aside from Broadway, there was the WPA Theater, the Group Theater, dozens of little loft theaters on Fourteenth Street—all of them alive with "social consciousness," European modernism, Depression realism, and sometimes outright Marxism. This was true in painting, design, and decoration as well. Radicalism and the arts seemed indeed to have merged, and Mason was in a continual state of responsive excitement, the two parts of the mingled dynamic seeming one to be as good as another. What, after all, did it matter if you worked in the arts or you worked in radical politics? It was all one, all feeding the same source, the same electric sense of life, the same live flow of politics, society, and art streaming together in an intensity of the world that was coming.

When Mason couldn't get work in the arts he joined the Communist Party. In the Party he experienced immediate satisfaction. Having been denied work in the arts, he felt that here, in the Party, what he actually *was*, was being used, fully taken up and taken *in*. He threw himself into Party work and rose quickly to become the branch organizer of a section in Upper Manhattan. In a curious sense, one could say the world had become a theater, the Communist Party was the drama upon the stage, and Mason became if not the set designer then at least a stage manager fully involved in the production: the revolution was around the corner, a new world was dawning, the fight against fascism was supreme, he was part of the future of man. The drama was tinged, for him, with a delicious edge of risk and danger fed by the feverish constancy of Party work and the shared conviction of all around him.

Nevertheless, Mason's social life remained for some time at a distance from that of the Party. He always felt vaguely ill at ease among *apparatchik* Communists. It seemed as though the men most devoted to the Party were also the narrowest; he remained in a state of emotional reserve and doubt. He kept telling himself that these doubts were the residual effects of his bourgeois background and in time, as his inner merger with the Party became more complete, they would evaporate.

The doubts never did evaporate. They continued to plague him. As the years went on they often nearly made him ill. He could not bear the Party hacks, the petty despots, his increasing unhappiness over the dictatorial characteristics of democratic centralism. He also hated his immediate political superior: a charming, intelligent, tyrannical man whose method of criticism was pure attack and humiliation.

There were hundreds of instances in Party life that caused Mason outright dismay. One night, for example, a meeting was opened by a speaker who said: "The subject for tonight's meeting is self-criticism. The first item on the agenda is the self-criticism of Mason Goode." Another time he was called down to Party headquarters and a Party functionary said to him: "I understand your sister is taking a course at NYU with Sidney Hook, and that she has 'questionable' friends. [For "questionable" read Trotskyist.] Perhaps you'd better stop seeing her." Mason stared at the functionary. "Stop seeing her?" he said. "What do you mean? She's my sister." The functionary looked up from his desk as though surprised that there was still something to discuss. "That's right," he said blandly, "stop seeing her."

Mason often felt the Party was foolish, embarrassing and, finally, dangerous; that more and more, as the years wore on, men like the functionary at headquarters and his own section organizer were the kind of men the Party was throwing up. He could not square this with his ongoing, Jeremy-induced, visionary sense of what the Communist Party was all about. And he did not square it, he simply endured it.

His love of painting began to live in a secret part of himself— a reserve part of himself, he thought. In time he came to realize the painter in him was not living in reserve, it was dying in exile. More and more, he could call up less and less those instincts, impulses, intuitions that had made him a painter, made him "see" the world and the life in it as a visual composition, a transformation of magic and serious fantasy.

One night in 1948, Mason attended a district meeting in Yonkers. The subject of the meeting was the expulsion of Earl Browder from the Communist Party USA. Having been expelled by the National Committee, Browder had now to be expelled by every district, section, and branch of the CP. This peculiar charade went on throughout the country and throughout the year.

The room in Yonkers was filled with men and women Mason had known for more than a dozen years. Across the room was one very particular friend. Mason tried to attract this man's attention, but he wouldn't look up, his eyes remained trained on the floor before him. The meeting began. The speaker talked passionately for more than an hour about Browder's betrayal of the Party. He went on and on about how this was the right, the necessary, the only thing to do. Everyone in the room began to look painfully uncomfortable. It wasn't necessarily that people liked Browder and didn't think he should be expelled. It was rather that most people weren't *sure*, and *therefore* didn't think this was the "right" or fully understood thing to be doing.

Mason looked around the room at all those faces he knew so well. Everywhere, the faces looked increasingly more torn, confused, hesitant. The voice of the speaker ploughed on. Everyone knew the decision had already been made, and each person who didn't rise to his feet when the moment came would be fixed in Party memory. The speaker called for a vote.

"One by one," Mason says, "and then two by two, and then six by six, everyone in that room rose to his feet. And then I, too, rose to my feet. Inside, I felt sick. Lost, betrayed, turned into an automaton. I watched my friend across the room. He wouldn't meet my eyes.

"Later, my friend and I went home together. We didn't speak of what had happened. Years later, I met him on a street corner. I said to him, 'Remember that night in Yonkers?' 'Remember!' he said. 'It has haunted me all these years.' In time, I discovered that nearly everyone in the room that night felt the same way."

In 1952 Mason Goode left the Communist Party. The doubts had not simply accumulated in him, they had accreted into a conviction of deformed life. Mason and his wife, Dorothy, left New York and settled in a small southern city. He would, he told himself, begin to paint again. But it was no good, and in a very short time he saw that it was no good. He could not begin to call up the impulses of the creative temperament that had once fed his visual imagination; they had atrophied, withered in him with disuse. The images he found himself putting down on the canvas seemed to be relentlessly controlled by the Marxist clichés that exercised mechanical power over his associative responses. He could no longer "see" differently. Mason quickly made his peace with what he realized was the permanent loss of his life, and found a job teaching in the art department of a small university in the town he was living in. He lived now in a state not of active well-being but of grateful relief. He felt free and at peace within himself for the first time in years.

In 1956 Mason was suddenly subpoenaed by HUAC. In that small southern town where he was living the headlines screamed the news: "Art Teacher Found to Be a Red!" Mason shakes his head in disbelief as he recalls: "They were the kind of banner headlines usually reserved for declarations of war or armistice." Overnight, his life was destroyed. He lost his job, his house was smeared with shit and swastikas, his wife received threatening phone calls, people he had known for four years turned away from him on the street.

"The irony of it all," Mason says softly, staring out at Puget Sound. "Here, I'm a painter. I become a Communist. I lose myself as a painter. Then I lose myself as a Communist. *Then* I get my head kicked in." Mason seems bemused by this calculation. Then he says: "Or *is* it ironical, after all? On the one hand, it seems as though I'd repeatedly lost everything because I was a Communist, including *being* a Communist. On the other hand, one could say: You were a Communist, and everything that happened happened as a consequence of that great and monumental fact of your life. *Including* the development of certain responses to life that could never have developed in any other way, and that you would not to this moment trade in for anything . . ."

Mason Goode is what it is all about: a man who has lived within the orbit of the political passion, its harsh and brilliant

rays reflecting off his soul, first nourished then deprived by the
language of the closed system; formed and deformed, shaped
by the narrow intensity, both hobbled and dignified by the power
of that decision taken in a moment of golden influence, a moment that spoke to a deep and most particular part of the man,
but not to the whole man.

Lou Goodstein and I were introduced by mutual friends over the
phone when I was visiting in New Mexico. We talked for a bit
and then agreed to meet the next day at a coffeehouse in Santa
Fe—the city halfway between Goodstein's home and my friends'
home.

"How will I know you?" I said to him on the phone.

"Well," he said in his soft, dark voice, "I'm small and thin, I
have dark eyes, longish grey hair, and my face even when unfurrowed looks anxious." The self-description was remarkably
accurate.

Lou Goodstein lives now in an adobe house on a hillside thirty
miles north of Albuquerque. Three days a week he goes into
town to take studio photographs of small children; in this manner
he supports himself and his wife, Clara. The rest of the time he
reads, works in his garden, does carpentry, and cultivates the
quiet he cherishes above all other things in the world. He is fifty-
seven years old; his dark eyes are beautiful, his grey hair poetic,
and his unfurrowed indeed anxious face is the face of a man
rich with inner life.

Lou Goodstein was born in Russia. He came to this country
with his father at the age of three in the midst of Russia's turmoil.
His mother, he was told, was "lost in the revolution." ("I didn't
realize until I was about twenty-five," Lou says, "that 'lost in the
revolution' was a euphemism for 'she ran out on my father.'")
His father was helpless with the child, and so Lou was placed
with conservative bourgeois relatives in upstate New York and
grew up there, physically fed and clothed, spiritually malnour-
ished. He entered, in those years, into a permanent state of spiritual hunger that drove him, ironically, to fail repeatedly at

whatever it was he was supposed to be succeeding at, thereby bringing down on himself more scorn, more neglect, when he desperately needed more friendship, more understanding.

He grew up and came to New York, and his father gave him a little money to enter City College. "It was Nineteen-Thirty-Five," Goodstein says. "The worst year of the Depression. Lawyers were selling apples on the streets, and I knew that I was lucky to be eating and living in a warm room. My father expected only one thing of me in return for this subsidy: I should *succeed*. I should become an engineer, a premed student, an economist, an English teacher, any damn thing I wanted, but something he could recognize as a bona-fide success. So I, of course, immediately set out to become a walking disaster. . . . I was lost, lost. See these kids?" (He looks around the room at the permanent dropouts who populate this as well as every other café in Santa Fe.) "They're in better shape than I was in Nineteen-Thirty-Five. They, at least, *think* they know why they're leading this *farshlepte* life. Me, in Nineteen-Thirty-Five, I knew only one thing: I was miserable. Living in solitary confinement inside my head. I wanted to succeed, wanted to do what I was supposed to do. Only I couldn't figure out what that was. Nothing made any sense to me, nothing. Succeed *how*? Where? When? For what? For who? Deep inside I was so lost I didn't even know I was searching.

"I began cutting classes, lying to everyone—my father, my teachers, everyone. I wandered the streets of New York living on apples and ham sandwiches. I guess in my gut I knew my father would have a heart attack if he could see me eating a ham sandwich, but I swear I'm not even sure I realized that at the time.

"But there is one thing about those days I am sure of, one memory I have that sticks like glue. I began haunting the movies on Forty-Second Street like every other miserable unemployed bum in New York in those days. I never even looked at the marquee to see what was playing. I simply bought a ticket every day and plunged into that fabled darkness. Then not only was 'realife' suspended, but very soon I began feeling wonderfully anesthetized. One day a Russian movie came on the screen. It was

Eisenstein's *Strike*. Inside of ten minutes I felt something elec-
trifying was happening on that screen. And inside of twenty
minutes I realized I was in the presence of a new world, a
place where some new sense of human life was stirring. And it
stirred me, it stirred me deeply. I came out of that movie feeling
alive for the first time in months, maybe years, maybe my whole
life.

"I went back to City, walked into the library, and got out every book I could find on contemporary Russia. Then I calmly
walked out of the school, went back to my room, holed up, and
began reading. I don't think I came out of that room for a week.

"Then I fell back into my old misery, and I wandered around
again for months confused, lonely, black depression of the soul.
I began flunking out of everything. They called me into the
dean's office. They said to me: 'Lou, what's the matter? Is there
anything we can do to help? You're such an intelligent boy,
what *is* it?' 'Nothing, nothing,' I said. 'There's nothing you can
do, I swear I'll do better . . .' And I'd try, I'd really try again.
For two days.

"One day during this time I ran into a guy I knew who told me
he'd joined the American Students Union, it was terrific, I should
join. So I joined. At the ASU, of course, I met people from the
YCL. They opened their mouths to talk and immediately the
memory of Eisenstein's *Strike* flashed before my eyes. They
were wonderful people, alive with the joy of ideas and full of a
burning sense of that new world I had glimpsed that day on the
screen. I began to feel rejuvenated. When I found the YCLers
I realized I'd been looking my whole life for 'my people,' and
here they were.

"But you know? It's funny, but I couldn't bring myself to
join the YCL. I hung out with them constantly. We lived a
wonderful life of nightlong discussions, picnics under the George
Washington Bridge, rides on the Staten Island Ferry, free con-
certs and theater, twelve-hour walks through Manhattan, and
always the talk, talk, talk. And yet, with all that, with all that
talk and all that comradeship I'd craved and now had, I had
lived alone inside my head for so long a time, there were thoughts
inside my head that—even with all that talk!—I somehow never
shared with my YCL friends. They were so sure of themselves,

so sure they had the answers to everything, and I just wasn't that sure. Something in me hung back.

"But," Goodstein sighs, his face looking more anxious than ever, "the times were relentless. Relentless. They kept accumulating around me, and finally there was no resisting them. On May Day, Nineteen-Thirty-Nine, I walked alongside my YCL friends. In the midst of all those marching thousands a group of men came down the avenue. They wore berets and foreign uniforms, and they carried a strange flag open like a blanket into which money was being poured. Behind them came an open car in which a blind man in uniform sat. The crowd swelled with joy. Tears streamed from the face of every man, woman, and child around me. I felt as stirred as I had at Eisenstein's movie. More so. I could feel the air vibrating with emotion, the emotion of thousands of people. I turned to one of my YCL friends and said: 'Give me a card.' "

In 1942 Lou Goodstein was drafted into the US Army. He lay on his bed with the draft notice lying beside him: scared, wretched, powerless. "In that moment," he says, "I became a Communist. I knew, ironically, that as a Communist I was supposed to be supporting the war. But all I could think was: 'It's *me* they're after. It's *me* this lousy fucking system is after.' "

The war for Lou was not simply terrifying—it was also absorbing. The experience was rich and complex. All around him human contradictions kept piling up. A sense of the dark forces of life entered into him. He began to brood on the idea of human destiny.

He came home in early 1946, and now suddenly he was a bit afraid to be a Communist. "Afraid!" he explodes. He leans forward across his coffee cup, the fingertips of one hand held together in the air before him, his dark eyes sparking. "I was in a state of *conflict*. But did I know that? Did I even know such a word existed? No. I did not know. All I thought was: I want to make something of my life, maybe it's dangerous to be a Communist now.

"Well, came May Day I marched. I simply couldn't not march. But I wouldn't put my uniform on. I'd heard that some guys I knew were planning to wear their uniforms and I remember thinking: They're nuts. Well, that was the year a thousand vets marched in their uniforms with their officers leading them. I was drenched in shame. That old emotional pull overtook me. I swallowed my misgivings and rejoined the Party."

From that time on he became a single-minded Communist. He went back to City College, graduated as an economist, and became an organizer for the Party. Occasionally waves of uncertainty would wash over him; when they did, he threw himself more ardently into Party work.

"You know," he says quietly, "there are people, if you met them today and mentioned my name to them, they'd say to you, 'Lou Goodstein? Very intelligent, severely Marxist, a thorough Party man.' But *oy*! Inside, I chafed continuously at the narrowness of the Party's authority. I hated the guys who said to me, 'What are you reading Faulkner for? Why do you go out with non-Party girls?'

"But still," Lou looks into his coffee cup, "the revolution was everything, and by now I had stifled so many contradictions there was no going back. When I married I married a Communist."

In 1951 the Party asked Lou to go underground and provide a refuge for an important, unnamed Communist. Lou immediately agreed. He and his wife left everything behind them in New York, explaining almost nothing to their relatives, bought a house in Pennsylvania, assumed false names and identities, and lived entirely unto themselves in this fashion for two years. Three or four times a year a man would appear and spend a number of weeks inside the house. They asked no questions, received no explanations. They never knew who he was or what he was doing. Twice the Goodsteins moved because they became convinced they were being watched.

It was during this period that Lou had his first intimate experience with the working class—he became a factory worker—and oddly enough the contact aroused his old conflicted sense of the complexity of life. "I learned the meaning of class, not in Marxist terms but in human experiential terms. Those men had a solidarity of experience that was foreign to me, and made me understand the word 'contradiction' as I had never understood it in the Party. There was the foreman who was buddy-buddy with a black worker, always walking with his arm around the black guy's shoulder, eating lunch together every day, and then talking to me about the shit-eating niggers taking over the world. And then there was the guy, a big bruiser of a man whose language was foul, a woman-goosing SOB, who, when my daughter was born and I was giving out cigars, he took one, started to walk away, turned back, and said to me, 'I hope you're not one of those bastards who thinks it's all the woman's job,' and delivered a lecture to me on what childbirth does to a woman, and how weakening and demoralizing it is for her.

"I remember thinking: My God, it's all so complicated out here! The Party doesn't know what the hell is going on out here, it hasn't got a *handle* on the American workingman. It would take me alone two lifetimes to figure it out. I was uneasy all the time I worked in the factory, terribly uneasy, I never felt at home there."

So, of course, since he was uneasy among workers and they reminded him of all his conflicted feelings about his identity as a Communist, in 1953, when the Party asked him to please close up the safe house, return to New York, and "go into industry," Lou Goodstein immediately said yes.

Going into Industry

"GOING into industry" (otherwise known in ironic Party parlance as "colonizing") is the phrase used to describe the Communist Party's practice during the Thirties, Forties, and early Fifties of sending Party organizers out to take up jobs as workers in the factories, plants, laboratories, and offices of America for the purpose of educating workers to class consciousness, converting them to socialism, and recruiting them into the Communist Party. Over nearly a quarter of a century thousands of American Communists spent the greater portion of their adult working lives "in industry." The collective history of the life and work of these CP "colonizers" is one of glory and sorrow.

While for the most part they did not convert American workers to socialism, and certainly they did not recruit them in any
significant numbers into the Communist Party, they most certainly did exert tremendous influence on the growth of worker
consciousness in this country and contributed vastly to the development of the American labor movement. Throughout the
Thirties and Forties, wherever major struggles were taking place
between American labor and American capital, it was almost a
given that CP organizers were involved. In the fields of California,
in the auto plants of Flint, in the steel mills of Pittsburgh, in the
mines of West Virginia, in the electrical plants of Schenectady:
they were there. They fought for the eight-hour day, the min-
imum wage, worker compensation, health and welfare insurance.
And for one glorious moment—during the brief life of the CIO
—they brought genuine worker politics to the American labor
movement. What happened to many of the organizers, in fact,
was that while they were unable to convert the nation's workers
to socialism, they themselves became gifted American trade
unionists.

Many of them, of course, did not. Many of them, like Lou
Goodstein, were painfully ill at ease "in industry" and remained
deeply dislocated throughout their years in the factories, plants,
and mills, where they went through the motions of organizing
for the Party but never made any real contact with the men and
women among whom they lived and worked. These are the people who Joe Preisen despised, and who John Dos Passos mythi-
cized: the CP organizer as spiritual isolate, living out his years in
exile—right up against the working class—as though doing confused penance for the sins of capitalism.

Lou Goodstein spent seven years working in an automobile
plant in Buffalo. "Buffalo," Lou sighs. "When I die and I come
up before the seat of judgment, there will be a book this thick
of my sins of omission and commission. Then there will be a book
this thick of the punishments I have already received. Then a
voice from above will be heard and it will say, 'All is canceled.
He lived seven years in Buffalo.' "

Lou is silent for a moment. Then his voice flares up in surprising defensiveness. "I *still* say sending us out was the right
thing to do." He is silent again. Then: "But we were the wrong

people. I could have worked all my life in the shop and I still never would have been one of them."

Karl Millens is fifty years old. He was raised in The Coops, named for Karl Marx, and was for twenty-three years a member of the Communist Party. Between the ages of twenty and thirty-seven he worked in industrial plants all over the Midwest on assignment for the CP. Today, Karl is an instructor in political science in a small community college in the New York area. He has written one book he was unable to get published and is now at work on a second. Publication, he says, is really a minor concern for him; he is happiest when sitting at the typewriter.

"The typewriter," Karl says, holding out his large, well-shaped hands, "is a machine that fits my hands. The machines I used when I worked in the plant, they never fit my hands. They never felt natural to me, the way the typewriter does."

Karl Millens is not bitter about his life as a Communist, but he is a sad man. He is divorced, estranged from many of his old friends, lives in a shabby one-room apartment in lower Manhattan, works at a low-paying, intellectually unrewarding job, and seems continually to be repressing a tide of emotional bewilderment that threatens daily to engulf him. It is visibly difficult for him to talk about the past. He is intelligent enough to know that if he could make sense of the past he would live more easily in the present, but he seems to have no confidence in the notion that he ever *can* make sense of the past. On this cold December night, however, he tries, he tries.

"Growing up in The Coops . . ." he begins vaguely. He passes a hand wearily across his wide forehead grown wider by virtue of a receding hairline. "It was like growing up in a hothouse. We were *the* hothouse kids of the Left. And like all creatures of the hothouse, we bloomed more intensely, more radiantly, precisely because the atmosphere was artificial. You know, in a very real sense America was a foreign country to us. Electoral politics meant nothing to us. But for weeks before May Day every wall, every storefront, every lamp post in the neighborhood was plastered with 'All Out May One.' And on the day itself the local grade school was empty. *That* was our election day, our July Fourth, our Hannukah, and our Christmas.

"I think almost every other Communist in America was more realistically involved with the country than we were. And more realistically involved with how they could best serve Communism in America than we were. We grew up inside a language and a culture that was so dense, so insular, and finally so abstract. It's incredible, when I think of it. We were all working class. Now, most working-class Communists didn't romanticize working. But we, having grown up inside the theoretical jargon of Marxist-Leninist thought, adopted the stance of middle-class Party intellectuals and conceived our mission as revolutionaries to join the proletariat as fast as possible. No matter that we really *were* halfway to being intellectuals, that we felt at home *only* talking theory, 'going into industry' was all most of us dreamed of from the time we were teenagers.

"God! That language. This was supposed to be a movement of liberation, but every time I turned around I felt more and more constricted. Constricted by my language, which was either acceptable or nonacceptable. Constricted by my actions, which were definitely either acceptable or nonacceptable. Books I should or should not be reading, thoughts I should or should not be having. . . . The Marxist-Leninist jargon was supposed to be evidence of high intelligence. But I found it put to uses of intimidation, and finally I felt it evidenced more a fear of life than it did of genuinely high intelligence. I remember when I left my wife and went into psychotherapy, I felt like a light had gone on inside my head. I saw a shape to my life I had not imagined before. When I tried to tell my oldest friend in the Party some of the things that were happening inside me, he talked to me as though I were counterrevolutionary vermin, fit only to be isolated in a laboratory or—under the right, the *correct* regime—taken out and shot. But all that came later, much later, these realizations of mine. First, I had to put in seventeen years in industry, serving the revolution around the corner.

"What can I tell you about the years in industry? They were, for me, slow, imperceptible, pointless death. I spent seventeen years working beside men I never had any intimacy or shared experience with, doing work which numbed my mind and for which I had no physical facility. Its sole purpose was to allow me to grow close to the men and be ready to move when a radically pregnant situation arose. Well, I was never close to the men and no situation arose, at least none *I* would ever know how to move into. I discovered very quickly I had no talent—repeat *none*—for organizing, for unionizing, for negotiating. I was slow-witted, clumsy on the uptake, half the time I didn't know what the hell was going on around me. When a real, a natural organizer arose among the men, not only did I see how far away I was from the action, I couldn't even encourage the guy in a radical direction. I'd open my mouth and out would come, I'm sure, I can hardly remember now what I said, some Marxist-Leninist formula. The guy would just stare at me, shake his head, and walk away. I know he liked me, but I'm also sure he thought I was retarded.

"I know that many people who went into industry were terrific organizers and turned out to be great trade unionists. But I have a feeling not too many of them came from The Coops."

There is at least one man in America who can, and does, challenge Karl Millens' conviction that no one from The Coops went successfully into industry. His name is Maurey Sachman. He, like Karl, is fifty years old, was raised in The Coops, and became a Communist in his teens. He received a college education, spent fifteen years working in a steel mill in Pittsburgh, and his story is as complicated as Karl's is simple.

Maurey Sachman and his wife, Paula, live in a small university town in Kansas. To anyone from the East or the West there is no word for this town but bleak; as far as the eye can reach and for hundreds of miles around the land spreads out in an oppressive, unbroken flatness; even when the sun is shining here, the atmosphere seems grey. From the edge of the town it feels as though one stands literally beyond the borders of the world. The university occupies the central space of the town—its campus quietly pleasant—and all around lie the "good" residential neighborhoods, the "less good," and the "bad." A deep puzzlement of the soul overtakes one: What is the point of it all? Why be rich or poor in this place? Over all the streets hangs the same off-the-map inertness.

The Sachmans live in one of the "less good" neighborhoods on a tree-lined street filled with large shabby Victorian houses. Instinctively, one knows that when you sell here you sell at a loss. The house I am looking for is a faded yellow with dull brown trim. The yard is full of weeds and the porch railing sags. The Sachmans live here with their four children because, while Maurey teaches history at the university, he has not yet received a professorial promotion and is, in fact, now locked into a tense struggle for tenure; half the people in his department love him, half of them hate him, his future here is up for grabs. Maurey himself seems to be enjoying the struggle, it clearly arouses old political appetites in him. Paula, however, seems bone-weary and terribly depressed by the uncertainty of their future.

Maurey is a tall, swarthy man; his face is handsome and powerful, the features strong rather than fine. His manner and speech match his face: they are open, warm, filled with an intelligence that is blunt rather than subtle. Paula Sachman is slim and beautiful, with deep-set dark eyes and the body of a dancer. She is one of those women who grew up wearing black stockings, silver jewelry, and her hair in a long ponytail. She still does, only now the ponytail is heavily streaked with grey. These two have been married for thirty years, and they have about them the unmistakable look of a couple who have been through the wars together.

In 1944, when he was twenty years old, Maurey was drafted into the army. Before he left for boot camp he and Paula were married. They had known each other forever, and now that the war had reached out for them they clung together in healing superstition: if they married surely he would come back alive. While Maurey was overseas Paula joined the Communist Party, this act somehow further ensuring in her mind their solidarity and their claim upon their lives.

Maurey returned in one triumphant piece and entered New York's City College, where Paula was already enrolled and active in the CP student group. He immediately plunged back into Party work, more than ever an intensely committed Communist. He did not, in fact, wish to return to school; he wished to go immediately into industry. The war had made him, if anything, more cynical about bourgeois education than he had been before and he was eager to enter into revolutionary "realife," but both his parents and the Party insisted he get an undergraduate degree.

While still at school—and now that Maurey was home safe—Paula began to chafe at the "hard-line" behavior of their fellow CP students. While the others were all studying history or political science, Paula was studying art, developing her early talents as a graphics designer. The atmosphere in the art department nourished in her an imaginative faculty that led her, increasingly, to question the black and white Marxist answers Maurey and his friends had for the innumerable uncertainties that now began to hover in her young mind. One day, while having lunch at the group's table in the City College cafeteria, Paula said to the leader of the group: "What do you mean, that's the objective reality? There *is* no objective reality in this case. Look at it this way . . ." And the two fell into a somewhat acrimonious argument about the situation under discussion.

The following week Paula was told that her presence was requested at Communist Party Headquarters. She was mystified and a bit frightened by this order to appear at the building on Twelfth Street. Maurey reassured her that it was all probably nothing with nothing, and accompanied her downtown on the designated day.

"I went up to the room I had been told to go to," Paula says, her face tight, her long slim fingers wrapped around her coffee cup as we sit at the kitchen table in Kansas twenty-six years after the fact. "Maurey remained outside in the hall. I went in and there were all our friends from school plus a man I'd never seen before. I noticed immediately that the chairs were arranged oddly: all in a circle with one chair in the middle of the circle. The strange man directed me to sit on the chair in the middle of the circle. I started to tremble. I took my seat and it began.

"I was being brought up on charges of insubordination and divisiveness, the man told me. What did that mean? I asked. Who was bringing these charges? The man nodded to the leader of our group. I turned to him and said, 'Jerry, *you're* charging me?' Jerry—I'd known him for years—didn't answer me. His eyes were cold and his lips pressed together, I hardly recognized him.

He nodded his head. 'What does that mean?' I asked. 'I've never said or done *anything*.'

"Then one of the girls in our group took out a notebook and began to read from it. It was simply unbelievable. I thought I was going to lose my mind then and there. She read out whole conversations that had taken place in the cafeteria at school. Conversations I could barely remember, things I supposedly said I couldn't remember saying, it all seemed so long ago and far away. She had been taking notes on my conversations for two years. Two whole years. I looked at her as though I'd never seen her before in my life. She had been my friend. We used to go back to the Bronx together on the subway. We'd talked about clothes and homework and our mothers, and all that time she'd been taking notes on me. It was like being in the middle of a nightmare I was never going to wake up from." Paula stops then and stares into her coffee. Neither I nor Maurey say a word. I continue to look into Paula's face, Maurey stares down at the table.

"I guess I *did* sort of lose my balance then for a moment," Paula goes on. "I began to scream, 'You're all crazy, crazy! If there's any justice in this lousy world it's *you* who'll be punished, not me.' And then I ran out of the room. I threw myself into Maurey's arms and said, 'Take me out of here, take me out of here. And never bring me back. *Never.*' Two days later I was expelled from the Communist Party."

Paula turns and stares at her husband, who continues to look down at the wooden kitchen table. Her stare is without expression: neither accusing nor ironic, only extraordinarily dry-eyed, as though all the feeling behind that stare had long ago drained out of her.

"Well," she goes on, "I was out, but he was definitely still in. I talked my lungs out to him. Days without end I tortured him. Trying to make him see what I had seen in that room, trying to make him understand what it meant, not just for now but for the future. For *our* future. I couldn't budge him. The revolution was everything.

"During this time another of our friends was put on trial and expelled. The guy nearly killed himself. I mean, really nearly committed suicide. He and his wife were our best friends, they'd been best man and maid of honor at our wedding and we at theirs. We sat around their kitchen one night, and suddenly he got up and left the apartment. Almost immediately we realized he'd gone up on the roof. Maurey ran after him and stopped him. He talked to him, pleaded with him, reasoned with him. He loved that guy. Just as he loved me. . . .

"But there was already a distance between him and us. We were out, and he was in. We were on the other side of some kind of wall inside his mind. We were . . . I guess we were somehow *unreal* to him already."

I look questioningly at Maurey who is being discussed as though he were not present. He waves my look away with his eyes, his expression indicating "This is Paula's story, she has the right to tell it any way she wants to."

"When Maurey graduated from City," Paula continues, "I was pregnant with our first child. He could hardly wait to leave New York and go into industry for the Party. I begged him not to do it, not to make me leave New York. I was twenty-two years old, pregnant, afraid to leave home. And besides that, I had just started to work in graphics design. I knew that if I stayed in the city I could make a career for myself, and that if I left I'd be tagging along behind him for the rest of my life. Nothing I said or did made a dent in him.

"I had a terrible pregnancy. In my seventh month I became bedridden. Maurey came home one day and said the Party had said to go to Pittsburgh. *Now.* We had a terrible fight. I screamed and cried. He just closed his face to me and left the house. I lay sweating on that bed in the Bronx. Maurey's father came to see me. He was beside himself. He said the Party was stealing his son's life, I must do something, I must stop him. 'You're the wife,' he said, 'stop him.' 'Stop him!' I screamed at the old man. 'Don't you know?' I said. 'Don't you know I don't mean anything to him? Not me, not you, nobody. Nothing but the Communist Party means anything! Forget it,' I said. 'You don't have a son anymore.'

"I gave birth alone. Maurey came home when the baby was a week old and he said to me, 'I'm staying in Pittsburgh. You want to come, come. You want to stay, stay.' Six weeks later I followed him to Pittsburgh."

The day after Paula told "her" story, Maurey and I took a ride out to a park on the edge of the town. The day was grey and wet, the air full of clean refreshing moisture. We got out of the car and breathed deeply, gratefully. We both felt, I'm sure, as though we'd been sitting in a roomful of stale air and cigarette smoke for days. We started up a path cut through the park's planted woods. For some time neither of us spoke, tramping along in pleasurable silence, looking at the sharply etched grey and black November trees. After a while we sat down on a rock placed at the top of a slight rise that looked down on the park's playground and out to the town's one factory sitting inside stolid nineteenth-century brick on the flat horizon beyond. Maurey gazed silently at the factory for a time. Then he said:

"Paula's right, of course. Everything she said is true. I was a gung-ho Communist, obsessed with the Party and the revolution. I couldn't see what I was doing to the people around me, the people I loved and who loved me, friends, family, comrades. There was only one way to act, one way to get things done, one way to serve the revolution. It was so deep inside of me I could taste it in my mouth, I really couldn't understand how they could see things differently. Nothing was as real to me as being a Communist. And then, you see, I had had a fantastic victory so early, the memory of it was like a blood transfusion in times of weakness for years afterwards. . . .

"Do you remember the Knickerbocker-Davis strike at City? Here were these two guys, these two professors paid by city taxes, teaching working-class Jews, making anti-Semitic remarks. The thing exploded like a bomb. It was an incredible issue at City. Feelings escalated and escalated, and finally the whole school went out on strike for three days. Do you know what that meant in Nineteen-Forty-Seven? To bring a school like City out on strike? It was unheard of. Everyone said the strike was engineered by the Communists. And," Maurey turned full face towards me and grinned deeply, "they were right. *We* did it. We prepared, organized, and led that strike. I couldn't believe it was happening. I couldn't believe we had actually done it. We worked our asses off thirty hours a day for weeks, hardly stopping to eat or sleep. And we did it. We brought them out on strike. All the time it was happening, in my head I was singing: It can be *done*, it *can* be done.

"I went into industry with the Knickerbocker-Davis strike ringing in my ears. I was twenty-four years old. I thought I was going to organize American steelworkers into the revolution like *that*. Oh, it might take me six months, a year, maybe even two years. . . . Ten years later my world was in ruins, inside and outside, and all I had probably done was help make a few more workers into cops for the bosses.

"It took a couple of years for it to begin to dawn on me, just ever so slightly around the edges, that I wasn't radicalizing anybody in the mill, that it was a full-time, maybe lifetime job just to make them see things in *union* terms, and what I was spending my life doing wasn't going to amount to a row of beans in larger political terms.

"But you know? And this is the thing, of course, that Paula doesn't understand, *can't* understand. I loved it. I loved working in the mill. I loved every part of it. The difficulty, the danger, the men, the machinery, the inhuman schedules, the whole process of turning out steel. I got to know that mill inside out. I knew how everything worked, where everything was kept, exactly how each job fed every part of the process, what it meant if one man worked two days running and another goofed off, how dangerous it was, what it meant all the way down the line.

"The thing was this: I was a damned good organizer, I helped build a strong local in that mill, I had real feeling for the place, the work, the men. In many ways, I had a good life there. But I never saw it in its own terms. I don't know if I ever *could* have, under any conditions, because that would have meant staying in the working class for the sake of staying in the working class, and that I'm not sure I could have done. For the Party I could have remained in the working class forever. But for myself . . . that was another matter.

"And, in a certain sense, that's the real tragedy of the whole thing. Not just for myself but for all of us. You see, the European Communists have always had the patience of the long view. Those guys could live out a whole lifetime working for something that might come in two, three generations. But with us, we lived with such a pent-up, explosive sense of imminent revolution. We could, and did, act often in such stupid, brutal ways because we imagined ourselves always in a revolutionary situation.

When we weren't at all. The result was that we had no foresight, no patience, no real understanding of how long and hard the road to socialist change is. And when it was all over for us the people we had hurt along the way came back at us hurling bricks and bats.

"The 20th Party Congress struck me like lightning. Here I was in Pittsburgh all those years, working like a son of a bitch in a steel mill, my wife bitter and angry all the time, my kids confused, me exhausted and harassed, my only contact with the Party the organizer who comes out from New York once a month and *he's* like a visiting mother-in-law, I gotta explain this jerk who talks like the Little Lenin Library to my wife *and* to the guys at the mill . . . and then Khrushchev drops this bomb."

Maurey fell silent at this point. He shivered for a moment in the late afternoon chill and huddled deeper inside his navy-blue parka. "Let's walk," I said. He nodded and we got up from the rock and began walking down the sloping hill toward the children's playground below. Maurey absentmindedly snapped a branch from a tree and began stripping its dead leaves as he walked. I remained silent, waiting. He went on:

"I don't really know how to describe what happened to me, to a lot of us, then. My own immediate response to Khrushchev's report was: What the hell does this *mean*? Don't panic. Hang loose. Wait and see. So I did just that. I made no move, I continued working, I hung as though suspended in air, like the moment between the time the shot enters the body and the body dies. Then, slowly at first and after a while faster and faster, I began receiving visits from guys like myself working in industry all over the area. From Jersey, from upstate New York, from Massachusetts. Everybody suddenly showing up in Pittsburgh and saying to me, 'Maurey, what do we do now?' As if *I* knew what we did now. But that wasn't it. Everybody knew nobody knew what to do, but everybody needed comfort real bad. Everybody needed to huddle and try to figure out what the hell our lives had been all about and what we do with them from here on in.

"So we began meeting, a whole bunch of us, in a kind of regular irregular way—in Pittsburgh, in Boston, in Philly. And talking. Talking like we'd never talked before. Years later, I discovered that guys in the underground began meeting after the 20th Congress Report in much the same way, and these guys—the Young Turks—became the dissenters who later ended up splitting the Party apart. Well, I don't think you could say we, the guys in industry, became dissenters exactly, we were really too confused for that, but let me tell you, there was a lot of pain and blood spilled at those meetings. People said things about themselves, their lives, the Party you'd never have dreamed were inside them waiting to get out. It was awful, simply awful. And yet, it was terrific, too. Exciting. Tremendously exciting to hear people rethinking their lives out loud.

"In a sense it came to nothing, those meetings. In another sense, of course, it was the beginning of the end. I didn't quit the Party or the mill. I stayed on for quite a few years afterwards. The world didn't end with a bang it ended with a whimper. The heart was just slowly leaking out of me. Paula knew, and for a long time she left me alone. The constant anger in her seemed to subside. She got very quiet. I think she was really very frightened by what was happening to me, to the Party, to the world she'd grown up in.

"But," Maurey laughed, a dry, wry laugh, "she managed to get it all back. The women's movement helped her, and the anger all came back." He fell silent again for another moment and didn't speak until we were once more settled in his car.

"In Nineteen-Sixty-Three," he said, putting the key in the ignition, "I went back to school. Boy, I hit those books like a madman, like a guy who's been out in the desert suddenly drinking water again. For three years I read day and night. I couldn't get enough. It was such a pleasure to be thinking again. I got the Ph.D. and here I am." He switched on the ignition and grinned at me. "*Still* scratching around." And he moved the car out of its space and onto the open road.

"But, no," he shook his head, "it's very different now. No matter what the outcome of this tenure fight, for instance, or any other fight of my life, for that matter. It can't really hit me where I live. It can't make me question the very core of myself. Can't make me lose my judgment or get confused about the reference points on the map inside my head. Nothing can do that anymore. My sense of survival is too solid. After all, it's been through the fire. What the hell in my life can come close to the years in the Communist Party? It's ridiculous. Nothing can make me question myself, my very existence, as those years did. And they were good years, damned good years, and the price I've paid for them, on balance, is an equitable one. No regrets, none at all. For Paula, of course, it's another question. And for Paula and me together, it's still another question. But that's it. That's where we are. And there's no place else we can be."

The Underground

IN 1951 approximately 2,000 American Communists went underground. The leadership of the Party had been arrested and put on trial in 1949, two dozen people were already in prison, and McCarthy was just over the horizon. The CP thought fascism was coming to America: that American Communists in wholesale lots would be arrested, imprisoned, exiled, perhaps even killed. It was decided that in order to save the Party the entire second echelon of Party leadership would be sent into hiding; that way, even if the top Party leadership was decimated there would still be a functioning organization, a "government in exile."

Between 1951 and 1955 these 2,000 experienced a life which—until the 1960s—was unknown in America: the life of an entire subpopulation on the political run from its own government, living in eerie exile ("strangers in our own country") for a period of years, cut off from their lives, cast adrift into a world without time, a place without content, an existence bereft of the connective tissue without which human life is mere survival, punishing in its crude loneliness.

One of these 2,000 was Nettie Posin, an organizer-at-large for many years for the Communist Party. In 1951, at the order of the Party, Nettie became "unavailable." She left her home, her family, her friends and disappeared for four years into drifting America. It was, she says, the very worst period of her life. She would much have preferred prison to the desolating loneliness of those years. To become a non-Communist melting into the people with everyone searching for her, to be ready at a moment's notice to leave everything behind, get on a bus, and disappear out of a town, to be able to confide in no one, to have to need nothing, to remain alone on the vast, disintegrating edge of life. "Better prison," Nettie says softly, "much better. It was a great mistake, a great error on the part of the Party. I'm surprised more people didn't go mad. As it was, many Communists were lost, many people lost *themselves*."

In the spring of 1974 Nettie Posin is a bookseller in downtown Los Angeles. She runs a small, cozy shop stocked with movement literature: Communist, black, women—you name the movement, she's got the literature. Nettie is still a Communist but, although she won't admit it directly, these days she stays alive politically more through the people who come into her shop than she does through the Party.

At sixty-five Nettie is a slim, athletic-looking, almost tomboyish woman: her hair is short, her stride is long, her clothes neat and very plain, her blue eyes earnest in her weather-beaten face. She looks straightforwardly self-sufficient, as though in fact she needs very little in the way of external sustenance, human or otherwise. However, her complicated history raises complicated questions about her appearance.

Nettie Posin was born in the Ukraine into a family of poor, politically disposed Jews. She had two sisters and two brothers; her elder sister Masha was her adored model for how to be in life. When the Red Army marched into the Ukraine Masha hung a red flag out the window and, for Nettie, that was it.

Nettie was seventeen years old when the Posins came to America. They settled in Chicago and Masha immediately joined the Communist Party. ("Did the other sister join, too?" I ask. "Oh, no," Nettie replies in perfect psychoanalytic innocence, "she was beautiful!") A year later, at eighteen, Nettie also joined the Party. For the next forty years she knew no other life than that of the Communist Party.

The Thirties was *the* compelling event for Nettie. ("Here you were hungry and unemployed, and *it wasn't your fault*.") She led a thousand demonstrations, was arrested twenty-eight times, and became involved in the deportation trials that have dogged her all her life in the United States.

In 1934, when she was twenty-five years old, the Party sent her back to the Soviet Union to become a trained organizer at the Lenin Institute. She returned to this country in 1936 and from that time on she organized: steelworkers in Gary, dressmakers in Los Angeles, electrical workers in New York.

In 1951, when the Party ordered her to become unavailable, Nettie was living in Los Angeles, as was her sister Masha and most of the people Nettie was closest to. She said good-bye to no one, left her apartment as though she would be returning that night, and simply evaporated into the Los Angeles smog: "When I disappeared I lay beneath rugs on a car floor. They took me to a bus terminal in a strange city. I took a bus to another city, then another bus to another city, and so it began.

"How can I describe those years to you?" Nettie says, as we sit drinking coffee in a little table-and-chair corner of her sunny bookshop. "At first, and for a long time afterwards, I did not question the Party's decision to send us into hiding. I, also, thought fascism was coming and that we—certainly as a party and most of us individually—would be wiped out. We *had* to make this effort to survive. It was the hardest 'assignment' of my life, but I accepted it.

"Then, as the months and the years wore on, I began to wonder what on earth it was all about. I began to lose my way—I was alone so much!—and my life, and the purpose of what I was doing became a dark and mysterious burden. I could not figure out why I was wandering around America like this.

"Can you imagine what it was like? I would land in a town, take a room in a boardinghouse and look for work, either by the day or by the week. I would live like that, entirely to myself, for a few weeks or a few months, and then I would move on. Something would happen, I would become convinced I was being watched, I would *go*. And then I'd have to start all over again. Collect again: a traveling iron, a pillow for my back, a pot of flowers, a shawl for the table, a few books and shelves, things for the kitchen and the bathroom. Do you know how many times I bought those things in four years? And how each time I set out to buy them I'd pare down the list by one item. I'd look at something in a store, something that I knew would make the atmosphere of my room a little more homey, a little more human, and I'd put it down and say to myself: What for? You'll only have to leave it behind.

"Why didn't I take these things with me when I moved? I'll give you one instance, and you'll know why. One day, I was living somewhere in the Midwest, I came home from work. As I started to turn the corner onto the street where my room was, I saw standing on the other side of the street at the far corner a man I'd known years ago in Rochester, a Party member everyone knew had turned informer. I literally turned on my heel and kept walking in the direction I'd been coming from. I never returned to that room. I left the city that day with five dollars in my pocket.

"When things like that happened it was terrible, terrible. Can you imagine what it means to arrive in a town with five dollars in your pocket? First, you have to look for a room where they don't ask for advance rent. You think that's easy to find? Then you have to find work right away so you won't be hungry. It wasn't so much going hungry I was afraid of, it was getting sick. I was terrified of getting sick. To know that you can't afford to get sick because you're afraid to go to a public hospital because maybe a cop will be there and will become suspicious of you. Oh, the depression these fears used to bring on!

"And the work I did. God, the work. You know, there's working-class life and there's working-class life. I'd spent my whole life among workers, in and out of plants, mills, factories. But then I was *organizing*, I was among my own, the work had purpose, meaning, connection. When I was underground I found myself working in places, it was like the nineteenth century. The silence in those places! The silence of people who don't even know they're workers, who are only extensions of the machine. And I could never break that silence. I couldn't talk to anyone, make friends with anyone, suggest something that would make that dumb intelligence start coming alive. Because then I'd call attention to myself.

"Once I was walking the streets of a town I'd just arrived in. I looked up on the main street and saw a huge sign over a factory building. It said, 'Plenty of work. Good pay. No experience or references necessary.' I went into the building. It was a tremendous factory, a hundred women sitting at sewing machines. They made clothes for dolls. You got paid by the piece and you could learn on the job. What the hell did they care if you worked a few weeks for ten cents? I said I knew how to run a sewing machine and they put me to work. Clothes for dolls! You could go blind in fifteen minutes, and in another fifteen lose two fingers in the machine. I looked at the clock when I started to work. After what seemed like hours I looked up at the clock again. Three minutes had passed. I worked that whole day, but the next day I couldn't go back. Not even for the few dollars I'd earned, I couldn't go back.

"Four years I spent like that. For my party. For international Communism. I grew numb and dumb inside myself. Three or four times a year I'd make contact with the Party, I'd manage to meet somewhere with one courier or another. They'd say to me, 'What's the matter, Nettie? You all right? You're not getting sick, are you?' After a while I could hardly answer them. But I stuck, I stuck.

"When I was finally given permission to come out, I called Masha in Los Angeles. I said to her, 'Do you know who this is speaking?' 'Yes,' she said. 'Well,' I said, 'how is your house these days? Is it clean?' 'Yes,' she said, 'it's immaculate.' So I came back to Los Angeles. I was walking up the street towards Masha's house. She came out and we fell into each other's arms in the middle of the street. Four years we hadn't laid eyes on each other."

Hugh Armstrong worked as a courier in the CP underground. It was one of his last assignments in the Communist Party, and the experience that led to his final break with the Party.

Armstrong is sixty-one years old. He is a large, handsome black man with a shock of white hair whose looks remind me of Bayard Rustin. He works as a sales manager for a large New England electronics firm, stays at good hotels when he is in New York, and dresses in well-cut conservative clothes. His manner is placid, easygoing, philosophical for the most part, only occasionally bitter. He tries very hard to place the political past in its proper perspective in his life but clearly it is a struggle for him to do so. He is now a passionate black nationalist, and the denial of black nationalism inherent in his years as a Communist often rises up in him to make him gag at the memory of that other life.

Hugh Armstrong was born in Cleveland to a father who was an educated hod-carrier and a mother whose emotional stability was powerful. He was one of six children. The family was desperately poor and food on the table every night was a touch-and-go affair for many years. The mother held them all together fiercely so that the poverty they suffered would be one of the body more than of the spirit.

Nevertheless, the father sank year by year into helpless despair and Hugh and his brother Ralph, the two smartest kids in the family, responded deeply to the father's complex and increasingly nihilistic sense of life—even while they yearned toward the mother's redeeming love.

In the late 1920s the father was arrested for running illegal whiskey; the police let him go on the condition that he leave Cleveland. When he left town Hugh and Ralph went with him. The father and his two sons came to New York and settled in Harlem. The boys, each in his own way, were by this time fairly wild. Neither one of them, says Hugh, could to this day tell you *exactly* why they did what they did but each of them embarked on a brief career of delinquency and petty crime. Each of them, he says, felt driven—wild, lost inside, wanting to press down on what felt like an open wound—almost as though he wanted to end up in jail, wanted to end up being beaten half to death some dark night at the bottom of an alley.

Harlem in the 1930s was alive with Depression and political animation: the Garveyites on one corner, the Anarchists on another, the Communists on still another. The two boys heard it all, dimly, on the edge of consciousness, as they went their angry, fighting way, but for a long time none of it sank in. Then, one day, they met a man who instead of yelling at them engaged them in conversation. He asked them why they were doing what they were doing and he asked them to think about it before they answered him. So they thought and then they answered. He listened for a while and then he said to them, "Listen, there's a woman I'd like you to meet. She invites a lot of people to her house, and I think she'd like to have you two come, also. Here's her address, come on over this Sunday."

The woman was Grace Tillett. She was an educated, well-to-do black woman whose house was a gathering place for talented, intellectual, and rather prominent blacks. In Grace Tillett's home, at the height of the Depression, all the ideas of the time were being discussed by the kind of black people Hugh and Ralph didn't even know existed. The two boys went up to Grace's house that Sunday and their lives were profoundly changed. The discussion going on excited them tremendously, and when they sought to enter it their half-formed, eager responses were considered, and even more important their raw native intelligence acknowledged.

They returned to Grace Tillett's house every Sunday thereafter. They stopped stealing and running wild in the streets of Harlem because suddenly they couldn't concentrate anymore on wildness, they didn't have the time, they spent the entire week talking over between themselves what had been discussed at Grace's on Sunday. A world beyond that of their claustrophobic pain had opened up for them: the world of their own minds.

The people at Grace Tillett's discussed everything: art, literature, philosophy, theater, the New Deal, Garvey, utopianism, anarchy, and socialism. What emerged most dynamically for the Armstrong boys was Marxism: Marxism and the Communist Party. At Grace's, they felt themselves at the center of things, and at the center of the center was the Communist Party.

In 1933, when they were nineteen and twenty, Ralph and Hugh joined the Party. In the twenty-five years that followed Ralph bolted in and out of the Party many times, but not Hugh. Hugh became passionately welded to the Party and to his life as a Communist; he rose in time to become the organizer of Mason Goode's section in the northern Bronx, wielding a fair amount of power and influence in inner Party circles. He left the Party in 1956 after the 20th Congress Report, feeling personally betrayed.

"All those years," Hugh says, "I always felt I wasn't being listened to as seriously as a white S.O. would be listened to. Oh, it was never anything I could actually put my finger on, just a feeling, a feeling that never left me, that kind of dogged me at the back of my gut. At the same time, I knew they needed me—after all, how many blacks did they have?—knew it was desperately important to them that I be soothed, placated, given extra attention. When it was all over that was the thing I remembered the most. That, I guess, is what made me turn on them in my feelings, made me think they were white men, after all.

"But while I was in the Party it was everything. The class struggle, party discipline, Marxist dogma, everything, everything. There was nothing you could ask me I didn't have an answer for."

What kind of a functionary was he? I ask. How would he classify himself?

"Oh," Armstrong says, crossing one neatly trousered leg over the other and running a hand through his beautiful white Afro, "I like to think I was kinder, more compassionate than some of the others . . ."

I nod my head, listening, waiting. I am remembering Mason Goode's description of his section organizer—Hugh Armstrong— as "a charming, intelligent, tyrannical man whose method of criticism was pure attack and humiliation."

In 1952 the Party asked Armstrong to become a courier in the underground. His duties as section organizer were allocated elsewhere, and he took to the underground road. "For the next three years," he says, "I lived out of my car. I carried a caseful of house appliances. In case I got stopped I was a traveling salesman. My territory was New England. I set up safe houses, a network of non-Party messengers (many of whom never knew what the hell they were doing), a foolproof telephone code system, and, of course, courier schedules. For three solid years I bought and sold houses, transported people by night and in secret, visited guys sitting for months on end in houses in the Connecticut woods . . .

"When I think back on it the thing that haunts me the most is the innocent people I involved, the people I pushed, bullied, nagged into helping me. If they had known what they were doing, if they'd been caught, their lives might have been ruined . . . But for the Party I was willing to ruin anybody, anywhere.

"I guess that's the thing that's stuck most in my craw. I like to *think* I was kinder than most, but it's not true. I wasn't. I was just like all the rest. I'm sure if I had had to turn my grandmother in it would have seemed like the only thing I could possibly do.

"But you know? If it hadn't been for the experience in the underground I don't think I ever would have seen that. The underground was so stark, so naked, so *driven* a business. The things we did were so mad. And nobody could see around it, not for ten minutes. Nobody could stand back and say, 'This is nuts. This is absolutely nuts. What the hell are we doing out here, playing cops and robbers in the woods?'

"That was so typical of the CP. The underground was the culmination of the theatricality, the self-delusion with which the CP embarked on the 'double life' of the 'professional revolutionary.' God! It was so ridiculous, when we were described later as this master organization of conspiracy. We couldn't conspire our way out of a paper bag. When people in the Party took aliases? Christ, at least half the FBI knew the real and assumed name of every CP functionary. And in the underground. . . . I know damn well we were running around like rats in a maze, with the FBI able to lay their hands on almost every one of us anytime they wanted to.

"Afterwards, it was so hard to remember the frame of mind that had made it seem the only right, real, reasonable thing to do at the time. All I could think about was the people I had endangered, the guys sitting out there going slowly crazy, the rigidity with which I acted out this half-imaginary war. And then twenty-five years of feeling patronized and used came crashing in on me, and I couldn't forgive, no I couldn't forgive."

One of the men sitting out there going slowly crazy was Bill Chaikin, who spent five of his twenty-five years in the Communist Party in the underground.

Chaikin lives on New York's West Side, runs a prosperous radio repair business, and looks much younger than his sixty-one years. He reminds me strongly of Maurey Sachman in the way that one is "reminded" by cruder or finer variations on a set of looks in the members of a single family. In this case the variations are all cruder. Chaikin's face is alive with the same kind of powerful good looks devoid of delicacy that characterized Maurey's face —only more so. His intelligence is as blunt as Maurey's—only harder edged—and his speech and views are also reminiscent of

Maurey's—only again, in a more extreme version. Unlike Maurey, however, he is now as passionate an anti-Communist as he was once a Communist.

Bill Chaikin, like Maurey Sachman, was born into the movement. He has never known life outside of the circle of the American left wing. His parents were both flaming Marxists who raised their son to become a professional revolutionary. Bill joined the Communist Party when he was eighteen years old, and rose quickly in the ranks to become the section organizer of the strongest CP neighborhood in Brooklyn. He was sent to cadre school ("Where I became a good Jesuit," he says with a bitter smile), and for many years administered his territory with a weighty sense of his place in the scheme of international Communism.

When I ask him—as I do everyone—how he would have felt if he'd been expelled during those years he replies that he can't even remember thinking about it because such a thing was unthinkable. "Could *I* have been expelled?" he says in dramatic self-mockery. "Never! Why how could *I*, I who was so thoroughly, so correctly indoctrinated be expelled? If you were expelled there was something wrong with *you*. But that you could never be me.

"And of course," he goes on, "the Party had a built-in method for dealing with the kind of situations that could lead someone to the edge of behavior that could get you expelled. You see, if you questioned anything, any decision, any bit of policy, any directive, why then *you* were the very one to implement that policy, carry out that directive. It was exactly like the church: every time you experienced a lapse of faith you prayed an extra hour, gave yourself an *extra* hundred lashes."

Chaikin's blazing bitterness can easily be traced directly to his very orthodoxy. All the way through this year I have found that those Communists who, consciously or unconsciously, said, "This far I go, and no farther," live in decent relation to their CP past; whereas, those who were most rigidly orthodox, those who were practically willing to commit murder for the Party, are those who now beat their breasts with a scalding Lady Macbeth–like inner revulsion, reflecting—still—the most neurotic element of idealism as it manifested itself in countless Communists. The failure, then as now, lies with understanding the requirements of the irreducible self, that self which when ignored or betrayed by ideology responds with panic-stricken cruelty.

It was the underground that turned Chaikin around, made him into a "Young Turk," the name given to the men who in the underground became the most unrelenting of dissenters; the men who in the years right after the 20th Congress Report demanded the kinds of structural changes in Party policy and Party authority that the Communist Party USA was constitutionally incapable of, and who—in 1956, 57, 58—left the Party in droves.

Men like Bill Chaikin who had been ferociously, expectantly active, now—in the ferociously *un*expectant idleness of the underground—fell apart. These men, living in isolation many of them for the first time in their lives, in occasional contact only with a courier or two, were very soon locked into themselves, and then into each other. In that isolation a terrible doubt about who they were and what they were doing began to grow. They had nothing to do but think. They had nothing to do but read. They thought thoughts they had not thought before, they read books they had not read before. They began to meet, some of them, and to discuss the thoughts and books.

Chaikin describes the conversations that took place in the underground as the most painful, most lacerating, most probing conversations of his life. "The men," he says, "took themselves and each other apart like wild animals tearing at open wounds. 'What the hell do you mean, Lenin said this or Stalin said that?' we would yell at each other. 'Bullshit! What does it *mean?* What the fuck does it mean, you son of a bitch?' "

And inside them grief began to flow, pure grief: the grief of loss, death, passion turned on itself. Not many people in the world have the courage to stare directly into the face of such grief, to bear its consequences in such a manner as to transcend it, come out the other side whole and free. Certainly, Bill Chaikin could not. His grief possessed him, twisted him about, he could cut loose from it only by performing a malforming amputation on himself.

It is strange to reflect that if these men had remained above ground, going their daily rounds, living their ordinary Party lives, none of this might have happened, and the Party's history might have been quite different. But as it was, the underground hurled these men into a black night of the soul. People like Lou

Goodstein and Hugh Armstrong took houses so that men like Bill Chaikin could lie awake nights in strange towns staring into the darkness of their political lives, drifting off finally into the bad dream of permanent self-exile.

What We Did to Each Other

THE underground brought to epidemic proportions something the Party had always identified as a threatening disease: self-doubt. Self-doubt was the infectious illness the Party sought to isolate. Self-doubt was at the heart of trial and expulsion, non-personness, avoidance of named carriers. Self-doubt was the feared heresy that induced in many Communists a kind of shameful behavior they would probably never in their lives have otherwise been guilty of.

Thus, in relation to certain kinds of memories, the Communists with whom I spoke were often like the Germans in relation to the Jews: nobody was there. Communists whose memories were letter-perfect with regard to everything else couldn't remember ever having had anything to do with anybody's expulsion, couldn't remember ever having brutally cut off relations with an expelled Communist, couldn't remember ever having presided over or been present at anybody's trial.

Arthur Chessler, for instance—the gentle, intelligent, thoughtful Arthur—softly, sadly told me no, to the best of his recollection he had never had to have anything to do with that ugly business. A month later Selma Gardinsky told me that Arthur had presided over her trial and expulsion. Marian Moran also led me to believe that she had been at a distance from trials and expulsions; again, six weeks later I was told of at least one trial she had presided over—a particularly ugly and unjust one at that—and I knew in that moment there were countless others she must have been involved in. Eric Lanzetti told me he had helped expel a "suspected Trotskyite" because Earl Browder wanted him out of the Party, and added that if he, Lanzetti, had stayed in the

Party and done things like that a few times more, he would probably be a bitter anti-Communist today.

In the 1950s—when the Party was under its severest attack in this country, when Communists were going to prison, when thousands were underground, when Khrushchev had declared Stalin a murderer of unimaginable proportions, when the American foothold was slipping away day by day—the Party's neurotic fear of self-doubt reached fatal heights, and the American CP became an Orwellian caricature of itself, disintegrating itself from within even as it was being destroyed from without.

"White chauvinism" ("racism" was not the term then in use) became the characteristic charge upon which this free-floating anxiety fixed itself; thousands of Communists were charged, tried, and expelled for being white chauvinists. The "evidence" upon which most of these charges rested was painfully ridiculous, indicative of the kind of mad suspension of reason that then prevailed. A kind of Swiftian upside-downness overtook the best people in the CP: the small became big, the Yahoos were in charge, the babbling abstractionists filled the tribunals. A Party member who visited her sister in Florida was accused of being a racist and was expelled; another served watermelon at a garden party and was expelled; a third did not invite a black Party member to sit down at his table in a restaurant and he was expelled. Those who called for reason were immediately suspect. And once the stigma of suspicion fell on you, you were lost; suspicion had become the mark of Cain.

But all this did not begin in the 1950s; it did not even begin in the American CP. Such behavior had a long history, a history built into the Party practices of international Communism that led directly back to Lenin. In 1907 at a Russian revolutionary congress in London, Trotsky and others begged: "European socialist parties work in the open. So should the Russian party." Lenin said no, the broad, open, tolerant base of Europe was nonexistent in Russia and therefore the Russian party must remain underground; underground, the only way the Party could survive was through strict, disciplined behavior any divergence from which would constitute a threat to the entire revolutionary movement.

Lenin was right—for Russia. But the Americans adopted his method as though it was self-evidently right for them too—when, in fact, their situation lay somewhere between the Europeans' and the Russians'. The sorrow and the pity of the American CP was that it never really understood or trusted the workings of its own country, and thus ricocheted continually off the walls of inorganic practices. These practices included an inconsistent relation to the idea of being an underground party in America; that inconsistency, in turn, heightened the Party's own social and political apprehensions, and made the fear of self-doubt a function of neurotic anxiety; that anxiety burst into flame in the 1950s, but it had been smoldering for thirty years.

Sam Russell is sixty-eight years old. He is a tall, well-built man with liquid dark eyes, thick black eyebrows, and a mass of silver hair that surrounds his face like an aureole. Sam lives in a small comfortable house furnished in 1930s leftwing-bohemian style on a tree-lined street in Madison, Wisconsin. Sam owns three houses in Madison besides his own. One night, in the course of our long visit, it began to rain and Sam rose saying he had to go and see to his property, a number of roofs would probably be leaking. I was startled and said: "Why, Sam. You're a slum landlord." Sam looked equally startled, then blushed and laughed. "They say," he replied, "that the Communists became landlords and the Trotskyists became professors."

But the irony seemed uncertain, while the discomfort seemed real and deep. Sam looked then—as he did so often during the time I spent with him—like a man who had lived in unnatural relation to uncertainty for a long time, dominated by a painful hesitation of the soul: a hesitation at whose center lay a frailty that took him by surprise again and again.

Sam Russell was born in the Midwest to middle-class Hungarian Jews for whom he was the adored, golden son. He grew up tall and beautiful, and possessed of a sensitivity that was almost talent. When he was twenty-one years old he went out into the world, a self-assured man striding into the landscape of his future. He had gone to college for two years but left, lured by the adventure of the waiting world and the spiritual respectability of the *Wanderjahr*. He knocked about Europe for a year or two, took an

Italian common-law wife, fathered a child, wrote a novel. Adventure palled, talent did not jell, a restless longing for a means with which to lead a serious life began to overtake him.

In 1928 a friend from college wrote, inviting Sam to join him in Palestine, where life was deep and dangerous. Sam took his wife and child and went. His friend had become an impassioned Zionist; he urged Sam to make contact with his own Jewish roots and join him in devotion to the great human drama that would certainly be unfolding in Palestine in the coming years. Sam searched his soul and found he was not and never could be a Zionist. The baby died in Palestine, the marriage dissolved, and the long wandering came to an end.

In 1931 Sam returned home to a Depression-destroyed family. The Midwest seemed bleaker than ever before, barren of all hope for the future. Sam convinced his parents a move was necessary, and the whole family journeyed to California.

California in the Thirties: alive with the Depression and the anxious excitement of the great radical stirrings. In the farm valleys headline strikes were taking place; on the waterfront heads were being broken; in the cities streetcorner orators from one end of the left political spectrum to the other galvanized the air. . . . Sam immediately felt drawn, quickening to the sights and sounds around him as he had never quickened in Palestine. A chord was being struck in him that had not been struck before.

He wandered into the I.L.D. office one day. A citizen's committee was being formed to go down into the Salinas Valley and get the facts in the strike going on down there. Sam volunteered to go. He spent a week in the valley, came back, wrote a piece about the strike that was better than the novel he had written, had it published in the *People's World,* and became "famous overnight." The PW asked him to write for them. He joined the staff of the paper and within a matter of months was recruited into the Communist Party. He had come to rest; he felt alive, full of his own found powers. He became persuaded (then and for life) that only as a part of organized Communism would he feel the pleasures of serious effectiveness. For the next ten years Sam worked hard and devotedly as a Party journalist.

When the CP developed the United Front after the German invasion of Russia all Communists were urged to work cooperatively with all U.S. agencies: even the FBI. One day Sam received a call from a man who said he was from the FBI. The man asked Sam for some information in relation to a story Sam had written the previous week. Sam replied that all he knew about the issue was in the story he had printed, but sure. . . . The man asked if he could see Sam's original notes. Sam showed them to him. As he had assured him: it was all in the story as it had appeared in the paper.

The man from the FBI continued to call Sam. They met a number of times; each time Sam gave him reports which were the basis of stories he was writing. It all seemed pointless but innocent to Sam. What the hell? he thought. The FBI *was* as dumb as the Communists all said it was. Then the man from the FBI began to press Sam for information about other Communists. Sam became suspicious. He went to the Party and told his superiors about the man from the FBI. The Central Committee in California became alarmed; it chastised and alarmed Sam. The chairman insisted he go to the FBI—with a Party leader—tell all, and discover the truth. This was done and, sure enough, the FBI had never heard of the man. Sam was confused and humiliated.

In 1943 Sam was drafted into the US Army. Ever since the incident with the bogus FBI man Sam had felt vaguely uncomfortable in the Party. He couldn't put his finger on it but something seemed wrong with the way people treated him now, almost as though he were not completely trusted. Now that he was about to go off to the war he felt he had to clear the matter up. He went to the head of the Party in California. He asked what his status was now in the Party. The Party head said: "Fine. Your status is fine. Don't worry about anything. Come home safe and sound."

Sam returned home in 1946 to find himself a pariah. Old friends avoided him, his job at the paper was gone, he learned about Party meetings only after they were over. He discovered that he'd been expelled from the Party in his absence and put on a list of suspected agents.

Sam demanded a trial. It was granted him. One of the members of the trial board was Marian Moran. Sam pled his case successfully and was cleared of all charges: nominally. Sam wanted the board to publish the findings of the trial in the *People's World*. The board refused. It also refused to readmit Sam to the Party unless he submitted himself to certain corrective measures. He was to join a "mass organization"; that is, he was to go to work for a number of years in a factory in order to "get back to the working class." This he would not do. Get *back* to the working class? Sam said. When the hell had he ever been in the working class? This order was nothing more than a directive to humiliate himself. Why was this necessary to prove he was a good Communist? He had been cleared. He was guilty of nothing. The trial board remained adamant on this demand. To them, Sam's insubordination was proof that he was, after all, worthy of suspicion.

So it was all over, his life in the Communist Party at an end. "I could hardly believe this was happening to me," Sam says softly, his face again taking on that expression of confused uncertainty, his large body suddenly seeming frail. "Fifteen years, and it was all over just like that. What stuck, bitterly, in my craw was that people I had known and worked with for fifteen years could so easily believe I was a government agent. . . . How was this *possible*? There was absolutely no proof against me. Needless to say, there could not have *been* any proof against me. And yet all my friends, everyone, turned away from me without batting an eyelash. I went through hell after that. The McCarthy years were murder on me. I was called up before a state commission, asked to testify, give names, threatened with contempt of court, had to leave California, start all over again in another part of the country. . . . But nothing was as terrible to me as that trial, it haunted my life for years. It *still* haunts me."

Legend, probably apocryphal, has it that when Lenin was asked what work in Russian literature influenced him most toward revolution, he replied "Chekhov's *Ward Six*." Chekhov's powerful novella tells the story of a doctor who feels spiritually isolated in the provincial town whose hospital he administers. The only man in the town whom the doctor finds he can talk to is an inmate of Ward Six, the hospital's mad ward. Although the doctor and the madman have many absorbing conversations the doctor never sees the madman as anything other than mad—that is, as less human than himself—and he remains essentially unmoved by the terrible condition in which the madman passes his days and nights, months and years.

The doctor himself grows more and more melancholy, more and more driven to act out his need. Eventually, the townspeople have him declared mad, events move swiftly, and one day the doctor is being dragged and shoved into Ward Six. As the door clangs shut behind him he realizes for the first time the full horror of what it is to be a human being caged. Chekhov's point, of course, was that the masters would not understand what it was to be a slave until they became slaves themselves.

Sophie Chessler—with all ironies properly noted—keeps reminding me of *Ward Six*. Sophie, wife of Arthur, devoted Communist for more than twenty years, lived with *some* discomfort over the question of other people's expulsions, but only when she herself became a pariah after separating from the Party did she experience the horror of "what we had done to each other."

Sophie is an attractive, dark-eyed, chain-smoking woman in her sixties who bears a striking resemblance to her husband. Although it is common for long-married people to resemble each other, among the Communist couples I have known this tendency to grow together in every way is really rather remarkable: duplicate expressions, gestures, language, political positions; it is this last, I think, that is the key—both cause and effect—to the oneness.

Sophie, like Arthur, was born into a family of poor Jews and, like Arthur, she early demonstrated an intelligence that was valued by her family. She graduated from Hunter College in 1928—a rare accomplishment for her time and her place—and became a schoolteacher. The Depression drew her to Marxism, and she attended classes at the Party's Workers' School. Arthur was her teacher. They fell in love, Sophie joined the CP, and they got married in the early Thirties.

From the very beginning Sophie was as dedicated a Communist as Arthur. She gave herself without stint to the requirements of Party politics, Party policy. There was, after all, only one way to be a revolutionary. Sophie's tone, like Arthur's, is low-keyed, reserved, and dignified, and in this somewhat remote voice of hers she remarks casually that had the Party expelled Arthur she would have left him; or, "If they'd thrown me out in the Thirties or Forties? Oh, I would have killed myself."

"It was curious," Sophie says thoughtfully, tapping a cigarette out of her package. "It wasn't that we didn't feel badly when someone was expelled. We *did*. Very badly. But Party discipline had at all costs to be upheld, defended. This was a fundamental no one questioned. And when someone was expelled it was because—and this we could always see *clearly*—Party discipline was being threatened.

"Now the thing is this: you felt badly, sometimes so badly you became nearly ill. But you got over it. It was exactly like a death in the family. You grieved, and then you passed out of grief. Because life had to go on. And you either believe everything and everyone in life is subordinate to life itself, or you don't.

"Well, it was like that. You grieved, and you passed out of the grief because life—that is, the Party, the revolution—had to go on. And no one—no one of us—was more important than 'life.' I mean, we could give ourselves up to it, but *it* could not be given up. It was just like that. The Party was equated with the life force. As demanding, as unquestioning as that.

"So you could feel badly when someone you'd known for ten, fifteen years suddenly became 'dead' to you, but you couldn't go any deeper than that. . . . In a very short time the person became unreal to you.

"I guess if I'd ever tried to examine my feelings deeply, which of course I never did, I'd have seen that by unreal I mean I couldn't *imagine* the feelings of the person who'd been expelled. I couldn't put myself in his place, I couldn't feel what he must be feeling. He was, I suppose, no longer quite as human to me as I was to myself.

"Arthur and I quit the Party in Nineteen-Fifty-Eight. For two years after the 20th Congress Report we'd hung on, trying to bring about what we thought of as reasonable change in the Party. It was impossible to do. So, finally, we quit. It was just about the hardest thing we ever did in our lives. We'd been through everything. Arthur had gone to jail—arrested in his own house at gunpoint, God what a morning that was, the kids screaming, my mother fainting—I'd lost my job, the children had lived in gloom and fear. . . . The Party had been our life, our life.

"The morning after we quit I went to the grocery store to buy some milk and bread and I ran into a Party member on the street.

When he saw me coming toward him he veered in his tracks and crossed the street. My first thought was: he forgot something back where he was coming from and didn't have time to explain.

"The second time this happened I felt a curious little twist go through me and I remember thinking, 'Is it possible . . . ?' And I rejected that thought immediately.

"But of course it not only was possible, it was what, in fact, was happening. I had become—literally overnight—nonexistent. The only people who remained our friends were the people who quit with us: at the same moment, in the same way, over the same issues. Everyone else disappeared. People stopped calling, stopped dropping by, crossed the street when we ran into each other. Sometimes, when they couldn't cross the street they passed by or looked into my face with glazed, unseeing eyes.

"One day I was in the supermarket. As I turned into an aisle of the store a woman at the other end also turned in. We glanced up over our baskets and our eyes met. She was someone I'd known since I'd been a girl. We had worked together in the Party many times over the years. We'd been extremely warm acquaintances, on occasion friends, intimates. I had liked her for her lightheartedness and she had liked me for my seriousness. Now, as our eyes met her face instinctively lit up and her hand came out in a greeting. Then suddenly, visibly, I could see it right there in her face, she remembered who I had become. Her hand came down and her face closed. She wheeled in mid-aisle, and you know how hard it is to turn around in a supermarket, and practically ran. I remember I stood there staring after her. I felt paralyzed. And for the first time I said to myself: My God, how came we to do such things to each other?"

Sophie lights her cigarette and takes a deep drag in silence. Then she says: "It was as though I had some contagious disease. Worse. I'm sure if I'd had black plague she'd have had more courage than she had that day in the supermarket. The *fear* in her face. . . .

"I went home that day and I began to think about myself, about my own history, about all the times I'd acted, if not exactly, still pretty much like my friend in the supermarket but had somehow never seen it quite like that before. It had never seemed the crucial matter it now suddenly seemed. Sure, it had been a lousy thing to live through, someone's quitting or being expelled, but it wasn't *that* terrible. Now, suddenly, it *was* that terrible. It seemed like the most terrible thing in the world, that people should have done this to each other, that we who were fighting capitalism because it dehumanized people had dehumanized ourselves in this way, and had lost the only thing that counts between people: the ability to see ourselves in each other."

Trial and expulsion from the Communist Party was, indeed, often terrible: an act potent with the terror of loss and unspeakable humiliation. The implication is always that it was only those being expelled who experienced the terror. But this is not true. Despite Sophie Chessler's classic testimony about how a Communist cut an expelled member out of his or her consciousness, there were countless people who suffered grievously over the expulsion of a beloved person and, in fact, were left more maimed than was the one being expelled.

At the age of sixty-three Tim Kelley looks like a Central Casting version of the utterly simple, utterly decent small-town American businessman he undoubtedly would have been—if he had not been a Communist. Sitting with him in his comfortable living room in a working-class suburb twenty minutes from the center of Chicago, I ask him what *he* thinks he would have been if he'd not been a Communist. Without a moment's hesitation Kelley replies: "A rich Republican. And probably one of the worst at that. I'd have been a Nixonite bastard, for sure." And he grins a wicked, self-mocking grin. He knows the qualities that made him a good Communist are the same as those that would have made him a stubborn Nixonite.

Tim Kelley was born in Kansas and raised in Denver. His father worked on the railroad, and his mother was a "rock-ribbed Republican": a good, principled conservative. His childhood was happy, unconflicted, filled with the simple rural pleasures of pure Americana. He grew up a man of exuberant energies and great good nature; he also grew up a classic American rebel of the "that just don't seem *fair*" school, and a natural organizer to the marrow of his bone.

In 1928 a talent scout from Hollywood drifted through Denver. Tim was by then a gifted athlete, the star of a local basketball team. The scout saw Tim play and invited him to come to Hollywood to play basketball in MGM college movies. Tim thought his fortune was made, and eagerly accepted the invitation. He married his high-school sweetheart and they went west. MGM used him three times in the year that followed, and that was the end of his movie career.

Tim drifted through Depression Los Angeles looking for work. He didn't know how to do many things, and many things were not available to do. He went to work in a car wash. At the car wash he worked in a long line of men who put in a ten-hour stint washing, running, hosing, washing, running, hosing. The owner had a habit of suddenly lining up a few extra cars at the end of the day and yelling, "Okay, boys, just one more, just one more," and the men would often find themselves working eleven or twelve hours while only getting paid for ten. One day Tim said to the men: "Let's everybody just quit cold at the end of the day. Throw down your sponges in the middle of a wash if you have to. But remember: *everybody do it.*" Tim gave the men courage and they all did as he instructed them. Within hours Tim was fired.

After that, he was a counterman, a security guard, a day laborer. Wherever he went, it was the same story: within fifteen minutes he was organizing the workers to defend their "natural human rights," as he says, and within thirty he was fired. On New Year's Day 1936 a friend of his wife's asked him what he intended to do with his life. Tim replied: "Get rich." Lots of luck, the friend said, and by the end of the day she had recruited him into the Communist Party.

Tim Kelley became a skilled trade-union organizer for the Party. Painters, construction workers, machinists, he organized them all. That was where his heart lay always: with organizing workers into the Party, the only organization in the world fighting to protect "natural human rights."

Tim loved the Party fiercely, simply. He could never understand Party or international politics. To him, the Party meant a generalized but deeply felt identification with all those who were "hurting" under capitalism. He was happy only among the workers, only organizing, only setting up a fight. Talk to him about "theory" and he becomes vague, but talk to him about the labor union battles in which he took part and the most amazing memory emerges: immediate, complex, fantastically detailed.

Tim Kelley was one of the Party mavericks: brash, boisterous, a lover of women, a monumental drinker. "Ah," Tim says wryly, lifting his glass of ginger ale to me, "the drink. Holymotherofgod, the drink. Even when it was killing me, destroying me at home, in the Party, everywhere, I couldn't stop drinking."

Why? I ask casually.

"I loved it!" Kelley beams at me. "Just loved it. I think nothing in the world ever made me happier than settling into a long night of drinking with a bunch of Irish union guys half of whom were in the CP. And there was one guy in particular, Johnny McWilliams, ah, drinking with Johnny was an *experience*."

How come? I ask.

Kelley leans back into his chair, the light glinting off his rimless glasses, a bemused recalling smile on his lips. For a moment he seems lost in time, forgetful of my presence, so deep is the mood that has suddenly descended on him. Then he shakes himself a bit and says: "Johnny was like nothing I'd ever known before. He was everything I was, only a thousand times more than I could ever be it. He was Irish, he was a drinker, he was the greatest union organizer that ever lived, and he was in the Party. He was black Irish, wild, with a reckless kind of poetry in him that drew the men like a magnet. When you were with Johnny, I don't know how to put it, you felt more alive than with anyone else, more like you could do or be *anything*. He had that gift of making you feel larger inside yourself, even when you were falling down drunk. If you were with Johnny you didn't feel like a damned fool, you felt like a *man*, like you'd done good work and had the right to be letting go. Ah, I loved him, I loved him fiercely.

"And what Johnny loved, more than anything else in the world, more than his own life, was the union movement. The union was home, family, church, and god to him. For the union he would have laid down his life, walked across hot coals, sacrificed his firstborn. I always knew that he wasn't a Party member first like I was, but I never really paid much attention to it, never thought it made any difference, *could* make any difference.

"In 1946 Johnny fell afoul of the Party, like a lot of other union people did. He got more and more agitated, felt the Party was selling out the union. He was getting sick over it, angry drunk, couldn't keep his mouth shut when he should have. I watched over him, tried to calm him down, but I didn't take it that seriously. Then one night, we were driving back late from a meeting outside of L.A. He told me he intended to challenge the Party at the next meeting on an issue that had just developed. I've forgotten now what the issue was, but I knew then that if he challenged the Party on this issue he'd be expelled. I protested, told him it was foolish to do this, what the hell was the point of getting kicked out of the Party? But he shook his head and said no, nothing could stop him on this one. I looked at him, I can still see him, hunched over the wheel of that old rattletrap, driving fast, his face turning black as the night. I saw that he was clenched up inside himself, almost beyond being angry, and I realized the meaning of what he was telling me, of what was happening here. I was overcome, I saw the future all in a flash, and I cried out, 'But you can't! How will we be friends?' He just looked at me, kinda like he felt sorry for me. But he never said another word. He just drove on into the city and dropped me at my house. And we ended our friendship then and there."

Kelley stops speaking. He falls silent for a long moment and then suddenly, right here in the middle of his quiet, orderly living room, his face falls apart and his large placid body begins to shake with uncontrollable sobs. Great tears spurt from his eyes, and he buries his face in his now-soft hands.

"Why do you feel so badly?" I ask. Softly, but I ask. "What exactly is it you are regretting just now?"

Kelley lifts his head. He leans forward slightly, his eyes narrow with an intelligence not visible until this moment. Steadily and very quietly he says: "It was the particular quality of that particular friendship. There's been nothing else like it in my life. Not before, not since." He stops, pauses, as though listening to find out what he's going to say next. Then he says: "I thought I couldn't have both the Party and Johnny . . . and I couldn't give up the Party."

Kelley leans back in his chair, wipes his tears away, composes his face. "Oh," he sighs, "we repaired the friendship years later. But it was never the same, never the same. I regret it all, I regret it now, I'll regret it till I die."

The Lure of the Disciplined Revolutionary Party

IN the fall of 1974, in Los Angeles, I spoke with two men, each thirty-four years old, who had joined the Communist Party in the early 1960s: the years when Sophie Chessler was at the height of her Chekhovian sorrows. The first of these was Larry Dougherty, an Irish Catholic born and raised in California; the second was Ricardo Garcia, a Dominican, born and raised in island poverty and family rebellion against the dictatorship of Trujillo. Both of these men had been drawn in their early twenties, at the height of the New Left's influence, to the Communist Party, lured by the still-magnetizing power of the disciplined revolutionary party.

Larry Dougherty in 1974 is possessed of a striking appearance that sets him markedly apart from the jarring grubbiness of the L.A. drive-in restaurant he has named as our meeting place. Tall, blond, athletic, Dougherty's looks instantly recall the perfect proportions of face and body that inform a Greek statue. Dougherty has as well a dreamy, otherworldly look about him; the peculiar stillness and grace of the saint, the idiot, the child is there in his deep-set blue eyes and his detached smile. His voice corresponds oddly to his appearance. It is low, soft, somewhat strained; it gives the impression that he is listening to a set of Platonic sounds in his head that he knows will only very imperfectly be reflected in the sounds that emerge from his mouth. But he takes the effort at duplication very seriously. He will try as best he can to give me the truth of his feelings about his life, his political being, his intensity of world.

Larry Dougherty was born into a broken, working-class home. Both his grandfather and his father were house painters; both his grandfather and his father drank; both his grandfather and his father were, in Fellini's famous words, "like dogs, they wanted to talk but all they could do was bark." It was Larry's mother who finally ran away from home. Larry and his brother continued to live with their father and grandfather: four men haunting the same rooms, together in brutal inarticulation, isolated in an aridity of the soul more life-destroying than poverty and ignorance.

Reading gave Larry pleasure and solace. More than solace, it gave him a sense of being he did not otherwise experience. This sense of being, he discovered, came not from poetry or fiction but from works of history and religion. Slowly, he began to grow attached to ideas. The first of the ideas that began to seem as though it could "explain" things was something he called "radical atheism": a sense of the wider meanings of Christian hypocrisies. In his early teens he was much preoccupied with a systematic anger at the church.

One night in L.A.'s Pershing Square Larry heard an Italian anarchist speak. The anarchist's all-encompassing social critique mesmerized the seventeen-year-old boy. He was drawn by a systematic explanation of the world that instantly made him abandon "radical atheism." He approached the anarchist as he was leaving his platform and walked out of the square with him, listening reverently as the anarchist went on talking. Larry became his informal student and remained with him for three years.

At the small junior college he attended he was a D student: he could not pay attention, the words and lectures drifted through open space, no fertile soil inside him for them to take root in. Then came the Bay of Pigs invasion. Overnight, he felt himself engaged. He and twelve others at the school put out a radical campus newspaper. Radicalism jelled and flowed into a sense of burning ethical issues. His intelligence cohered, and he worked day and night on the paper. The campus responded violently to the paper, its response electrified him, and in that electrification the permanent revolutionary in him was born.

During this time he met Marian Moran who persuaded him toward Marxism and urged him to join the Communist Party. He was much drawn to the idea, but hesitated to join the CP; he feared to risk his "future."

In 1960 Larry was drafted. He left the country and went down to Costa Rica. There: riots. He became embroiled: something in

Latin America had reached into him, striking a chord deep within. He was arrested and deported. When he arrived in Texas the FBI was waiting. He was arrested again, thrown into prison, and brought to trial. Prison was traumatizing: solitary confinement, homosexual assault, fear and darkness, the loss of much weight. That decided him on his "future" in America. He came before the army board with Marx and Lenin in his hands. The army declared him a "hard-core Communist" and rejected him.

Now, he thought, America had done everything to him that it could do. He marched down to CP headquarters and joined. He remained in the CP for six years, three of them on the National Committee. He left for the age-old reasons, but he describes his leaving in the voice and language of his own generation:

"It was impossible to talk to them. Open debate was unknown among them. We, the young ones, weren't used to that. They tried to go easy with us. Expulsions were no longer the order of the day. But it was no use, it was like coming up against a stone wall. We tried to show them how removed they were from the working bases of the country. They didn't know what the hell we were talking about. Then came Czechoslovakia. Here, they kept talking about self-determination, and here was Czechoslovakia, and they were defending it! They were old, old. And I think they hated us for being young. They'd been organizing for years. What the hell did *we* know?"

Dougherty clasps his strong, gentle hands gracefully across the dirty formica-topped table and, his voice keenly quiet, says: "But the pleasures and rewards of working within a disciplined revolutionary party were very great. Nothing else around me could have given me what the CP gave me. It was a wonderful and terrifically interesting life I led in the Party. I learned things, saw things I could never have learned or seen anywhere else. People came to the section organizer with all their problems, the life was extraordinarily *knit*, and I grew as a result of it all, I grew."

He hasn't the heart, now, for another Party life. He looks back on the last twelve years of his life and he says sadly: "What, after all, has it accomplished? I don't want to look back on the next twelve years and say the same thing. . . . So, I'll try to write a bit, and keep moving in the Third World."

Dougherty drifts continually through Latin America. He loves the continent the way only a blond, repressed American can. He's been in prison in Ecuador, Argentina, Chile, Mexico: blindfolded, handcuffed, tortured. He knows he can end up on a dirt road with a bullet in his head. He says all this with an uncanny detachment. The sense of disconnection in him is acute, removal at the center of his lonely American soul, socialism and the beautiful brown people filling the void.

I ask him why he is particularly preoccupied with Latin America. His answer nearly makes me fall out of my chair: "American imperialism will fall only when the Third World rises. American imperialism depends on Third World markets and exploitation. When they disappear the American economy will fail. Then the objective reality will come into line with revolutionary readiness. And that is what I work towards."

Objective reality. Revolutionary readiness. After all this, pure forty-year-old CP jargon. And all of it spoken out of what I suddenly realize actually *is* the face of a Greek statue: the eyes blind, the lines strong and mute, the chained stillness of unknowing life imprisoned in the helpless beauty of this young American body.

Dougherty is—still, and again!—right out of *USA*. That disconnected, drifting underside of American life Dos Passos made metaphoric in his Wobbly, hobo, Depression images still lives in the flesh; that mute American longing to which the CP spoke and, on occasion, still speaks, is here, alive in Larry Dougherty.

But now is no time for the Party to come to the aid of American loneliness. Dougherty probably will end up dead in a silent, dusty, sun-drenched patch of weeds somewhere in Central America with not a soul in the world to mourn the ceasing of his existence: for the connections he has made are sadly out of joint.

When Ricardo Garcia was four years old his grandmother stood him on a table in a café in their village, and his penis was dipped in a glass of water, and everyone around the table drank from the glass. He was the ultimate male child, the golden center, the adored phallic future. In him the hopes of the race would live again, the bitter burden of his people perhaps be laid down at last.

In this story of Garcia's something clarifies for me. Psycho-analysis of Communists has commonly declared that it was the man or woman with no center, no developed ego, who joined the Communist Party. Garcia, though, has a strong center, as do many of the Communists I have known. Like Eric Lanzetti, like Marian Moran, like Arthur Chessler, like countless others, Garcia was the golden child, the adored being. It was that strongly loved center that fed his capacity for moral outrage. That capacity is oddly coupled with a spring of sweetness flowing deep within him. Like Lanzetti, Moran, Chessler, and others, Garcia is a deeply sweet person; his sweetness is at the center of his Marxism. His sweetness made him join the Communist Party—and then leave it. It precludes his ever becoming a professional anti-Communist.

Ricardo Garcia was born in a village in the Dominican Republic and raised in poverty and Catholic love and strictness. His father and his uncles were Communists living in underground resistance to the Trujillo dictatorship. His parents went off to the capital city when Ricardo was a boy and he was raised by his grand-mother, the central, powerful, matriarchal figure of his child-hood. Ricardo ran wild as a child and his grandmother—a devout Catholic who made two-hundred-mile walking pilgrimages and was named the holiest Catholic on the island—beat him literally every day of his life. But, Ricardo says, he understood. Those were the rules of the game: she dipped his penis in water and drank of the water, she beat him for the good of his everlasting soul.

When he was fifteen his parents divorced. His mother remar-ried and he went to the capital to live with her. He was still wild, still a flaring rebellion in his gut. There were political meetings at the house, and once a man rose, a glass in his hand, and said, "Down with American imperialism." Ricardo said hotly, "Why do you say that? The Americans are good." The man explained. But Ricardo would not hear the explanation, only the anger in his belly . . . at what he was not quite certain.

His mother and her new husband came to New York. Ricardo came with them: still wild, still running amok, now pain, fever, a kind of madness in him. When he was twenty they discovered a tumor in his brain. He was operated on, and his life immediately changed. The anger and wildness disappeared, calm and intellectual steadiness replaced them. He returned to school and became a passionate student of physics and mathematics, finding great beauty in the discovery of natural law.

Concurrently, though, other, older stirrings began to awaken in him. In the hospital he read a Spanish translation of a Russian novel called *Man Does Not Live by Bread Alone.* He began to see the world in social terms, and he ached and was tremendously excited. Next, he went to the house of a Dominican woman whose daughter he was interested in. In this house he met an old Spanish War vet. One day Ricardo and the old man began to talk. Ricardo was deeply moved by the purity of soul he found in the old man and he found himself saying: "I want to do something useful. I want to help humanity." The Spanish War vet said to him: "If you want to help humanity there is only one thing for you to do. Become a Communist." And he put Karl Marx into Ricardo's hands.

Marx was fireworks. Suddenly, Ricardo saw that just as nature was governed by laws so was society governed by laws, and the law from that day on was capital versus the proletariat.

At this point, Ricardo recalls, he remembered that "when my grandmother was dying she called the whole family to her bedside. My mother, father, sister, aunts, uncles, everyone. We all stood around her, and she described the process of dying to each of us. She instructed each of us to let her hold us in her arms. We each did. And then she told each of us she would return now to the earth and to god. And then we laid her upon the earth. And only then did she die. Now in New York I was twenty-four years old, and I remembered my grandmother's dying, and I said to myself: 'All this she did for Jesus. I will do the same for Marx.'"

Ricardo joined the Communist Party in New York and remained in it for nearly ten years, having quit only six months before I met him. Throughout most of those years he edited the Spanish section of the *Worker.* When the paper folded and reemerged as the *Daily World* the Spanish section was reduced to one page and Ricardo quit in anger.

"But," he sighs, "of course, it wasn't because of that. It was for years of senile leadership and American chauvinism. They kept wanting me to go down to Santo Domingo and teach them how to be Communists. Jesus! The people at home would have kicked my ass from Santo Domingo to New York. They knew more about being Communists than I would ever know."

Why did he remain in the Party so long?

"Because," he says, his dark face lighting up, "they gave me the beauty of discipline, the deep pleasures of analysis, the excitement of organizational ability. They *gave* me my Marxism. I had come to them a wild, excited boy, ready to make the revolution, armed only with my first glimpse into Marx. With them I learned to *penetrate* Marx. I learned, through the long years of patience and self-control I had to practice in the Party, the deeper meanings of socialism, all the ways in which the socialist view may apply itself to our life. I know, I know, it was the Nineteen-Sixties, and the cry of the times was 'do your own thing.' But this slogan did not speak to me, I could not find my way through it. The young American radicals around me with their long hair and their self-consciousness, they were a thicket, a jungle of words and attitudes I could make no real sense of. To me, they were anarchic, I could not see their actions leading to anything. The Party was real to me, the Party with its long history, its deep structure, its ties to international Communism. *This*, I thought, is the way, the only way to bring change to this lousy rotten world, to end this capitalism that eats the lives of my people.

"Now, of course, I see the American Communist Party is nowhere. It can give me nothing. But this certainly does not mean that I am no longer a Communist. On the contrary, the American Party experience helped me clarify for myself the meaning of my life's work. I consider myself a child of the Cuban Revolution, and a lifelong Marxist in the service of the Third World. My immediate plans are to leave America, go to Puerto Rico and, for now, work with the Independentistas. . . . Then, we will see. It's a long life, and a big world, and the teeth of capitalism will certainly not be pulled in *my* lifetime. There is much work to be done, and I go to it now with a full but free heart."

Larry Dougherty and Ricardo Garcia are, to the largest extent, anachronisms as American Communists (Dougherty much more so than Garcia). Nevertheless, they embody the enduring pull of the CP, and reflect on its powers of evocation deep within the political human soul. The lure of the disciplined revolutionary party—the power and meaning of the highly structured organization within which one can give idiomatic shape to political yearnings either too inchoate or too large to bear in the void that is independent action for most people—that is what the Communist Party has been in the history of radical longing. That is what "living it out" has been for most Communists; that is what was so hard to give over, to abandon and walk away from.

After all was said and done, Sam Russell said, "I *still* believe the only way I could ever be effective in this world is as part of an organization as large and structured as the Communist Party." And the power of regret in his voice was strong enough to stop the heart.

CHAPTER FOUR

They Went Back
into Everywhere:
Varieties of Aftermath

JUST AS American Communists came from every sort of life and condition so they have returned into every sort of life and condition. They had been every kind of American before they became Communists, and they became every kind of American once they ceased being Communists. They became again rich, poor, urban, suburban, intellectuals, laborers, private men and women. For the most part, they became again Americans who live at a "reasonable" distance from their politics. Many of them still consider themselves socialists but most of them are about as politically active as liberals—that is, they pay more attention to the work they do and to their family lives than they do to the stir of world events. They are on the whole excellent workers, superior in their capacity for achievement, and they occupy large and admirable spaces in nearly every sphere of American life. They are professionals of every stripe, artists, labor organizers, businessmen and women, academics, service and government workers. They belong to the ACLU and the PTA, and they give money to Ralph Nader. In short: they are model Americans.

However, none of them are the same *kind* of American they had been before. Today, whatever else they are in their lives, they are all ex-Communists. This piece of identity is a reference point on the map of being as stable as the compass needle pointing north is to an explorer seeking his bearings. It is *the* vital experience by which nearly every one of them gauges the subsequent course of his or her life, the success, failure, clarity, murkiness, sense of shape or shapelessness: the where, who, or what he or she is in the world. For better or worse, love it or hate it, idealize the memory or revile it, having been a Communist is the experience to which each one of them still owes a moral accounting.

When I asked Arthur Chessler how he felt about his life now, he answered, instantaneously and with an extraordinary note of relief in his voice: "I feel free. Free to think what I like, to accept or reject an idea, free to have a discussion that isn't resolved, isn't necessarily going some-Marxist-where, free to pursue my own thoughts." Yet, in the end, he quoted Sartre, who couldn't live with the Party or without it, saying softly and with pain: "Something endures, something endures."

When I asked Maggie McConnell—helplessly cheerful Maggie, temperamentally the diametric opposite of gentle, dour Arthur —how *she* felt about her life now, she instantly said she mourned the loss of the CP in her life and would do so until she died. She spoke scornfully of the people who had accused her of failing to grow up, failing to stand on her own two feet, and she said: "Did the Communist Party get me from one crisis to another? *Life* is a crisis. Maybe you can say the Communist Party got me through the crisis that is life." And yes, she went on, she honored the Party for that, and would give ten years of her life to have another Communist Party arise tomorrow so that she could once more live out the crisis that is life with meaning and dignity.

On the other hand, there were many who shook their heads sorrowfully and said no, they didn't think they could ever give themselves again to another party, they had learned certain things that precluded such devotions. Jim Holbrook, for instance, when he was asked how he felt about his life now, said quietly: "I try to be kinder to people. I try to cause as little pain as possible and live in peace with myself." Holbrook spoke for many Communists when he said that, many who have come to value personal relations as they had not in the past, and who live with a keen and penetrating remorse for "what we did to each other." Yet, in the end, Holbrook said: "The Party gave me Marxism. Everything in my life flows from that simple fact, everything returns to it. No matter how far I may seem to stray from any recognizable relation to that fact, it is there inside me. It is the center of my gravity, sooner or later the arc returns on its course to that center. In that sense the Party will live inside me until I die, and I remain accountable to it."

There are as many different kinds of ex-Communists today as there were Communists yesterday. "The idea," as one Communist said to me, "that once we were all *there*, and now we are all *here*, is wrong, dead wrong, willfully wrong. It is a political convenience to have it so, and like most political conveniences it is at a great distance from the truth." The political convenience of which he spoke turns, once again, on the monolithic view of Communists anti-Marxists choose to hold: a view that makes it easy to abstract and wipe out the complexity of the experience, to ignore and deny that powerful root of political passion to which its origins are tied.

The passionate experience had streamed through the Communists, like fire and ice, burning and freezing, permanently altering, shaping them into Americans with a long cultural memory and an historic sense of self. Within that context, individuals responded in vastly differing ways, absorbing the experience toward a multiplicity of emotional and psychological ends. In 1974 I spoke with a number of Communists who were as impressive for the ways in which they had become ex-Communists as the ways in which others had once become Communists. Just as they had come from everywhere they had, indeed, gone back into everywhere: both as Americans and as Communists.

Politics Without the Party Is Unthinkable

JEROME Rindzer is a wealthy Arizona surgeon with an intellectual bent and an enormous appetite for work. He is attached to a large city hospital in Phoenix, teaches in a residency program, takes welfare patients, does medical research, and attends to an overburdened private practice. Rindzer is fifty-seven years old. A fast-moving, stocky man with an expressive face and a shock of grey-black hair, he grew up in the New York working-class Left and was a member of the Communist Party from earliest youth. Although he had gone to medical school in his twenties he did not give himself wholly to medicine until he left the Party in 1956. However, he attributes his enormous capacity for work entirely to his years in the Party.

"The Party experience, for me," says Rindzer on a sunny afternoon in May, "was not one of living for a future time, or in any sense of 'rising above myself,' as that phrase is ordinarily used. On the contrary, morality for me and for the people I knew was being the absolute best that we *were* at that time, in that place. If I was a doctor, it was my duty as a Party member to be the best doctor I could be. *That* was my obligation, that was my Communist morality. We really were too poor to adopt the anti-intellectual stance taken by middle-class Communists. We did not despise the professions. On the contrary, we thought comes the revolution we're certainly going to need doctors, and we'd damned well better have them within our own ranks.

"The Party taught me how to think, how to take and allocate responsibility, how to develop my own skills. What the Party taught me I applied to my medical work. Everything I am today," Rindzer grins, making a mock salute to the flag, "I owe to the Communist Party."

What Rindzer is today is a total nonstop doctor. His life is as dominated by the practice of medicine as it once was by the practice of Communist revolution. He does not, he says, know how to do it any other way. "And besides," he adds, shrugging his shoulders with the first sign of weariness I have seen in him after hours of talk, "there *is* no politics, anymore. Ideology is dead, and without ideology there is no politics."

What exactly does he mean, I ask, by the words "ideology is dead"? Rindzer looks at me for a long moment, his eyes growing moody, his lower lip tucked over his upper lip, his right hand moving absently across the surface of a pencil he repeatedly stands on end and lets fall onto his desk. Then he says:

"I'm not one of these Old Lefties that hates any revolution that's not his revolution. I'm really not. When the Sixties burst on us I didn't start cursing the kids out, I listened hard to them. Dammit, I *wanted* to listen, I thought maybe through them it could start all over again for me. But it was no use, no use. For me, they were like a throwback to the *Narodniki*. They were a bunch of middle-class anarchic kids with no base, no structure, no sense of history, no program, no party, no nothing. I didn't know *what* the hell they were all about, and I still don't know. They would, I thought, just burn themselves out, nothing would come of all the tumult. And, to my sorrow, I was right.

"Yes, I know," he leans forward across his desk, his eyes looking puzzled, "they call themselves Marxists. Today, *everybody's* a Marxist. But what the hell does that mean? People I call liberals call themselves Marxists. What do they *mean* by that word? I haven't been able to figure it out yet. Are they revolutionaries? Do they concentrate on the takeover of the capitalist means of production? What's their plan? Where's their discipline? What makes them different from the disgruntled man in the street? How are they different from the ordinary guy who says they're fucking us in Washington? You tell me. I'll be damned if I can see it.

"It seems to me there's no ideology in the New Left. It seems to me theirs is only the politics of despair not of disciplined action. I don't think they understand world socialism at all, neither its struggle nor its history. They don't know the difference between socialism and totalitarianism, they think it's all the same, they reject Soviet Communism wholesale, as well as capitalism. Throughout the Sixties they never wanted to see what they could learn from us, the Old Left, all they wanted to do was yell 'dirty Stalinist' at us, and I grant you, most of us did pretty well, too, so far as yelling and name-calling was concerned. We acted as ugly and as stupid as the kids did. But *still*.

"It's all too amorphous for me. If I wanted to join the Left today, I wouldn't know how, where, what. The relation between ideology and party and political action is crucial. There must be *structure*. Without it, everything falls into a vacuum, dissipates itself in the atmosphere, accomplishes nothing. Worse: it becomes anarchy and anarchy leads to fascism."

Rindzer falls silent. Glances out his window. Plays with the venetian blind behind him. Looks around his book-lined office. Then he says:

"So for me there's no politics anymore. The years when I was a Communist, bar none, were the best of my life. The relation for me between the personal and the historical was intense, deeply felt, fully realized. Now, I live an entirely personal life, removed from the larger world. I feel no interest in anything beyond my work. I work hard, I'm proud of the work I do, I consider it an obligation to take as much responsibility for the medical profession as I can, but that's it. The world is smaller, colder, darker by far for me than it was when I was a Communist. . . . That's a funny thing to say here, isn't it?" He laughs, waving his hand toward the brilliant Arizona afternoon. "I've made my peace with my life, but I have no illusions that I live a life of larger meaning."

Grace Lange is a maker of quilts and ceramic objects who wears her hair pulled back severely and gathered into a knot at the back of her head. Her face is bony, her features chiseled, her arms and hands powerful. Her grey eyes are neither young nor old, only deeply mature, and the intelligence in them holds the key to this woman and her surroundings. It is a calm, attentive intelligence, a controlled and controlling intelligence that, very nearly, seems able to will order in the universe it surveys.

The large studio in which we sit on a rainy afternoon in September is located in one of Berkeley's poorest neighborhoods. The walls and floorboards are bleached grey-white with age and scrubbed clean to receive the clear north light that comes in through the tall windows in great unshadowed blocks. The room itself is a composition of space and light with the power to arrest and focus attention. Within the design of the room are grouped objects, tools and artifacts which also form designs. At one end of the room stands the potter's wheel; behind the wheel shelves hold a dozen pots; beside the wheel on a rough table lies clay in varying stages of readiness: wet and gleaming, dry and powdery, the colors white and dun and burnt sienna; on the wheel sits a perfect mound of clay waiting for the touch of the hands that will shape it into a form of useful beauty.

At the opposite end of the studio stand four large frames across which are stretched the quilts that have brought Grace a moderate amount of fame in Berkeley. What is instantly striking about these quilts is the use of classic American designs as a basis for the creation of new designs: somewhat like the beauty of a jazz variation on an old American melody. Beside the freestanding frames is a table upon which lie the materials for a fifth quilt. Next to the table is a drawing board to which is tacked a large sheet of tracing paper with various designs sketched on it.

Against the wall facing the windows, in the center of the fifty-foot-long room, is ranged Grace's "living quarters": a daybed, two comfortable sagging chairs, a long low table on which sits at all times a pot of fresh flowers, and a screened-off kitchen. Grace awakens in this bed each morning at six, sits up with her back pressed against the whitewashed wall, observes her domain, mentally sketches out the work for that day, and rises to take her place in the disciplined design of her life.

Grace Lange is sixty years old. She was for more than twenty years a section organizer for the Communist Party here in California. She is the daughter of New England Yankees, raised in a harsh, unyielding land where life went forth under the impetus of stoical self-discipline. Stoicism, for Grace, is the supreme human virtue. She associates stoicism not with endurance but with creation. It makes, she says, for the discipline out of which comes freedom, the patience out of which comes a valuable piece of work, the structure out of which comes civilization. It was Marxism and the CP, she explains, that *gave* her the stoicism into which she had been born. After years of rebellious denial of the life which had formed her she was able, through the Party, to put to gifted use the hated self-control that had been her parents' heritage.

"Marxism stirred me deeply," Grace says, leaning back in one of her two chairs, crossing her long, blue-jeaned legs on her low table. "It struck chords in me as deep as the remembrance of New England. It transformed the memory of those isolated human efforts, made my parents' lives a thing of beauty. Simply understanding their lives through Marxism lent them a beauty in my eyes. Clarity, purpose, seeing them in the larger design, that was beautiful to me. The act of understanding was an act of creation. The discovery through new materials, so to speak, of the hidden content.

"Marxism was the transforming stuff, the new color, the new space, the new texture, the one that brought to the surface the life until then obscured. Do you know what that means? That's what the artist waits a lifetime for, that newness, that particular discovery that catalyzes inner sight, makes you 'see' like you've never seen before. . . .

"But the *tool* with which to shape the stuff of Marxism, the vessel with which to give it form, the frame within which it could, and without which it never could, make its statement—that was the Communist Party.

"Marxism was like that clay over there." Grace gestures. "The CP was like the wheel. And yes, I, then as now, was the artist whose life was being served by the rightness of material and form come together. Yes, I always felt like that. I never felt myself a tool of the CP. On the contrary, the CP was *my* tool, *I* was the living purpose to which the joining of form and content was put. I was the mighty *one* using Marxism and the CP to express the newfound wonder of self, world, being."

She lifts a cup of coffee to her narrow, shapely lips. When she has sipped and put the cup down on the table, she goes on: "That's what politics was to me, the power of that joining. The thrill of seeing one become through the other, the idea through the structure, the structure through the action. And the whole of it disciplined, each by its own properties, own functions, and, together, by the grand design that only a disciplined existence could form.

"Malraux once said, 'The greatness of a living personality lies precisely in the link between thought and action.' He said that because he was an artist and a revolutionary. And I always felt I knew exactly what he meant. It was beautiful to me, extraordinary, exciting, that relationship between Marxism and the CP.

The two *together* were the design that lifted new life from old patterns. Therefore, I bent myself with pleasure to the 'disciplines of the wheel,' so to speak, knowing that if I didn't learn to work within its limits, understand *its* properties, I would never have the benefit of seeing the design stand whole and clear, alive with newly created life.

"But," Grace shrugs, "when the clay slipped from the wheel, and the wheel was spinning empty on its own axis, well then, it was time for me to turn away and form a living design elsewhere."

The question I have for Grace is: Why, when the CP failed for her, and she set out to find another "living design," did she turn from politics to quilts? Why has she remained sequestered inside this studio while all around her, in the streets of Berkeley, throughout the Sixties, a new sense of politics was forming, a new idea of social revolution. Why has she not felt revitalized by the student or feminist movements, for instance, and the political ideas they have brought into our lives?

"Yes, yes," Grace sighs, "I know what you mean. Don't you think people have been trooping in and out of this studio for the past ten years asking me that very same question? 'Grace,' they come and say, 'we need you.' 'Grace,' the feminists say, 'don't you see we're offering you a new politics, a new way of seeing things, something better, fresher, more alive than the old Marxism, the old rigid CP.'

"Well, frankly, no, I don't see it. Oh, of course, I see that the students, the blacks, the women have taken hold of the political meaning of their own lives, and they are pushing on all of us questions and angers that we, in the Old Left, only barely had a handle on. And, of course, I support it wholeheartedly. It's a wonderful, exciting thing to see happen. But . . . it's not for me. *I* can't get a handle on it. I can't see my way into it.

"Consciousness! they yell. Self-realization! they yell. I don't know what that means. Oh, I know with my *head* what that means, but I don't really know what it means. Is that politics? I say to myself. And if so, *where* is this politics? Where and how does one begin to become political today?

"So they say, 'It's an atmosphere, it's a way of thinking. Self-understanding is a political act today. Remaking yourself from the inside out is a political act. Advancing the general consciousness of the country is a political act. Marxism itself,' they say, 'is just the way a whole lot of people are thinking and talking and writing today. That's *it*, Grace. Don't you see?'

"No, I don't see," Grace says quietly. "I listen. I nod. I agree. Then a voice comes rushing up from the subterranean depths and it says: 'But where is your plan? Where is your discipline? Where is your structure? How do you join thought and action without a structure? How do you make a revolution without a plan, without discipline? What the *hell* are you people talking about?' "

The afternoon is fading, the brilliant north light vanishing from the studio. Grace and I replace our coffees with scotch. We remain silent for a bit in the gathering darkness. Then Grace lights a cigarette, inhales deeply, and says:

"I guess I'm an old-fashioned ideologue. For me, discipline *is* freedom, ideology *is* specific, organization *is* crucial. Without these tools, these structural means, I don't know how to perform or produce. I *sense* that there is a new world out there, a new and important idea forming itself, perhaps even a new step in the human struggle is being taken with this cry of 'consciousness.' I sense it, but I don't feel it. It doesn't speak to me in my gut. It doesn't give me new sight. . . . So I make my quilts and my pots. Here in the studio I fashion a kind of structure I understand and within which I can function. And that's it. That's how an ideologue without an ideology goes on."

David Ross, like Jerome Rindzer and Grace Lange, has also discovered in the years since he left the Communist Party that he is a permanent ideologue. The realization has struck him with force over these past seven or eight years; he had imagined himself otherwise, so angry and bitter had been his leavetaking of the Party and his belief that ideological dogma had very nearly destroyed his life.

David is fifty years old. He is a physical chemist who lives and works in Boston. He, like Jerome Rindzer, was also raised in the New York working-class Left. David's wife, Marilyn, comes as well out of that world. Marilyn goes a long way toward explaining much about both of them when she tells the following story on a Saturday afternoon in April over coffee at their kitchen table:

"Last year we visited my cousin, Georgie, in Chicago. He's forty-eight years old, the director of a Jewish community center, a terrific social worker, he was involved in the movement for years. We talked about all sorts of things, mostly family stuff, for a long time. Then the conversation turned to economics and politics. God! You should have seen it. The entire atmosphere changed in an instant. Suddenly, everybody resettled themselves in their chairs, grabbed for their cigarettes, lit up, and then leaned forward and started *talking*.

"It was a direct throwback to my childhood. The moment when somebody asked a question and my father said, 'Let me explain.' And then he gave you The Word, The Truth, The Marxist Explanation.

"And I loved it. I loved it when my father did that. I could make sense of things then, and above all I wanted to make sense of things. If I could just understand things then everything would somehow be okay.

"I never felt again what I felt in childhood until I came to psychotherapy. Psychological insight was to me in adulthood what Marxism was in childhood. I know, I know, everybody says insight is not what therapy is all about. But it was for me. Psychological insight, at a certain time in my life, allowed me to *live*. And that's just how I felt as a child when all confusions were explained over the kitchen table through the Marxist explanation. It allowed me to understand, and if I could understand I could live."

David Ross, who wears rimless glasses and a nervous smile, was a member of the Communist Party between 1941 and 1956. He and Marilyn have known each other since their teenage years, and he shares to the very largest degree her perceptions about the role Marxism played in their lives. He would go even further than she goes for his position was not that of Marilyn but rather that of Marilyn's father. He was not receiving the explanation, he was giving it.

"For sixteen years," David says, "I was suffused with the dogma of Communism. It was the air I breathed, the food I ate, the wine

I drank. My studies, my marriage, my friendships were all strained through the liquid flow of Marxist thought before they entered my brain and my feelings. That flow seemed to me alive with chemical being, essential matter. It contained everything necessary to life.

"In 1956, after the Khrushchev Report, the flow dried up, and I found myself living in a world that for me had turned arid, barren and bitter as gall. I ceased functioning entirely. I had become so confused I literally didn't know whether or not to cross the street when the light turned green. My work fell to pieces. And Marilyn and I," he lays a hand on his wife's arm, "nearly fell to pieces, too. I entered psychotherapy in true desperation.

"Well, psychotherapy was for me quite different than it was for Marilyn. Or perhaps I should amend that statement to: I *thought* it was different. It seemed to me that my life was opening up to my own inspection in a way I could not have imagined possible. The reality of the subconscious hit me like a ton of bricks. To have to rethink the *meaning* of love, the *meaning* of friendship, the *meaning* of systematic thought . . . it was dynamite.

"I learned a great deal and I feel, without question, that psychoanalysis not only saved me from breakdown but allowed me to rebuild my life and to value, *philosophically*, the concept of internal integration above social integration. And above all, to try to deal with the contradictory notion that internal integration depends to a large degree on the ability to let everything go, to risk the shattering, scattering process of taking into myself the idea that human experience is characterized by an utter *lack* of system. For me, that was the worst. This idea at first brought total despair. But then, in time, it brought freedom, a large measure of freedom."

David stops short, as though suddenly at a vital loss. How to say what he must now say? He struggles to go on.

"When the Sixties hit and the New Left exploded I felt instinctively that many of the things they were saying, and then many of the things the women were putting their fingers on, were deeply related to the new kind of knowledge psychotherapy had given me. And then I saw that my new knowledge was no match for my old knowledge.

"I could not accept the New Left as genuinely political. This simply was not politics to me, and it never would be. Without structure and organization it was gossip. I found myself longing again—longing? hungering!—for a cohesive world of ideological explanation such as the one that Marxism had provided me with. I knew I could never feel passionately about the new movements as I had about the old, I realized that the CP had provided me with a sense of comradeship I would never have again, and that without that comradeship I could *never* be political. . . . Something within me rejected violently this new way of being political. The fragmentation, the loneliness of it all! Marxism had been transcendent. But, I now realized, it had been transcendent only because it was linked intimately, for me, to the life of the CP. Without a CP, without that structure surrounding and containing it, there was not that extraordinary amalgam that made a political *life*, that raised the meaning of politics to a higher power. The idea of politics as simply a diffused consciousness linked only to personal integrity was—*is*—anathema to me."

These people—Rindzer, Lange, Ross—are the permanent ideologues of a very particular stripe among the Communists, those for whom politics without the Party is unthinkable. They pass now for apolitical or nonpolitical, but in actuality they are deeply, inflexibly political. They know, many of them, the limitation and danger of political life as they conceive it. They know better than anyone in America that structure, leadership, organization can quickly become dogma, tyranny, authoritarianism. They know that the idea of "freedom through discipline" walks a dangerous tightrope. All this they know, but they cannot *feel* what they know, they are compelled to feel otherwise. They are governed by an emotional frame of reference that cannot be wrenched from the socket of an old and passionate experience inextricably bound up with disciplined structure.

Often, this emotional reference produces grotesquerie. It was once at the heart of what was worst in the Communists, it is now at the heart of what is worst in the ex-Communists.

The Anti-Communist Communist

IN *The God That Failed*, Louis Fischer made the following observation:

> Among the ex-Communists . . . there is a type that might be called the authoritarian by inner compulsion. A changed outlook or bitter experience may wean him from Stalinism. But he still has the short-comings that drove him into the Bolshevik camp in the first place. He abandons Communism intellectually yet he needs an emotional substitute for it. Weak within himself, requiring security, a comforting dogma, and a big battalion, he gravitates to a new pole of infallibility, absolutism and doctrinal certainty. He clings to something outwardly united and strong. Often he deserts Communism because it is not secure enough, because it zigzags and flipflops and thus deprives him of the stability he craves. When he finds a new totalitarianism, he fights Communism with Communist-like violence and intolerance. He is an anti-Communist "Communist."

Max Bitterman, sixty years old in 1974, was for almost twenty-five years a functionary of the Communist Party. Bitterman left the Party in 1956, wrote a scholarly history of American Communism, and subsequently became a teacher of political science. I read Bitterman's book in early 1974, was much impressed by its thoughtful measured tone, and I wrote to him, telling him of the book I was trying to write and asking if he would care to talk about his life with me. He wrote back immediately and said, "Come visit me this summer on my farm, and we'll have a good long talk." So, in August I took the train up to Vermont to visit Max Bitterman and his wife, Laura, and subsequently passed three of the strangest days of that highly volatile year.

The Bitterman farm was very large, consisting of a number of parcels of land that had been bought piecemeal, most of them at Depression rates, over a thirty-year span. On the farm stood three houses, all built by Bitterman himself and scattered beautifully on the hillsides and woodlands of the property. The houses themselves were very lovely, a testament to Bitterman's skill and taste. The first house built was the one the Bittermans lived in, the other two were rented out. That summer three men were living in the house on the hillside visible from the Bittermans' kitchen window, and a young relative of Laura Bitterman was living in the house in the woods.

I arrived at noon on a hot sunny day, having been dropped at the back door of the first house on the land and told by the taxi driver, "This is it." I knocked at the door. No answer. I pushed the door. It gave way, and I entered the kitchen. Silence, no one home. Yet, I puzzled, they'd been expecting me. Well, I'd just wait. I put down my bag and walked into the living room. The interior of the house was even lovelier than the exterior. High beamed ceilings, oaken walls and floors, huge fireplace in the living room, deep beautiful space in the kitchen, plants, walnut tables, early American sofas. I was more than prepared to like the people who lived here.

At one o'clock the door burst open and a woman came flying into the kitchen where I sat waiting. "Oh, I'm so sorry," she said breathlessly, "the car broke down, the neighbor's children, Max wouldn't let the older boy, I had to go, do, wait, see . . ." She babbled on without a halt. "That's okay," I said quickly, "really, perfectly okay. I've been just fine here, just fine." She calmed down then, threw her car keys on the counter, and abruptly asked me what I'd like for lunch.

The woman was Laura Bitterman, Max Bitterman's wife of thirty-five years, and her appearance was as strikingly disordered as her entry into the house had been. Her hair, dyed an inappropriate blonde, looked like a hank of hay sitting on top of her head. On the other hand, her body was lovely, slim, and strong. She had Isak Dinesen eyes and a transforming little-girl smile, the eyes and the smile trapped in a bewildered, sorrowing network of aging wrinkles. Her movements were jerky, disconnected, touching. From the very beginning, Laura Bitterman seemed to me both beautiful and slightly deranged.

Laura said: "Max is working on the house up on the hill. He'll be in for lunch." At exactly one-thirty, when lunch was on the table, Max Bitterman walked through the door. His appearance was as surprising to me as Laura's had been. I had expected a dark, solid, warmly bulky man. Bitterman was small, thin, almost wizened. His skin, hair, eyes were nearly colorless, all a kind of washed-out grey. His eyeglasses threw off the reflecting light, making him blind when he looked directly into my face. His voice, when he finally spoke, was hard-edged and shot through with casual sarcasm, its tone, I realized quickly, permanently, insistently bitter.

I also realized quickly that Max Bitterman was going deaf. Within a few hours I realized that Laura, too, was going deaf, and within twenty-four hours after that it struck me that this condition was the objective correlative of their lives.

"Well, well, Laura," Max said that first day at lunch, not looking at either of us, "so the younger generation has seen fit at last to come and sit at the knee of the elder. Maybe there's a trick or two they can *still* learn." His voice dripped scorn. I was so startled that for a moment I remained silent.

"Mr. Bitterman," I said, raising my voice carefully, "I'm not quite the younger generation. I'm thirty-nine years old. I was raised in the Old Left. I have never held the Old Left in contempt as those ten years younger than myself did."

It was as though I had not spoken. "Yes, yes," Bitterman said, spreading his napkin and lifting his fork, "you sit there making theories, and you don't know what the hell you're talking about. All those theories, based on history that's just words to you, *words*. To me and my generation, it's blood, our blood. We were *there*. We lived through all these things you're. . . ."

"Max," Laura blurted out, "she's not saying anything of the sort. Max, you're not listening to her."

It was as if *she* had not spoken. Bitterman went on in this fashion throughout the lunch. Both Laura and I subsided quickly into silence. I could see by the way she shrugged her shoulders ever so slightly and bent calmly once more to her food that Laura's interruption had been a reflexive twitch, not a form of expressiveness she expected to have honored with a response. (Afterwards, when I was thinking about their both going deaf, I saw it had all been there in the first hour of our meeting. He hadn't heard any voice but his own in thirty years, so why not go deaf? She hadn't heard any voice but his in thirty years so, indeed, why not go deaf?)

When the lunch was over Max rose abruptly and said he had to get back to "the work." In the doorway he flung at me, "We'll talk this evening, young lady. Meanwhile, see if you can't make yourself useful around here. We all work here, you know. There are no guests around here."

Laura raised her coffee cup to her mouth and gave me a radiant little-girl smile. "He doesn't mean it," she said. "He doesn't realize how his voice affects people, that's all." I stared at her, not speaking. I wanted to say, "I don't understand. Where is the man who wrote that book? Where is the man who wrote that letter? Are you telling me the self-absorbed creature who just walked out of here is *him*?" But since I was not quite prepared to say that to Laura Bitterman I said nothing.

"Come on," she said good-naturedly, "I'll take you for a drive, show you the village, the countryside, then we'll come back, have a good dinner, and afterwards you can get what you came for."

As we rose from the table an enormous rumble shook the house. I jumped. Laura laughed and said, "Don't worry, it's not an earthquake. It's just 'the work,'" and she pointed out the window. I looked out and saw a huge machine digging into the earth beside the house on the hillside above us. "That's Max's project for the summer," Laura went on. "He's digging out a new foundation for the house and making a garage and a ter- race above the foundation. I begged him not to do this, the work, the noise, the tenants, the whole summer destroyed. But he said it was *necessary*, and once Max thinks something's necessary, that's it. The whole world can go down the drain right in front of him, if it's *necessary* he does it. I guess in some ways that's a good trait . . . good for the revolution, anyway . . ." she finished, her voice trailing off strangely.

We left the house, climbed into Laura's little blue car, and drove off to the village, where Laura collected mail at the post office, bought some wool in a knitting shop, stopped in at the hardware store to ask if Max's order had come in, and did her supermarket shopping. Everyone in the village knew her and greeted her kindly. Afterwards, we drove out into the country and Laura showed me a lake, a castle, a wooded stream, a stretch of pine forest. As we drove we talked. I asked her many questions about herself, her life, her marriage, her own years in the Com- munist Party. She drove and talked in the same way that she looked and acted: now jerky, now smooth, now disconnected, now coherent, now warm and imaginative, now confused and somewhat crazy.

By the end of that afternoon Laura Bitterman had become for me the prototype of The Wife of the Great Revolutionary. She made me "see" what I had only been slowly perceiving throughout that year: where women were concerned the Communist Party reflected not the rewards and abuses of the democratic impulse but the rewards and abuses of the elitist impulse. Women who were "the brilliant exception" often rose higher in the Party than they could in any other part of American life, but women who were simply ordinary beings were often more subjugated in the Party than they were in ordinary American life. In the name of the revolution, women like Laura Bitterman suffered untold abuses, and remained with their spirits damaged beyond repair.

Laura was the daughter of dynamic, difficult, self-absorbed parents: impassioned socialists who rode roughshod over themselves, each other, everyone around them. Laura's brother, Saul, knew how to defend himself and engage his parents' interest at the same time. For Laura it was otherwise. An imaginative, sensitive, entirely unintellectual girl, a talented dancer, her gifts went unnoticed, unprized.

Politics for Laura was a diffused atmosphere all mixed up with modern dance, wall posters, intense schoolmates, and a sentimental rush of feeling for "the people." She wanted to dance, but all around her in great waves rose up her parents' socialist ardor, the Depression, the fight against fascism. She was stirred and confused. She resisted joining the Communist Party because all she wanted was that the world should be soft, pretty, and loving, not mean, cruel, and political. One night in 1934 at Columbia University police on horses drove wildly into an antifascist demonstration. They formed a wedge and drove the students to their knees, cracking their heads as they fell. "Now?" a friend of Laura's cried wildly to her. "Now, will you join?" And she did.

The revolution and the Communist Party was for Laura, more than any other single thing, the men in it who dominated her life: her father, her brother, her husband. She had known Max Bitterman from childhood on, and when she married him she married herself for life to her emotional fears, to her frightened (exploited) conviction that Max and her father were large figures involved in mammoth doings while she was an insignificant creature who should be grateful to be standing on the edge of this great human drama they were taking part in.

In 1954, while Max was in Russia for the Party, Laura was brought up on charges of white chauvinism and threatened with expulsion from the CP. She denied these charges violently and fought bitterly with her accusers. When it came to it, she dreaded the loneliness of expulsion. She nearly went mad, she says. Her brother, long out of the Party, had said to her: "Leave them. It's an insanity, the whole thing is an insanity. And, after all, what does it matter anymore? Leave them." But Laura could not. "I said to him, I *must* fight this. This is my Party. My husband is in Russia, the FBI is after all of us, they're throwing me to the wolves!"

If Max had been in America in 1954 he probably would have stood by, watching Laura's trial without a word spoken or a finger raised. And Laura would not have been too surprised. "You know," she says, "we had one child, a son named Michael. All of our life together Max said to me, 'Politics first, Michael second, you last.' And in Nineteen-Fifty-Four it was still, unquestionably, politics first."

Some years ago Laura entered psychoanalysis. Max threatened to leave her. "It was the one time nothing he said or did mattered," Laura says. "I felt like I was fighting for my life. I was in such pain I don't think I even heard him. He realized I was beyond him, he couldn't get at me. So he was impressed and frightened. So that was the end of his leaving me." She had been speaking in rather a monotone, but now she turned to me and between clenched teeth said: "And what I got out of analysis was, afterwards, I could say to him 'Don't you *talk* to me like that!' "

But in the last five years, she went on, all the fight has gone out of her. Within these years her brother and her son had died —both of them suicides. She and Max now live in a state of armed truce.

It was late afternoon when we returned to the farm. The sun had disappeared and suddenly a thick rain was falling. The house was silent, empty, rain-darkened. Laura and I sat down in the living room, shaking ourselves dry. She stood by the fireplace. In the strange half light she turned to me and said: "I have always feared being abandoned. And I was right to fear it. My father died and left me, my brother died and left me, my son died and left me." I felt cold listening to her.

At six o'clock Max walked into the kitchen saying, "Where's dinner? Where's dinner? Workingmen must eat, you know. Well, young lady, did you make yourself useful this afternoon? Laura, has she been useful or has she spent the day being a social parasite like most young people today?" No answer was really required. These sentences were spoken not to me but at me as Max continued on to his bedroom where he remained secreted for the next half hour while Laura hurried to get dinner on the table.

As we were eating Max said, "We're going to visit Gino and his wife tonight." He turned to me and beamed. "One of my young workers has a new baby he's dying to show me. He insisted we come tonight. You know, the people in the village all love working for me. They know its a *real* project when I put them to work, and they love me for giving them real work."

Laura and I stared at him. Then Laura burst out, "Max, you can't *do* this! She's come all the way from New York to talk to you. You can't drag her around like this."

Max continued to eat, saying brusquely, "Nonsense, nonsense. Plenty of time, plenty of time. After all, she's not taking the train first thing in the morning. Plenty of time to talk. And besides, it's just as important that she see the people in the village. Give her a taste of real life. Let her see how the little people of this world live. None of these New York intellectuals know what real life is like. Give her an education."

By now, I was feeling spellbound by Max's behavior and wondering how far he would carry this incredible manipulation. I nodded my head silently, and we continued our meal while Max delivered a lecture on the beauties of the earth-moving machine he had rented: the implication being that it was a magnificent machine because he had chosen it.

At eight o'clock we got into Laura's car and drove the ten miles into the village where we stopped before a small frame house on a tree-lined street and got out as a young, dark-haired man opened the door with a baby in his arms. Max greeted him effusively and we all entered the house, Gino and his sweet-faced wife ushering us into their formica and naugahyde living room.

There then followed two-and-a-half hours of the kind of ut-terly boring, pointless chitchat that passes among people who have nothing in common and no real reason for being together. Gino and his polite wife seemed slightly confused throughout the whole time, and I realized this visit had been Max's idea not Gino's.

We returned to the house at eleven, having driven back in total silence. In the house we all sat down in the living room. Max flung his body onto a sofa, lifted his legs onto a coffee table, leaned his head back, and took off his glasses. He sighed, rubbed the bridge of his nose, and then said: "Communism was the work of the devil. Do you believe in the devil, young lady? Well, you damned well better. Because Communism was the work of the devil. Couldn't have been anything else. The things we did, the lies we told, the lives we destroyed, the deaths we were responsi-ble for. Nothing else but the devil could have made us do that. All these people you're running around talking to, I bet most of them are telling you what a wonderful life it was, how Com-munism was the best thing that ever happened to them. Don't you believe it. Liars, every damned one of them. Liars, cowards, opportunists. Most of them not even really Communists. Most of them goddamned fellow travelers, if you ask me. Anyone who wasn't an open Communist like I was is a fellow traveler in my book. And then all those goddamned cowards who ran like sheep in Thirty-Nine, and again in Forty-Six, Forty-Seven. And all those opportunists who stayed on through Hungary, Czecho-slovakia. Can you beat that? Staying on through Czechoslovakia? Well, what can I tell you? It was an evil business, an evil business. You put that in your book, young lady. It was an evil business."

Without another word Max rose and left the room. Laura and I remained sitting together without speaking. Finally, she went silently off to bed and then I did, too.

I remember lying in bed that night thinking two things: One, what Bitterman shared with too, too many Communists—only in his case more madly virulent than in most—was the scorn and hatred for anyone who had left the Party either thirty seconds earlier or thirty seconds later than he had. If they left earlier they were cowards, if they left later they were opportunists. Only if they saw the moment when he left as *the* insupportable moment were they duped but still righteous people. Two, as Bitterman delivered these infuriated bitten-off sentences one could see the rage choking him was actually snuffing out his intelligence: short-circuiting the ability to think, wiping out the long line of analytic connection necessary for clear sight.

The next day was an unbelievable repeat of the previous day. In the morning Max said, "After lunch." At lunch he said, "Later this afternoon." In the afternoon he said, "After dinner." I determined that I would leave early the following morning no matter what occurred that day.

In the afternoon I wandered up to the house occupied by Laura's young relative, a graduate student in his late twenties named Mort. Mort was the son of Laura's cousin and had known Max and Laura all his life. He was studying for his orals that summer and Max had rented him the house "cheap." Mort invited me in for a cup of coffee and as we sat in the wood-paneled kitchen of the little house he said to me, "How's it going? Can you still stand the sight of Max or have you just about had it?" I looked at him, laughed gratefully, and said, "Tell me." Mort leaned back in his chair, stretched out his long legs, and said:

"Well, I guess Max is just about the worst man I know. He has absolutely no sense of or respect for other human beings. The revolution is everything, people are shit. It's been like that since I can remember. He destroyed Laura's life for the revolution, and then when the revolution failed him he turned on the CP like a vicious animal. He is eaten up alive by his own anger, and it's from inside that anger that he posits reality. No matter how blindly he arrives at the idea that something is real, right, and necessary, once he does there's no stopping him. Like the good Stalinist he still is," Mort grinned, "he moves forward like a bulldozer, and woe to anyone who stands in the way of the historic necessity.

"Take this business this summer with the foundation for that house up on the hill. Well, the whole thing is ridiculous. There was no need for that foundation, the house had been standing

solid for ten years. This summer because he has nothing else to
do, Max decides the house *must* have a foundation. Everyone in
the village is laughing at him. He'll tell you they love to come and
work for him because it's real work. Right? Hasn't he told you
that? Well, it's just not true. They come to work for him when
they finish their other work, that's why it's going so slowly.

"And then there's the men living in the house. Mind you, he
rented that house to them. Those guys work all night, sleep all
day. Well, how much sleep do you think they've been getting
this summer with that machine digging the house out from under them all day long every day this month? I thought Laura was
really going to go over the bend this time. She cried and yelled
and waved her arms like a lunatic, begged him not to do this to
the tenants. Max set his face grimly and said the work must go
on. Mad, mad, mad. The whole story of Max Bitterman is just
mad."

That evening after dinner Max rose from the table while I was
still drinking my coffee and said, "All right, young lady, let's go,
let's go. You want to talk? Let's talk now." And he walked out
of the kitchen. I hastily put down my cup and followed him.
He led the way to a remote part of the house and opened the
door to a room that looked like the classic room behind the store:
small and dusty, piled high with books, papers, cartons, junky
furniture. Max sat down at one end of a ratty sofa, motioned me
to sit on a broken-down easy chair facing him, and waved me to
begin, adding he really didn't know what else there was to talk
about, he'd told me everything yesterday. My heart sank.

"Max," I said doggedly, "I'd like you to tell me about your
early life. Tell me how you remember the early days. How you
became a Communist."

"What's to tell?" Max said curtly. "It was Depression, fascism
was coming, a blind man could see what was coming, I became
a Communist. There was nothing else to become, that's what
you became."

"Where were you born, Max? Was your family political? How
did you grow up?"

"I grew up in Brooklyn. My father was religious. I discovered
Lenin on my own at sixteen. By the time I got to City College
I knew more political history than most people ten years older

than myself. They were stupid, all stupid. But *I* beat it into them. By the time they got through with me they knew what it was all about. And that's about it. College, the YCL, the Party, I was a professional revolutionary from the first. That's it. I don't know what else I can tell you. I told you everything you need to know last night." He bit off these sentences in that infuriated voice of his and fell silent. I could just see him at eighteen, one of those snotty, sneering leftist kids: the Max Bitterman of today in embryo.

I could hardly believe this was it. He actually had nothing more to say to me than what he had just said. My frustration split its skin. "Max," I said, "why did you invite me to come up here? My letter was most explicit. It told you exactly what I was doing, and what kind of interview I expected from you. Not only have you steadfastly refused to give me that interview but you have manipulated me shamelessly for two days, you have made me follow you around like a dog on a leash, you have called me young lady about three hundred times, you have acted as though my time had no value. Why have you done this?"

Max Bitterman stared at me as though I had suddenly lost my reason. "I do not know what you are talking about," he said, and he got up and walked out of the room.

The next morning we shared a silent breakfast. Throughout the meal Max clearly was uneasy. Something had happened which I think he truly did *not* understand, but he had felt the weight of my displeasure and it somehow seemed necessary to him to deal with it. I should have known that dealing with it meant triumphing over it. He rose from the table and walked to the door. On the threshold he paused, turned to look back at me, raised a finger, and, his eyes gleaming with appreciation at his own intelligence, said, "Communism was a response to the loneliness of the universe." I stared after him as he walked out the door, and behind the sound of his words echoing in my ears, I heard Laura's voice saying, "I have always feared being abandoned."

At noon Max and Laura drove me to the train station. As we stood on the platform waiting for the train to New York Max said, "Well, well, young lady, always glad to be of service to the younger generation if I can. It's most important that you understand these things, most important. If you need any more help don't hesitate to write or call or come visit again." I stared at him. Then I said, "Thank you, Max. That's very kind of you." As I boarded the train, Laura grasped my arm. In a low, steady voice she said, "Be kind."

The Wounds of the Past

SIXTY miles from New York, at the edge of a small lake in New Jersey, stands a sprawling wooden house, its weathered shingles grey-brown, its trim grey-blue, its overall look cozy-shabby, as though the people who own the house live in it rather than attend to it. The rooms inside fulfill the promise outside: the furniture is comfortably worn, the rugs clean but threadbare, the living room lined with book-filled shelves and bare of decorative objects, except for plants and six framed 1930s woodcuts.

Arnold and Bea Richman live in this house. They have lived here for thirty years. The three children they raised in this house are grown and gone. The meetings, parties, and political gatherings that once animated this house are also gone. Only Arnold and Bea remain.

Arnold and Bea, both in their late fifties, were members of the Communist Party for twenty-five years. They, like other people whose lives fill the pages of this book, were both raised in the New York working-class Left. Between the middle Nineteen-Thirties and the late Nineteen-Fifties they lived the life of professional radicals, and in the Nineteen-Sixties, in their late forties, they remade their lives. Again—as with many other Communist couples whose lives are here traced—the decision to live such political lives was primarily Arnold's not Bea's, and they have had to live with *that* knowledge, as well, these past fifteen years.

Today, Arnold works as a biologist in a research laboratory twenty miles from this house and Bea works as a school secretary in a high school fifteen miles in another direction. They are both handsome people with the map of their lives etched on their faces. Arnold is tall, slim, athletic, with a well-shaped head and a shock of coarse grey-brown hair. His body is full of easy grace, and as he walks across a room I can easily see traces of the boy he must have been, reaching high to send a ball into a net in a Brooklyn schoolyard. There is nothing of that boy, however, in his face. The lines in Arnold's face are shockingly deep. They pull down the corners of his nose and mouth as though the entire face is being dragged relentlessly toward some long-repressed gravity of the soul. The eyes above the lines look caged. They are large, brown, liquid. If they were gentle Arnold would look like an intelligent bulldog, but as they are sad he looks like an intelligent beagle.

Bea, on the other hand, is all nervous angularity, spare flesh on good bones, quick movements, darting eyes. She moves with the grace of a high-strung cat rather than that of a tranquil athlete. The shape of her head is amazingly like Arnold's—as is the texture of the thick grey-brown hair surrounding and softening her face—eerily increasing the ever-present incestuous look of people long married. Bea's face, however, is neither sad nor gentle. It is flat, tight, compactly held together. Not bitter, not malicious, not brittle. Only tight. Smooth and tight. As though if it were anything else it would shatter into a thousand fragments.

These two are not friends. In the sense in which the word is usually used they do not appear even to be intimates. On the other hand, the sexual bond between them is palpable. No doubt there is a dynamic relation between the absence of friendship and the presence of sexual electricity; but the Richmans exude an atmosphere of peculiar isolation, as though they are bound together in mysterious circumstances, living in the motionless eye of the electric storm, and one wonders what it really is that keeps them together.

I spent two days in New Jersey with the Richmans. Arnold picked me up at the train station and we drove through the black and grey November countryside to his house. Arnold drove expertly, with a smooth fine knowledge of the road, and talked continuously as he drove. His talk was warm, expansive, filled with an unbroken ease of speech. He spoke of the countryside in which he lived, gave me a little history as we passed through the village, told me something of the lab in which he was working, and of the school in which Bea worked.

"Bea has become a real force in that school," Arnold said proudly. "She's a militant feminist now and boy! do they know it in that school." He turned toward me and grinned. "You know, you can't keep a good organizer down. She's got those secretaries fighting for equal pay, bosses making the coffee, no more friendly pats on the ass, and promotions from within.

"The women's movement has done wonders for Bea. Wonders. And it's terrific. She's her own person now. *Really* her own person. You know, in the Party we talked a good game about male chauvinism but," a deep shrug of the shoulder, "the fact is, all the years in the Party, *I* was the hotshot organizer and Bea . . . she was my wife. Now, it's really different. And nobody could be happier about it than me. She is definitely *the* political half of the Richman family now."

We drove up to the house, and as we got out of the car the door opened and Bea stood in the doorway. Arnold reached for my bag and Bea said crisply: "Arnold, she's not a cripple, she can carry her own bag, and I'm sure she'd prefer to do so."

Arnold froze in midmotion, looked uncertainly from his wife to me. I laughed and said, "Bea is right, Arnold. But I take it in a friendly spirit." I picked up the bag and we all entered the house.

"These men," Bea said, shaking her head. "You tell them and tell them and tell them. But does it sink in? It does not. A hundred years it'll take to sink in." Arnold remained silent. Bea reached up, patted his shoulder, and kissed him on the cheek.

"Well," Arnold said, "I don't know about you two but *I* could use a drink." Bea and I walked into the living room and sat down, Arnold brought a tray of ice, liquor, and glasses from the kitchen, and our visit began.

For the next two days we three talked nonstop. Eating, walking, sitting by the fire, driving to the market for groceries: we talked. We talked about the Communist Party, about the Richmans' lives now, their children, the women's movement, the political atmosphere in America today. Arnold's voice was uniformly soft, moderate, full of chastised wisdom. Bea's was constantly setting the record straight.

Arnold spoke movingly of his years in the CP, of what the idea of revolution had meant to him, of how powerful and total the world of the CP had been for him. His words were eloquent, his sentences full and rich as he spoke. Then his voice fell, and he said: "Of course, we made a lot of mistakes, a lot of mistakes, and we've . . ."

"Mistakes!" Bea's voice broke in harshly. "*Mistakes*! Arnold's mother was expelled from the Party in Nineteen-Fifty-Three for white chauvinism. White chauvinism! She was a 1905'er. She'd been in the American Party thirty years. She went to visit her sister in Florida, and she was expelled for white chauvinism. We sat in that room in open hearing, a hundred people must have been crowded into that room, Mrs. Richman was *beloved*, and listened to this insane trial proceed. I clutched Arnold's arm and I said to him, 'Arnold, do you see what is happening here? Do you understand what they are *doing*? This is *Animal Farm*, Arnold,' I said to him, '*Animal Farm*!' But did he listen to me? Another three years it had to go on."

Arnold remained silent for a long moment, his brows drawn together as though his head was hurting him terribly, and then he said: "She's right, she's right. What can I say? It took Khrushchev's revelations to make me 'see,' as Bea says. So, *nu*? What can I tell you? You think you just walk away from a lifetime? Just like *that*?"

"What I want to know," Bea barreled on, "is how come so many people were thrown out for white chauvinism but not one goddamned Communist was ever thrown out for male chauvinism?"

Arnold's head remained bowed. He lifted his eyes to me and said wearily, "She's right, she's right." He smiled gently at his angry wife and repeated softly, "When she's right, she's right." Which, I added silently to myself, is every day of your life these days.

So it went for a day and a half. Clearer and clearer it came: he had beat her head in for twenty years with the revolution, she would beat his in for the next twenty with feminist retaliation. Bea would exact retribution, Arnold would take his punishment.

On the second day, at lunch, in the midst of a welter of words, Bea made some passing crack about men raping their wives. Suddenly, Arnold leapt up, upsetting his lunch on the table. His face went white, and with barely controlled anger he spat out: "All right! *Enough* already." He stalked from the room, the door slamming shut behind him. Bea and I stared wordlessly at the door. Silence filled the room with cubic force, and then the silence seemed to fill the whole house. All around me, the house grew sad, shabby, intensely still. An eerie isolation seemed to descend on us, as though suddenly we were sealed off from the world beyond this room. I felt: "This marriage is held together by the wounds of the past. A world of strained remorse, controlled forgiveness, is at the center of things here. Everything hangs on a thread, a thread that is perpetually ready to snap at a moment's notice, but one I think that never actually will."

Late in the afternoon Arnold drove me to the train station. We had some time before the train was due, and we took a walk through a nearby winter-brown field. Arnold walked with his head down, kicking at loose clumps of dead grass. Then he said:

"You ask me how I feel about the Communist Party. Do I love it? Do I hate it? Am I an anti-Communist? That's like asking me do I love my mother, do I hate my mother. What's the difference whether I love or hate her? She's my mother. I am bound to her by ties stronger than love or hate. Well, that's the way it is with me and the Communist Party. Probably more so than with my mother. It is my *history*. To hate it, to deny it, to turn on it is to wipe myself out. I cannot do that. So I live with it, I live with it. It rises up and bites me? I live with it. It torments me? I live with it. In some sense it's like I walk around with this gaping wound inside me, holding myself together. But I do it. I walk around, and I hold myself together." Arnold's eyes came level with mine and he said: "And that's why I don't leave Bea. Because she knows what's going on inside me." His voice went husky. "She *knows*."

Arnold's brows came together as they had the day before, the motion expressing pure pain. "And," he said, clearing his throat, "I think that's why she doesn't leave me, either. Who else in either of our lives could ever understand the history each of us walks around with? And how could either of us live without the other being there to recognize that history? That would *really* be lonely. . . . And that, God help us, is what holds us together. So what does that mean? What kind of an ex-Communist does that make either of us? You tell me."

"I Lost More Than I Got"

MAX Bitterman sits in unyielding judgment upon his life as a Communist, Arnold Richman abdicates judgment entirely. In relation to the past, one lives in a state of aggressive fury, the other in a kind of wounded stun. Between these two extremes there stands a variety of Communists who, while far from Bitterman's rabid anti-Communism nevertheless frown on Richman's withdrawal, and of themselves conclude: "I regret nothing, but I lost more than I got." Three such Communists are Morris Silverman, Carl Peters, and Dave Abetta.

Morris Silverman is sixty years old and runs a prosperous life-insurance business in Denver, Colorado, where he has lived for the past ten years. He is a small, silver-haired man who wears rimless glasses, "natty" clothes, and speaks in a low, unvarying monotone. His movements, like his words, are economical and ungrudgingly to the point. One feels instantly that this man is fair rather than generous, that moderation has become a way of life, and that there is a ledger of debits and credits in his mind into which all actions, emotions, and convictions are relentlessly entered.

Silverman was born and raised in the Midwest, the son of prosperous German Jews who sent their son to college so that he could inherit America. When Morris joined the Communist Party in 1935 his parents were confused and alarmed. "The *Communist* Party???" his father said to him. "What is that all about? In America, you join either the Democratic Party or the Republican Party. That's how you rise here, no? What has the Communist Party got to do with anything?"

Silverman, like Arthur Chessler and like countless others, says (and in almost the exact words that Chessler used): "I didn't join the Communist Party because of starvation or Depression. I joined because a new world was coming, and I wanted to be part of it. And if you wanted to be part of that world in 1935 you became a Communist."

He was twenty-one years old, a college senior who had majored in chemistry. In his last year in school the Party asked him to leave his studies and his hometown, and take charge of the CP organization in another state in the Midwest. Morris knew he had become an extremely skillful organizer, and he was flattered that the Party recognized his achievement. He experienced this request to become a full-time organizer as a reward, and unhesitatingly agreed to go. He became and remained the head of the organization in that state for twelve years.

Silverman removes his glasses from his nose, polishes them carefully, replaces them carefully, and says quietly: "Was the work I did valuable? I really have no way of knowing. You see, I loved doing it. I loved it because I was good at it. Now, after all these years, I really don't know whether I loved doing it because it was valuable in and of itself, or if I loved doing it because I was good at it. The two became and remained one and the same for me." He stops talking for a moment, clasps his smooth white hands together across his neat desk, smiles a small tight smile, and goes on:

"And that, you see, is the problem of the CP for me. I was such a *good* organizer, and I so loved being good at my work, that I think I went on being a Communist long after I actively felt or thought about what it was I was organizing for. My revolutionary zeal had, I think, left me sometime during the Second World War, but the years simply ground on without any real review of purpose for me. I was what was known as an 'influential figure' in the Party. That's how I was treated, and that's how I acted. The tragedy, if that's what one wishes to call it, was that I never inspected the meaning of that term . . . until it was too late, much too late.

"Now, I do not hate the Communist Party," he says, his lips tightening yet again. "Nor do I regret my decision to become a Communist. But no, I do not think if I had it to do over I would again become a Communist. And I say that for a number of reasons.

"To begin with, there is the question of the objective meaning of our work in America. We thought we were the only ones who understood the meaning of social and political repression in America. We kept *saying* we were the only ones. But we were wrong, totally wrong. There was a large democratic movement out there. *It* has always saved America from fascism, not us. When, in the Nineteen-Sixties, I began to look and really *see* America, I felt as though I was emerging from a twenty years' sleep, from some incredible fog I'd been living in all my adult life. It was awful, just awful. . . .

"And then there is the question of my own life. I could have been a scientist or a scholar. I'm not proud, you know, that I'm a businessman." Silverman falls silent for a moment, and when finally he speaks it is in a tone of outburst he will not again repeat in my presence. He says hotly: "But we *despised* the intellectuals! And when I got out it was too late, too late."

Aggression has pierced the surface of repressed ambition. Moderation is a terrible strain. How angry he must really be! How frightening his own anger clearly is to him.

He pulls himself together and says softly: "I do not regret the choices I made, but certainly I lost more than I got out of my years in the Party."

Carl Peters is a tall, gaunt man with a headful of black hair streaked with grey and ironic blue eyes that seem to belie his sixty-six years. He lives in Minneapolis where until last year he made his living as a skilled electrician, plumber, and carpenter. Now he has retired to write a history of his grandfather's life and times.

Peters' speech and movements contrast sharply with his youthful appearance; they seem terribly aged, extremely slow and deliberate, as though Peters fears the physical consequences of any sudden motion. . . . After I had talked a while with him I began to wonder if it was indeed age that was the cause of this physical deliberation, so great was the sense of emotion barely under control I felt operating in this man.

Peters is a true native son. His grandfather was a pioneer trek-

ker to the West in the 1840s, and his father a Western wanderer
in his turn. The children grew up moving continually: poor,
rootless, semiliterate. "But," Carl grins on a May evening at his
home in Minneapolis, "we were held together like all good American families by the 'normal' prejudices. We hated Jews, blacks,
and foreigners. That made us know we were better than all the
rest, even when we didn't have a pot to piss in."

Carl left home early: a tall, glowering boy mad at the world
and not knowing why. He was in those years a laborer of every
sort: logger, powder monkey, machinist, dishwasher. He fought,
drank, and stayed mad.

But the generations had had an effect; whereas his grandfather
and father had worked and cursed, Carl worked, cursed, and
read. By the time the Depression was at full tilt Carl's head was
stuffed with the literature of Utopianism, the Co-Operative
Movement, the militance of the Wobblies. In 1934 he met a
Communist who told him, "Nothing will be different until the
workers run the country." That made a lot of sense to Carl,
and he joined the Communist Party.

Peters was a Communist for thirty-four years. He left the
Party only after the Russian invasion of Czechoslovakia. He says
flatly Czechoslovakia was "objectively" the last supportable moment for anyone to have remained in the Party; all those who
left the Party earlier were opportunists, all those who remained
in the Party after Czechoslovakia were sniveling sheep. He feels
compassion for none of them, not for anyone on either side of
the 1968 demarcation point that glows in the dark in his head.

Peters admits he's been angry all his life. He was angry before
he became a Communist, he was angry while he was a Communist,
he's angry now. As a Communist he defended hotly what he
"believed in," and defied recklessly whoever or whatever opposed him. To this day there are sisters and brothers he doesn't
speak to because of the fury their opposition to his political life
aroused in him. And, he adds grudgingly, he also made a lot of
enemies in the Party. Perhaps he should *not* have behaved in
quite so gung-ho a fashion but, he amends quickly, he didn't
know any other way to be. "After all," he says, "you either
believe in something or you don't. If you believe in it you've got
to give your all to it. Your *all*."

It was during the Second World War that his first uneasiness began, secretly, to steal over him. He moves restlessly in his chair, his blue eyes glitter with irony, and he says: "It was the rapid advance of the Nazi Army into Russia that did it. Not a shot fired. Not a hand raised against them in the Ukraine. I was stunned. I thought, What the *hell* is going on over there? How great can things be if the Ukrainians are practically welcoming the Germans into Russia? That stayed with me a long time. I didn't talk about it, none of us talked about it, but it stayed with me, nagged at me, I couldn't get rid of it throughout the war. . . ."

However, he pushed down his doubts and went on with his life. Crises in the CP came and went but Peters remained grimly "true." Even the Khrushchev Report in 1956 was supportable. Of 1956 all he has to say is: "I always thought those who left the Party had been suspect for years."

In the mid-Sixties he made a trip to Russia and Czechoslovakia. His first look at Russia startled him. He couldn't get over what he saw there: "The incredible, insufferable bureaucracy! I kept thinking: Is this what we've been fighting for? Is this what it's all about? My god, it's a thousand times worse here than in any Western country. What the hell has it all been for? To have overthrown one suffocating apparatus for another? It was just godawful to me. I was in a rage day and night.

"And then, and this was even worse, this was what really gave me nightmares . . . one day, at a collective farm, I saw two workers being bawled out by a foreman. Why, if I'd been bawled out like that in the U.S. I'd have slugged the foreman. But those Russians, they just put down their heads and took it. I couldn't forget it. It just stayed in my mind. I'd wake up nights and see those Russian workers before me all over again, their heads down, this sonofabitch of a foreman yelling at them.

"Then I went to Czechoslovakia, and it was really beautiful there. The people, the atmosphere, the whole sense of the place, it was terrific. Like a breath of fresh air after Russia. It really *was* socialism with a human face." Peters breaks off and shakes his head. "What a phrase. 'Socialism with a human face.' Can you beat that? I mean, when you stop and think about the *meaning* of that phrase.

"And then the Russians march in, declaring Czechoslovakia is in the hands of the counterrevolutionaries. Well, that did it for me. I mean, maybe if I hadn't been there and seen for myself what Czechoslovakia was really like, maybe then I'd have been able to swallow it. But as things stood, the bile in me just overflowed. I left the Party then, and I was very bitter for a long time afterwards. I felt I'd wasted my whole life."

I ask Peters if he still feels that way, if he now regrets his life as a Communist. He instantly shakes his head vigorously and says: "Not a bit of it. It was a rich, adventurous life. I learned things, lived vitally, had experiences I'd never have had otherwise. The Party really *was* at the center of the times in the Thirties and Forties. People were really moving then. Searching, insistent, hungry to hear and see everything. And there I was, an ordinary working stiff, in on all of it just because I was a Communist. No, those were good years, good years, I wouldn't trade them for anything. I feel sorry for the young radicals today. They'll never have what we had.

"But the thing is this: I'm still angry. I'm sixty-six years old, and I'm still angry. And that hurts. You know what I mean? You know what I'm talking about?

"You might not believe this but there was a time when the anger left me. During the really good years in the Party. It was remarkable. Life was wonderful then. I thought the anger was gone for good. I thought being a Communist had done it for me. Then after my trip to Russia and Czechoslovakia it all came back again, and it's never left me since.

"I've learned a little bit about what that anger in me is all about. I look around at other people my age. They're not angry. They're at peace with themselves. And you know why? It's because they know who they are. All those years I spent being a Communist these people spent getting to know who they are. I thought being a Communist had done it. But I was wrong. I was fooling myself. Now, we're all in our sixties, and a lot of people I know are free inside themselves, and me I'm still fighting mad. When I was young that anger was good. It was a force that got me moving. Now, it's like a millstone around my neck. So in that sense I feel I lost out. I feel I'm paying now in spades for those good years. It's like, emotionally, I took out the wrong life insurance, gave my money to a hustler, and now I'm sitting here old and broke."

Dave Abetta—whose emotional balance sheet also records a loss— is a sixty-four-year-old lawyer with a good private practice in Seattle which he has carefully built up over the past fifteen years. Before that, he was for the twenty years between 1936 and 1956 a lawyer for the Communist Party, one of the men who spent long weary years of his life in the courts defending the Smith Act defendants, the Hollywood Ten, and a host of other people who were hauled up before the bar of American justice to show just cause why, as Communists, they should not be prosecuted as enemies of the state.

Abetta is a swarthy, baldheaded man who, when I meet him, is wearing a rumpled grey suit and sitting in a small, dusty office at a desk overflowing with books, papers, and briefs. The most striking aspect of Abetta's appearance is the expressive patience that fills his melancholy brown eyes. One glance reveals a world of lived and unlived life behind that patience.

Dave Abetta brings into sudden focus for me something that has been nagging at the edges of my mind for a long time now: the difference between the lawyers of the Old Left and the lawyers of the New Left. The lawyers of the Old Left have always seemed to me to have about them a patient, hardworking manner, as though they were people with a humbled sense of the long haul rather than an excited one of the revolution around the corner. New Left lawyers, on the other hand, have almost always struck me as being arrogant, self-important, "insider" types who behave as though the revolution is their personal responsibility.

Looking at and listening to Dave Abetta, I realize that in the Old Left the lawyers were bunched together with the intellectuals and the "bohemians": necessary and appreciated comrades, but definitely subordinate in power and respect to those doing the "real and important" work, the political work. Today, given the absence of an organization on the Left, the lawyers are the kind of people who thirty years ago would have been functionaries in the CP, and as such arrogate to themselves that contemptuous righteousness which passes for revolutionary fervor and which surfaces in generation after generation on the Left.

Dave Abetta still considers himself a socialist, still believes that socialism must ultimately replace bourgeois capitalism in the civilized countries of the world, still believes that his years in and around the CP were the very best years of his working life. "To work in context," he says, "is without doubt the most satisfying and effective way to work. For me, the CP was an irreplaceable context. Every case I fought, every brief I wrote, every legal decision I took part in was enlarged by the structure within which I worked. That structure made me think better, act more deliberately, see further than I would have otherwise.

"Now, of course, there are lawyers who have always worked the same way within the context of the American democracy. Darrow was such a lawyer. He *believed*. Believed in the system. His mind was powered by that belief, by his sense of outrage when the system betrayed itself. That outrage focused him, gave him a point of view which directed his thought, his research, his lightning connection. I always loved Darrow for that, for the seriousness with which he practiced the law.

"But for me," Abetta smiles gently, "that context was Marxism and the CP. They gave my work a meaning and an intensity it will never have again. I loved the practice of the law in those days in a way I find remarkable to contemplate today. The law then was as beautiful to me as poetry, as mathematics, as the pyramids of Egypt or the biological construction of the human body. A marvel, a true marvel."

Abetta locks his hands together behind his head, leans back in his swivel chair, and raises his legs to his piled-high desk. "No," he says, "I have no regrets, no regrets at all." He falls silent for a moment. Then he sighs and says, "On the other hand, I have no passions either, anymore. None at all."

For a long moment neither of us speaks. Then Abetta says softly: "You see, the work was all. Nothing else in my life made a dent in me. The work and the CP. Only that. My friends fell by the wayside, my family fell by the wayside, music, books, the whole variety of human pleasures, human exchanges outside of politics, all went.

"I lost the ability to develop personal relations. I don't know how anymore. My family never forgave me. My children are strangers to me. *Polite* strangers. But strangers nonetheless. There is a coldness between me and my wife that will never thaw, I think. How could it? All those years I shunted her aside, or patted her on the head, or locked myself up in my office for days on end. . . .

"I try to talk to her now. I really try. But it's no use. I don't know how. I *think* I'm doing all right, I think we're reaching each other. Then suddenly she turns away from me with such a remoteness I know I've been talking into a vacuum. The distance is too great. It can't be bridged anymore."

Abetta falls into a kind of musing stare. Absentmindedly, he removes his feet from his desk, unlocks his hands, and allows his swivel chair to come upright. His eyebrows come together in a frown, his face indicates clearly the effort to collect his thoughts. Then he says:

"I guess in that sense I must say I lost more than I gained from being a Communist. My inability to live among people, to live inside my own skin, is the great reality for me now. The past is something of an abstraction. I did not bring anything out of it that links those years with these years. There is no sense of integration, of continuum, for me. There was me then, and there is me now, and the two don't seem related.

"Somehow," Abetta grins sadly, "that doesn't seem quite right. Having lived my life in the service of the humane ideal, it seems to me I should feel more human now not less so. And this is not the case, not the case at all."

"Communism Was Part of the Journey"

DIANE Vinson is a remarkably beautiful woman who looks fifteen years younger than her sixty-two years. Her body is slim and lithe, her hair burnished and abundant, her blue eyes clear and serene, her head held at an angle of attentive repose. An actress for more than forty years, fifteen of them spent in the soul-destroying limbo of the blacklist, Diane is today the director of her own acting company and a graduate student in psychology at Columbia University. Life is full for Diane, alive with the dramatic pursuit of self-knowledge, a pursuit her twelve years in the Communist Party enriched immeasurably. Psychologically, she stands at the opposite end of the spectrum of ex-Communists from men like Max Bitterman, Carl Peters, and Dave Abetta.

Sitting on a velvet sofa in her Upper West Side apartment on a cool evening in June, Diane rearranges the folds of her purple and gold caftan, raises her eyes slowly to mine, and says in the thrilling voice of the trained actress: "My love of the theater and my attraction to the Communist Party stem from the same impulse: the creative impulse. The impulse to live through my actions. To recreate myself. To find myself in that which embodies the common psyche of man, the binding commonality, the archetypal experience."

I stare, disbelieving, at her. What on earth do these sentences mean? Does she really use such language *naturally*? Diane catches the meaning of my stare. Abruptly, her manner changes. Amusement quickly crowds into her serene blue eyes, an earthy laugh escapes her throat, and she says: "No shit. I really feel that way."

This exchange clears the air. I laugh, nod my head, and settle down to hear the political life story of a woman alive with contradiction: on the one hand, possessed by the actor's need for self-dramatization, on the other hand, filled with an earthy honesty that not only prevents her drowning in her own rhetoric but delivers shrewd insights into the meaning of her experience as well.

Diane Vinson was born and raised in Kentucky, the oldest of seven children born to a country schoolteacher and a farmer. The family was dirt poor ("*Dirt* poor," Diane says evenly), and the children worked in the fields every day of their growing-up years. The life was brutal, but there was gaiety and closeness in the family, the inexpressible moody tenderness of country people alive to each other in their mutual need. Everyone worked from dawn to dark, but on Sunday the father played the violin and the children acted out Sunday-school sketches for the entertainment of all.

Somehow, money for a first year was scraped together, and

Diane was sent to college. Her father expected her to become a teacher and return to the little red schoolhouse to help her mother teach, but when Diane went off to Kentucky State College she knew she was never going to return to the farm. She had been happy at home but when the door to the world opened she stepped unhesitatingly across the threshold.

At college Diane discovered that she was an actress; the discovery was magnetizing; theater became and remained the abiding passion of her life. Tent shows, traveling circuses, vaudeville, high-school shows and college revues, community theater, revivalist carryings-on, burlesque, the New York stage—it was all theater, all spilling itself across the world for her, bringing to consciousness an inner expansion of disturbing proportions. She began to perceive within herself lights and darks, shadows and images, an unexplored continent of the self she had had no previous knowledge of. The theater for Diane was that uncanny ingredient: the catalytic force in whose presence the experiencing self flickers to life.

After college she joined a traveling circus show, and within a year had made her way across the country to New York. In New York she connected immediately, and worked steadily in the theater almost from the moment of her arrival in the city.

In 1940 Diane came under the influence of a Russian dramatic coach. He had defected from the Soviet Union because, he said, he could not "breathe" in Russia. Nevertheless, Marxism glittered like mica-schist in him, and he began to teach Diane how to interpret roles from a class-conscious position. She responded instantly to the Russian's teachings. Marxism seemed a new and enriching way to speak to unresolved, barely acknowledged conflicts battling within her.

"You see," she says, "the New York theater was not really what I wanted. I had never wanted fame or fortune from the theater. I wanted my soul to grow. I wanted inner clarity. I wanted to *understand*. The theater for me had been a marvelous laboratory in which the culture of my own self was to be cultivated.

"I experienced Marxism through Sasha, the Russian teacher, as a tremendous excitement, new equipment for the laboratory. He made me see the *world* as a theater, the social struggle as the drama of the ages. Politics became a method, an interpretation of the drama. A new fire was lit in me, and I saw myself taking part in the revolution of the future as the logical next step in the education of myself that had begun with my work in the theater."

Diane has been speaking and gesturing elaborately, her hands and eyes contributing to the mythic sense of self her words have been creating. Now, suddenly, she stops and a lightning-swift change overcomes her. Her eyes go flat and hard, and when she speaks again her husky voice has a steel edge to it. The tough, knowing country girl replaces the sophisticated New York actress and she says:

"There was something else to it, though. Something else that came rising up in me, hot and angry, when I heard Sasha speak. I saw the farm again. I saw my father's hands, black and twisted from all those years in the fields. I saw the ghastly weariness in my mother's face. All those kids. All that work. All that rotten, never-ending poverty that had made her look fifty when she was thirty. And I looked around at all my middle-class friends in New York and I thought, 'What do they know? What the *hell* do they know?' I didn't know I was so angry until Sasha. Angry? I felt murderous!"

In 1941 Diane joined the Communist Party, and shortly thereafter married the CP functionary assigned to organize the actors' union of which Diane was already a member. As a Communist she attended Party meetings, took instruction from her organizer husband, returned to her union and, she says, amused and triumphant now, "I was very effective!"

For the next twelve years Diane Vinson was a Communist who was also an actress. She gave herself over, freely and fully, to the drama of Marxism as it lived itself out through the CP. Her work in the theater, in the actors' union, in the Party became one. An integrity of being informed her life; that integrity produced a thrilling sense of power within her.

"They were good years," Diane says thoughtfully, "very good years. Rich, alive with the sense of everything coming together, a fusion of world and being that made you drunk with life. And the bond created through work done in comradeship. What a powerful bond that is! I never understood that properly until the Communist Party.

"Then, after some years, something began to happen inside of me. The learning process seemed to come to an end. I never did know exactly when or where, or under what circumstances, it happened. But it did happen and, imperceptibly, without my knowing it consciously, things began to come apart for me in the Party. I became intensely unhappy, uncomfortable among my comrades, balking at everything—assignments, discussions, directives, the lot.

"I struggled desperately to let them know what was happening to me, unconsciously begging them to help me help myself. They didn't know what I was talking about. And they were harsh, most harsh with me, telling me that this was all *personal* and, therefore, trivial. That I should be more serious, more dedicated, a better Communist after all than that, to be so concerned with something as frivolous as my *feelings*.

"This response sent me into despair. I began to realize that I was no longer sure what my genuine experience was from day to day, as opposed to my *rhetorical* experience. I began to feel isolated. Then I looked with new eyes on life within the Party. I saw more and more that these people, my comrades, did not know themselves what they *actually* thought and felt about things, and had not known for many years. Their identification with the Party had become so complete, so absolute, they no longer knew the difference between their own finite selves and what I could now only call party dogma. These perceptions made me even more desperate. I felt I had lost my way terribly. Who was I? What was I? Why was I here? What did it all mean?

"And of course, irony on irony, it was through the Party itself that my need to answer these questions became more urgent, more compelling than it might otherwise have been. The very fact that in the Party everything personal was suppressed and despised began to make it impossible for me to ignore the personal. The more they told me not to pay attention to the personal, the more I found myself thinking about my unhappiness. It's odd to think that if they had been clever enough to give me even a bit of understanding, I might have remained a Communist god knows how long.

"In the midst of all this soul-searching, in 1953, I was suddenly called before the House Un-American Activities Committee. Everyone and everything went mad at the same moment. My husband, the Party, my work, America—everything went up in smoke in one hideous moment. I went before the Committee, took the Fifth Amendment, and endured their hammering away at me. They asked me many questions about my 'foreign' connections, 'foreign' influences, 'alien' thoughts and activities.

"That was my one good moment. I stood up very dramatically, head held high, Hester Prynne on the block, and announced I was American, gentlemen, as American as you are. Everything I am today *America* made me." Diane shakes with laughter at this point. Then she sobers up:

"But when I walked out of that room my life was changed for good and all. I realized I had answered as I had not out of loyalty to the Party but out of loyalty to my own integrity. I knew I was no longer a Communist.

"But it seemed I was no longer an American either. At least not to the people who could have given me work. It is almost impossible to communicate to you the Kafkaesque quality of the blacklist. First of all, no one ever admitted to the existence of the blacklist. No one ever told you you were not getting work for political reasons. Ever. So you would go for an audition. In the morning you'd be assured the part was yours, and in the afternoon or on the next day a phone call would come saying a mistake had been made: the producer had dropped dead, the part had been deleted, the show was postponed. Two weeks later, of course, you would read the announcement of another actress having been signed for the part. This went on month after month, year after year. You knew what was happening, but it ate away at you, anyway. You couldn't help it. Especially not if you were an actor. Somewhere inside you a voice kept repeating, 'It's because you're no good, if you were good enough they'd *have* to give you the job.' Your nerve simply began to disintegrate. The humiliation was indescribable.

"Those were terrible years, and for a long time I couldn't pull myself together. I left the country. I went to Europe and remained there for three years. There was always someone in Europe willing to give work to a blacklisted American actor. So I worked, but Europe was not real to me, the time spent there was time in limbo.

"When I came back I decided to set my life on a new course. I entered psychoanalysis, took it very seriously, began to read and think as I never had before. I began to *see* my life. I thought back to the time when I had left Kentucky. I saw how the enclosed space that had been my life there had widened when I left, and continued to widen until the opening that had meant freedom and possibility became a yawning void into which, finally, I fell freely. With no foothold, no ledge to grasp onto. I saw then that I would have to learn to live in that vast open space with nothing but my very own self. That I must become my own foothold, my own anchoring ledge.

"Do I regret the years in the Party? Never. My dear, my life has been a long journey into myself. My years as a Communist have been an invaluable part of that journey. They taught me things about human identity I would never have learned otherwise. *Really* taught me. I learned from the Party the tragedy of identifying your entire self with anything outside of yourself.

"I also learned from the Party the depth and height of human aspirations and how, inevitably, those aspirations take on a shape that forces you to identify with things outside yourself. *That's* the painful contradiction. That's why much of what happened to the Communists is not evil but tragic.

"There were many, many people in the Party who sought the essential experience even as I did. Good people, people who were marked by the deepest of human longings. Genuinely tender people who felt intensely for the suffering and deprived of the world. My husband was one of them.

"He was an emotionally flamboyant man, in his own eyes 'a tragic figure.' He was typical of the politically astute, emotionally ignorant party functionary. There was in him, as in many of them, an incredible ego, a brashness of political ambition he did not admit to, a harshness of behavior committed in the name of the revolution. But with all that, he hungered. He was deeply moved by the spectacle of injustice under capitalism, he felt himself engaged in an enormous drama of human will and intelligence to defeat the dark forces of life.

"Now, that is a powerful feeling. It is impossible to overestimate its influence on the human soul. It is very *difficult* to arrive at the point where you can see this feeling operating in an illusionist structure. The feeling soars through you, convinces you that you are experiencing yourself as never before. To see that the self is in fact *not* developing, but rather is being stifled? When it *feels* exactly the opposite? That takes a lot of living, a lot of living.

"My years as a Communist were born out of my need to experience myself, and they ended out of the same need. I could return to the theater with new strength, new knowledge, new independence, and work within it better than ever. I could be myself, and still act. I could not be myself, and still be a Communist.

"But, oh, how moving all that is to me! How integral to the discovery of the self that Marxist passion had been for me. And yes, for many, many other people I have known. Sasha was right. The social struggle *was* the drama of the ages. And yes, he couldn't 'breathe' in Russia."

"It Was the Best Life a Man Could Have Had"

THE English Communist Claud Cockburn wrote in his autobiography:

> When I became a Communist, it never crossed my mind that Communism was going to solve all the problems of humanity. I did not think, even, that it would do more than a little good here and there. I did think that without it the crack-up of civilization everyone spoke of was going to occur sooner rather than later. I saw Communism, that is to say, as essentially a conservative force—a means of conserving civilized human values. Nor do I now regard that assumption, or gamble, as having been merely ludicrous. I still quite often meet people who tell me, quite sincerely, that they "simply cannot understand" why or how I should ever have become a Communist. Their incomprehension can suggest that perhaps they have never looked closely at their own political faces in the mirror of our times.

Almost from the first moment I begin speaking with Anthony Ehrenpreis the memory of these words starts crowding into my mind. That is, the *sense* memory: the tone of Cockburn's voice, the particular sound of the man behind the words, the humor and aloofness, the intellectual worldliness. All these are recalled vividly in Ehrenpreis's presence.

Anthony Ehrenpreis is sixty-four years old. He is a tall, bulky man with a thickness of iron-grey hair that falls to either side of his face from an uncontrollable part in the middle of his head, and his craggy features bear an uncanny resemblance to those of the English actor Peter Finch. The eyes are long and grey, remarkably wolflike. The face is commanding—marked by strength, dignity, and intelligence. The manner is also commanding—simultaneously inviting and distancing. Marc Antony among the rabble. A complicated man, this.

Ehrenpreis was for many years a distinguished book editor. In 1950 he went to jail for refusing to answer the questions put to him at a HUAC hearing. When he emerged from prison eighteen months later it was to discover himself blacklisted from his profession. For the next ten years he scrounged for a living. He did free-lance editing at home, wrote two books under a pseudonym, did occasional work for obscure university presses or left-wing periodicals. In 1963 he was offered a job at a major publishing house, and was thus returned to professional respectability. Last year he retired to a farm in northern Pennsylvania that had been left him by his father: to read for *pleasure*, and to write his own history of the times he has lived through.

Anthony Ehrenpreis was the son of wealthy, cultivated parents—the mother Italian, the father German—who came to this country in 1920 to escape the disorder and melancholy of Europe after the First World War. The democracy was good to them. They prospered financially and emotionally and, like de Tocqueville, found the New World uncultivated but wonderfully alive.

For their handsome, intelligent young son, Anthony, it was otherwise. Unaccountably, he was a brooder. The boy brooded endlessly on the human condition. The parents considered Anthony's mental preoccupation unhealthy and tried repeatedly to interest him in the pleasures of life as they experienced them—

tight-knit family life, a rare love of books and music, a Germanic appreciation of work and order, a Victorian sense of the obligations and satisfactions of personal achievement, as well as of the religious beauties of nature. The boy responded—he was open-hearted and loved his parents—but something kept him apart from them, his soul somehow absorbed by a sense of being they did not share.

On a late afternoon in December, with the winter light thinning in the sky outside, Ehrenpreis lifts a book down from the library shelf above him as we sit in the large, comfortable front room of the farmhouse. The book is *The God That Failed*, and to my astonishment I see that his copy is as well worn as my own. He thumbs through the book and, finding what he is looking for, tells me that here, this passage expresses perfectly what he felt as a young man in the early Thirties. The book is open to Stephen Spender's section, and the passage Ehrenpreis reads is the one in which Spender is describing how he first came to Communism:

> My sense of the equality of men was based not so much on an awareness of the masses as on loneliness. I can remember lying awake at night thinking of this human condition in which everyone living, without the asking, is thrust upon the earth. Here he is enclosed within himself, a stranger to the rest of humanity, needing love and facing his own death. Since to be born is to be a Robinson Crusoe cast up by elemental powers upon an island, how unjust it seems that all men are not free to share what nature offers here; that there should be men and women who are not permitted to explore the world into which they are born, but who are throughout their lives sealed into leaden slums as into living tombs. It seemed to me—as it still seems—that the unique condition of each person within life outweighs the considerations which justify class and privilege.

Ehrenpreis returns the book to its place on the shelf and laughs. "Spender, as you know, reversed himself on the Communist Party in the name of this very insight. He came, after the Spanish War, to feel that the Party was as much the enemy as class and privilege. . . . I, however," he adds softly, "did not." He falls into a brief revery and then, shaking his head as though to clear it, says:

"This sense of the loneliness of the universe was overpowering to me from boyhood on. I have tried to figure out where it came from, why I should have felt so, living in the midst of my family's good, kind life, but I can't, I can't. My father was a wonderful man, a big bear of a man who would hold me in his arms more tenderly than my mother did, crooning to me—I must have been three, four—'*Toni, liebschen, liebschen.*' It was as though he would hold me above the earth forever, never letting it soil my feet, or my heart, for that matter, as though this precious boy of his would be forever protected and yet, of course, now that I think of it, forever held apart from other human beings.

"My mother, a beautiful woman too intelligent to be *really* vain, would laugh and say softly, almost mockingly, 'Hans, you are ruining that child.' And my father would become embarrassed and put me down quickly. There was a formality in them that worked two ways: on the one hand, I often experienced it as creating an emotional distance between me and them, on the other hand, it was a source of tremendous security, it had civilizing powers that put everything in the world in its place and kept it there.

"I remember as though it were yesterday my first conscious awareness of the loneliness of life in the midst of this plenty. My father had a sister, Mady, who had married badly and 'ruined her life.' Her story was a classic. She had fallen in love before the war with an American adventurer, married him against her family's wishes, and been disinherited by my grandfather. Mady followed her husband romantically across the sea. In America he promptly abandoned her. By the time my parents arrived in America Mady was already a broken woman, sick and prematurely old, living a life two steps removed from destitution. My father, of course, immediately put her on an allowance and made her welcome in his home. But the iron laws of Victorian transgression had been set in motion and it was really all over for Mady. You know what it meant for a woman to have been so disgraced and disinherited in those years? She had the mark of Cain on her. She would live, barely tolerated, on the edge of respectable society for the rest of her life.

"A year after we arrived in America, I was eleven years old, a cousin of mine was married out of our house. We lived then in a lovely brownstone on New York's Upper West Side. The entire house had been cleaned and decorated for the wedding. Everything sparkled and shone, from the basement kitchen to the third-floor bedrooms. In a small room on the second floor the women gathered around the bride, preening, fixing their dresses, distributing bouquets of flowers. I was allowed to be there because I was only a child. There was a bunch of long-stemmed roses lying on the bed, blood-red and beautiful, each rose perfection. Mady walked over to them. I remember the other women were wearing magnificent dresses, embroidered and be-jeweled. Mady was wearing only a simple white satin blouse and a long black skirt with no ornamentation whatever. She picked up one of the roses, sniffed deeply at it, held it against her face. Then she walked over to a mirror and held the rose against her white blouse. Immediately, the entire look of her plain costume was altered; the rose transferred its color to Mady's face, bright-ening her eyes. Suddenly, she looked lovely, and *young* again. She found a long needle-like pin and began to pin the rose to her blouse. My mother noticed what Mady was doing and walked over to her. Imperiously, she took the rose out of Mady's hand and said, 'No, Mady, those flowers are for the bride.' Mady hastily said, 'Oh, of course, I'm sorry, how stupid of me not to have realized that,' and her face instantly assumed its usual mask of patient obligation.

"I experienced in that moment an intensity of pain against which I have measured every subsequent pain of life. My heart ached so for Mady I thought I would perish on the spot. Loneli-ness broke, wave after wave, over my young head and one word burned in my brain. Over and over again, through my tears, I murmured, 'Unjust! Unjust!' I knew that if Mady had been one of the 'ladies' of the house my mother would never have taken the rose out of her hand in that manner.

"The memory of what had happened in the bedroom pierced me repeatedly throughout that whole long day, making me feel ill and wounded each time it returned. Mady's loneliness became mine. I felt connected, as though by an invisible thread, to her alone of all the people in the house. But the odd thing was I never actually went near her all that day. I wanted to comfort her, let her know that *I* at least loved her and felt for her. But I couldn't. In fact, I avoided her. In spite of everything, I felt her to be a pariah, and that my attachment to her made me a pariah, also. It was as though we were floating, two pariahs, through the house, among all those relations, related to no one, not even to each other. It was an extraordinary experience, one I can still taste to this day.

"I was never again able to address myself directly to Mady's loneliness until I joined the Communist Party. When I joined the Party the stifled memory of that strange wedding day came back to me. . . ."

Ehrenpreis pulls himself heavily from his chair and walks across the room to a massive, old-fashioned sideboard where a small bar is set up. He picks up a bottle of scotch, raises it questioningly in my direction. I nod, and he turns back to pour drinks for both of us. I watch him. His gestures are economical, graceful, and innately authoritative. Ehrenpreis is dressed in a black-and-red-checked flannel shirt and farm denims, but I can just as easily envision him in a suit of grey worsted, or Ivy League tweeds, or black tie. Whatever the history of his feelings may be, he is pre-eminently a man of the world, a man who can control his unease with the proportion that comes of aristocratic beginnings applied to hard-earned wisdom.

Ehrenpreis walks back across the room, hands me my drink, lowers himself into his chair, takes a sip of his own drink, and stares off into space for a moment, his grey wolf's eyes emptied of all expression. Then he says: "The Communist Party was never all things to me in the manner in which that expression is commonly used. I was a member of the Party in good standing for nearly twenty-five years, and certainly it was as true for me as for almost all other Communists that an emotional distance grew up between me and the world beyond the Party. It was exactly as Koestler has described it in discussing what happens to those living inside 'the closed system.' Somewhere he says that he disliked a number of people in the Party but they were his kin, and he liked a number of people outside the Party but he no longer had a common language with them.

"All that is true, it was as true for me as for anyone else in the Party. Nevertheless, it is also true that I think I always saw certain things clearly. I saw all the bullying, all the petty despotism, and all the real horror of being tied to the Soviet line. I saw all the abuses of power within the Party for which it has been justly reviled, and I knew that if the American Party ever came to power there were many in it who would eagerly have purged and killed, imprisoned and exiled.

"I knew how barbaric much of it was. I knew because I had the memory of my parents always alive within me. My parents had been the most civilized people I ever knew: kind, intelligent, worshiping order and moderation, all things graceful and beautiful, dedicated to avoiding the brutalities of life through the beauty and goodness of 'gentle' daily behavior.

"The question of how they made their money? Who paid for it? What the social meaning of that payment was? Those were distressing and unseemly questions one simply did not ask. After all, the consequence of asking those questions would be to bring chaos and cruelty into the world, phenomena to be avoided at all costs.

"My parents were the kind of people who fill the pages of Thomas Mann's novels. Mann, with that formidable, all-seeing intelligence of his, had understood their world perfectly, and described it in the kind of detail that gave it tremendous historical weight. Mann described neither in sorrow nor in anger. He simply saw clearly and deeply. And what he saw was that while there was much in that world that was invaluable, its time had come. Posed against the goodness of my parents' world was Mady's humiliation, rising up from the dark hidden center, pushing through with a speed and momentum that of necessity would smash the world as we had known it.

"Now, the thing is this. Between Mann's time of maturity and *my* time of maturity what had changed was not the quality of the insight but the urgency with which that insight came to serious men and women. Mann saw as clearly as we did the meaning of human loneliness at the center of the bourgeois world. But what he observed with philosophical distance we experienced with a sense of imperative. That, as far as I can see, is the difference between Mann and Marx, the difference between the nineteenth century and the twentieth. That imperative became the characteristic emotion of our century, and for better or worse the Communist Party embodied it.

"So, here I stood in my youth, poised between these two worlds, each with its mixture of barbarism and beauty, falling finally to the left because to the left lay the future while to the right lay the past.

"And it was the difficulty of *realizing* that future that held me to the Party when those I felt closest to, most sympathetic to, fell out by the thousands. People like Spender and Gide and Silone were always the ones I felt myself most attuned to. As the horrors of Stalinism mounted, and these men and many others like them fell either into morbid depression or deep anger and left the Party, I began to feel myself acutely isolated.

"But what I could never get out of my head was the example of Erasmus and Luther. When Luther exploded on the scene Erasmus welcomed him with open arms; his hope of humanity lived again in the German priest. But Luther was a tiger. Ferocious, driven, often bestial. Erasmus turned away from him with the bitterness that only a sense of betrayal can produce, and he said finally, 'Wherever Luther goes literature dies.' Well, literature did not die, and Luther changed the face of the world. Only it took a couple of hundred years for that to become apparent. While it was happening it looked like a scourge. . . . But who among us would now rather that Luther had not lived?

"So it was with me and the Communist Party. And so it is to this day. Through all the worst years in the Party I felt—as I do today—'This is a mighty beast we have got hold of, this idea of socialism. It has brought to the surface elemental pain and need. It has got hold of *us* now but if we hang on and ride the beast we will have hold of it, and then a new day will dawn.' The Party at its worst, Stalinism, state socialism, the lot, was the beast thrashing about. Chekhov had said we must squeeze the slave out of ourselves drop by drop. That idea speaks to a process of civilized patience, an order of highly controlling intelligence. But fifty years of Communism in the real world have taught us that human transformation does not come about in this manner. The first impulse of the powerless upon seizing power is not generous it is murderous. The slave aroused is at first a beast, Plato's man coming out of the cave blind, awareness exploding in terror and fury. But in time, in time. . . ."

Ehrenpreis gets to his feet once more and moves restlessly about the room, swishing the ice in his glass. He peers into the glass and walks again to the sideboard where he pours another inch of scotch. He returns, settles into his chair once again, and goes on:

"You know, it is very fashionable these days to equate fascism with Communism. Same totalitarian methods, same police states, same concentrated power, et cetera, et cetera. To this sort of thing I can only reply with the words of Eduard Benes, the Czech prime minister who said: 'Communism and fascism may look the same but they are far from the same. Fascism is like a raging fire that destroys everything and afterwards nothing grows again. Communism is like a raging flood that also destroys everything, but afterwards life is renewed and flourishes.'

"For me, the rise of the Italian Communist Party is the earth renewed. I have great hopes not only for the Italian CP in and of itself, but for its meaning in the long struggle. It represents holding on, holding on. No matter what the Italians do or do not accomplish within the next twenty or thirty years, they will provide a link between the Stalinist past and the unknowable socialist future. And that is of vital importance. Inestimable importance."

Ehrenpreis's grey eyes grow warm suddenly and filled with open affection. He smiles deeply and says: "For myself, it was the best life a man could have had. I feel that as a Communist I have lived at the heart of my times. The most problematic sense of man's life is embodied in the history of twentieth-century Communism. It was through Communism that, in our time, one could grapple most fiercely with what it means to be a human being. Four-hundred years ago it was through Christian doctrine and the politics of the church, but in our time it was, without question, through Marxism and the Communist Party. For my money, it still is."

The Political Emotion Embodied

ON A brilliant blue-and-gold day in October I am walking across the campus of a large state university in the Midwest with a tall, thin man whose boyish face lights up readily as people greet him warmly on every hand. We walk down the tree-lined path from one Gothic stone building to another; a student calls out, "Hello, Professor Edel"; a colleague stops to say, "Boris, I've been meaning to call you"; a secretary lays her hand on his arm and says, "Professor, I need your signature on . . ." The man walking with me responds with affection, courtesy, and care to each claim on his attention. "How are you, Bob?" he calls back. Or "Oh? Something important? I'll be home this evening." Or, "Yes, yes, I know. This afternoon, I promise."

At last we reach the building we are heading for, enter under an arched doorway, walk down a corridor lined with student bulletin boards, and open the door of a large office bright with the light streaming in from two leaded-pane windows at the far end. The man sinks down into the swivel chair at his desk, motions me to a chair beside the desk, and excuses himself to make two telephone calls to people who have been waiting all day for his reply to earlier calls.

Boris Edel is fifty-three years old. He is a tenured professor of theoretical physics at this university, highly respected for his work and much beloved for his person. He is, in fact, known among the students as Boris the Good. Sometimes Edel can hardly believe that life has turned out so well for him.

Boris is the son of Isaac Edel who, for thirty years, was the state chairman of the Communist Party in one of the large northeastern states. Isaac's reputation for Solomonic wisdom and beauty of spirit had earned him the title of "most saintly man in the CP." And, indeed, many who knew him speak even now with reverence for his goodness. His sons, Josef and Boris, idolized him. In another time and place Isaac and his sons might perhaps have been distinguished Talmudists. In this time and place they were devout Communists.

From the time of earliest memory, Boris was impatient to take his place beside his father in the organizing structure of the Party. While still very young he had already exhibited his scientific bent and his prodigious capacity for scholarship. But scholarship outside of politics and political theory was a game to him, with no meaning in and of itself. It was, of course, beyond imagining that a time would come when the application of academic logic to Marxism would seem as much of a game as it then had applied to abstract science.

When Boris finally got to college he instantly became the leader of his school's YCL branch, and soon wanted to quit school and become a full-time YCL organizer. His father said, "No. Become *something*. That way you'll never be a burden to the Party or to yourself." On the other hand, Boris now laughs, when he would fantasize out loud about what he hoped to accomplish in the movement his father would admonish him: "That is not for you to decide. The Party will decide what you will do."

Boris graduated with a BS in physics, and immediately entered the Party as a full-time organizer in the YCL. By this time, however, America had entered the Second World War and Boris was soon drafted into the army. He served abroad during the war, and when he returned home it was to become the founder and leader of the Party's final youth movement.

The 20th Congress Report in 1956 sent his world crashing. For many Communists Khrushchev's revelations had been the straw that broke the camel's back; conflicts, doubts, and inner erosions of faith had been slowly accumulating, and now the final disintegration simply occurred. For many, though, the Report came like a thunderbolt and carried with it the effects of trauma. Boris Edel was one of these. His faith had been not only perfect, it had been the manifestation of a sense of world that was all-precluding. For Boris, international Communism was not *a* world it was *the* world. To be told that Stalin was a paranoid murderer was akin to Oxford intellectuals being told by Darwin that they were descended from the apes: it constituted a blow of universe-shattering dimension.

"We could not believe these things were true in the USSR," Edel says gently, "and when we discovered they *were* we realized we had built our world on mud and shit, there was no foundation for our lives."

In the midst of terrible struggle, both internal and external, Boris fought with himself and with his Party, and realized he would have to remake his life. Edel, like Bill Chaikin and Arthur Chessler, was one of that fatally diversified group of dissenters within the Party who in 1956 made a tremendous, anguishing attempt to turn the American Party around, to make it see that if it did not now learn, truly learn that it must become independent of the Soviet Union, it was doomed. The dissenters failed.

They failed, partially, because they were not united within themselves; hopelessly fragmented, unable to bind up their own separating wounds, they could not become an effective force.

Edel takes off his glasses, leans back in his swivel chair, places his left ankle on his right knee, runs a hand swiftly through his grey-black curly hair. Thoughtfully, he begins to wipe his glasses clean and, as he does so, he says: "For me, the question was not one of personal betrayal—like for the Max Bittermans who beat their breasts and put on hair shirts and said, 'All these years I have been telling lies.' For me, the question was: How could this have happened? And it is a question that remains unanswered, and haunting, to this day. The great unresolved issue was and is: How do you have leadership, organization, and discipline (which I still believe you must have), and still retain democracy, avoid cruelty and contempt for human beings?

"Yet, even though I concentrated on this question, it was all so incredible, all so overwhelming. . . . The sheer *dimension* of Khrushchev's accusations. . . . And everything that has happened in the socialist world since 1956. Certain things in my world were unthinkable. For instance, that socialist countries should arise and fall into conflict with each other! That was unimaginable. That I could never have predicted. We built our world on logic. And this was supremely illogical. The shock has been enormous.

"And yet, when I left the Party I did not think I was leaving for good, I certainly did not think the Party would disintegrate out of American life. I thought it was a period of transition, that I was going off to think out these questions, and that I would return to work again in my movement. Of course, it did not work out that way."

Isaac, who did not leave the Party, was entirely supportive of Boris' decision to leave. His brother Josef, on the other hand, was not. They walked the streets of New York and they quarreled. And finally Boris said to his brother: "Mark my words, in ten years I will be in a position to be entirely true to my past, and still be effective."

Boris says now he really didn't know what he was talking about when he said that, he was speaking half out of intuition, half out of yearning, entirely out of a bravado that masked the deep despair he felt beginning to descend on him.

He returned to science by way of seeking a period of hibernation in which to lick his wounds without being stared at. At the age of thirty-five he reentered the university and threw himself with blind relief into the exhausting life of the graduate student. Some four years later he was graduated with highest honors, and at the age of forty entered upon a second distinguished career, this time in academic science.

In the mid-1960s, to his utter amazement, Boris found himself once more deeply embroiled in American politics. One by one, the universities of America began to explode with violent discontent. When it came the turn of Boris' university he casually got up one day at a student rally to preach reason on both sides; instantly, the natural leader in their midst was discovered and hailed.

"It was crazy, absolutely crazy," Isaac Edel's son says with an embarrassment that makes him look more boyish than ever. "I had absolutely no intention of getting involved in what was happening on the campus. But everybody seemed to be going nuts at once, and after all, it wasn't as though I was a novice at political quarrels. I could see certain things happening to each side, the administration and the students, and nobody else seemed to see them. I thought I'd just inject a little reason in the whole business. Well, they were all so grateful for someone who simply refused to vilify either side that overnight I became a campus hero."

Other people on this campus insist there was a little more to it than Boris' modest explanation allows. They say he mediated student-administration quarrels with wisdom and compassion when everyone else was rendered useless by rage and frustration; that he was totally on the side of the students, and yet at the same time refused to see the administration crucified; that he recognized the bind in which the whole university was caught, and communicated a large, distancing sense of things that was immensely healing.

"In many ways," Boris says soberly, "they were terrible years. People said and did cruel, outrageous things to one another. Friendships were smashed, irreconcilable differences established, the bitterness that only politics can cause ran rampant.

"But in other ways they were wonderful years, too. That headiness of people discovering themselves to be political animals was everywhere, in the very air you breathed. And for me . . . Well, for me it was a very good time, indeed. I came alive again. It was that simple. After so many years in limbo, I came alive. I confirmed what I had always known: that I was a political creature through and through.

"Science is quite marvelous. Absorbing. Beautiful. But it doesn't hit me where I live as politics does. To be involved with people in a political enterprise, to feel that particular comradeship, to watch people *becoming* in such an atmosphere, that is to feel the world being made anew. There is nothing in the whole variety of things done and made that can make me feel the beauty of human beings, of life itself, as political work can. That is what the CP always was for me. That's what it was for my father.

"And yes," Edel beams at me, "there was the satisfaction of seeing the promise I made to my brother all those years ago finally being fulfilled. I was as radical as ever, as true to my past as ever, and in a position to still be effective. It felt damned good. I felt as though I'd vindicated not only my own life but my father's life and the Party's life as well."

Something in all this, some peculiar note struck, prompts me to ask Edel what his personal relationships have been like during these past years. What is the nature of the friendships that have evolved out of the university years?

Edel looks shrewdly at me for a long moment. Then he nods his head at me as though he's been reading my mind, and grins. "I don't have any," he says. "Not really. No, I don't think I have personal relationships." Edel then startles me with a bit of real self-knowledge, rare among the Communists.

"It's odd," he says, making a tent of his hands, his head brooding slightly over the tent. "Often, since the Sixties, people come to see me with personal problems. A failing marriage, the discovery of homosexuality, you name it. They come because they remember me as a warm, sympathetic guy in the midst of everyone else's anger, and they're sure I'll be sympathetic now, too. . . .

"I know they don't go away *sorry* they came. But I also know that they won't be back. Somehow, I can't give them what they came for. I can't make them feel I've been there, too."

Edel looks at me as though he's puzzling something out in his own mind, something that he finds extremely interesting, uncanny even, but also slightly shocking. "I've come to realize," he says slowly, "that my deepest emotions are engaged only in a polit-ical context. It's as though people are *real* to me only in political engagement. Sometimes I think that's true even for my wife. I've really no way of knowing. Our political life is so deeply inter-twined with our personal life, always has been. It *is* our personal life. I mean, I'm not sure what else there is. I'm not sure what else there is *apart* from politics. . . ."

I stare wordlessly at him for a very long moment. Boris Edel is the perfect embodiment of what is most striking in the Com-munists: the gift for political emotion highly developed, the gift for individual empathy neglected, atrophied. In Boris, as in most Communists, the experience of all things human lives primarily through the political act.

Radical politics, for Edel, is the construct through which is per-ceived, on a heroic scale, the idea of man. To that idea he is pas-sionately attached. Through that idea—the idea of humanness—he experiences the act of being human. In the presence of that idea the goodness in him is stimulated into being, and he connects: he loves.

The limitations of such a dynamic are obvious, the power and beauty equally obvious. The idea of man—as distinguished from the actuality of the individual—is one of the two great ways of loving life. In the Communists, this idea—however often per-verted, however often corrupted—operated passionately. Narrow, intense, potent, it achieved in them mythic proportions.

"I'll Tell You What a Communist Is"

ERIC Lanzetti—like Anthony Ehrenpreis—is one of those Communists for whom the words "take the long view" are not a piece of Party jargon. It is elemental nourishment for an in-tellectual life rooted in a vision of world socialism heaving, lurching, sometimes hacking its way into the jungle of human consciousness. For Lanzetti, fifty years of state socialism in Russia (which, he is quick to remind you, have *included* thirty years of socialism in Eastern Europe and China, and twenty in Cuba) are but a moment in the centuries-long struggle it will take to make the philosophic teachings of Marx a genuine human reality; a moment that, with all its murderous wildness, all its abuses and thrashing confusion, has been of unavoidable necessity. In this context Lanzetti is fond of saying of Gerhard Eisler, the famous German socialist: "When Eisler was dying I was in Germany, and I went to visit him. I leaned over him and I said, 'Tell me, Gerhard, what have you learned?' The old man lay back, exhausted, and almost whispering, he said, 'I have learned how hard it is to build socialism.' "

Lanzetti is widely known on the Communist left. For one thing, his was a *cause célèbre* in the 1950s. His indictment in 1947 aroused wide sympathy and made him famous overnight. For another thing, his attachment to Communism burns as fiercely today as it did thirty years ago. However, there is a twofold curiosity about Lanzetti's relation to the Communist Party: one, he was a member of the Party for only three years; two, many people, both on the Left and on the Right, think he's been a general in the CP underground for the past thirty years. This disparity—taken as a whole—is an important clue to the dual nature of Lanzetti's devotion to Communism and/or the Communist Party. The following "excerpts" from Lanzetti's life illustrate this duality perfectly.

In his unpublished autobiography Lanzetti has written:

As an ex-Catholic I was attuned to and resentful of orthodoxy but I went along because I thought the party was politically effective. This decision, a sharp and conscious one, was literally forced on me (at the time of the Soviet-Nazi Pact). . . . I sat in the rear of the hall, restless at the way the Pact was being presented. . . . The stress was on peace and I knew that line was imbecilic. It was obviously a storm signal for war. . . . When no one made this point I stood up. . . . I had hardly spoken two sentences when the district organizer cut in with a venomous attack, not only on my ideas but on me personally. I was accused of disrupting and undermining the party. I was a Trotskyite, a bourgeois lickspittle, possibly an FBI agent. . . . I was stunned, still standing, by the unexpectedness of the attack, but particularly by its viciousness, out of all proportion to what was involved. What I didn't realize at the time was that the venomous edge was due to the insecurity of the organizer. . . . This vicious form of attack against me I had seen used in England against Trotsky. It is a method to reduce one's opponent either to annihilation or subjugation, a method derived directly from Lenin, who used it as a deliberate tactic: "I purposely choose that tone calculated to evoke in the hearer hatred, disgust and contempt. . . . That tone, that formulation, is not designed to convince but to break the ranks, not to correct a mistake of the opponent but to annihilate him, to wipe him off the face of the earth."

I had three choices: walk out of the meeting and the party; make a fight and get thrown out; keep quiet and sit down. I kept quiet and sat down. . . .

Later on, Lanzetti writes:

The Pact played a significant role in my education and in my Communist career. For at the very same time that it strengthened my confidence in Stalin's adroitness it eroded my dependence on his ideology. It showed me, abruptly and vividly, how far advanced was my intellectual *rigor mortis*. I had become a prisoner of my ideology and it wasn't going to happen again. . . .

Thus, although he initially left the Party in 1941 in order to run a popular front agency *for* the Party, Lanzetti knew he was never again going to put himself under the authoritarian control of the CP. But he never made it public knowledge that he had left the Party—not even during the bitter years that included indictment, prison, and frantic financial difficulty—and to this day the question of Lanzetti's Party membership remains a matter for speculation in many quarters. For, if you meet him today and in his presence you attack the Party or Stalin or the Soviet Union, he flies into a passion and cries: "Don't talk to me about the atrocities of Stalin! He only killed Russians! We kill *everyone*. Don't talk to me about Vietnam, the energy crisis and Watergate, and then dare to tell me what is wrong with the people and the Party and the movement that I represent and will belong to with honor as long as I live."

In time it becomes abundantly clear that Lanzetti is a Communist with a deep, fluid sense of the spirit of the movement but a developed human distaste for the narrow meanness of its doctrinaire politics. This duality has, in many ways, isolated him. To many people he is an apologist for Stalin, to others a hopeless revisionist, to still others an idealistic maverick. To many people in the American Communist Party, today—because of his obvious independence—he comes perilously close to being "an enemy of the working class." The long view has taken Lanzetti out on a limb where often only the most courageous sway.

There is about Eric Lanzetti a remarkable wholeness of being; he is the most perfectly integrated Communist I know. Everything he has learned in a long eventful life—about himself, others, the nature of human experience, the multiple causes of change—flows into his politics. He has paid careful attention to the evidence of his own senses; that evidence continually shapes and re-shapes his observations and responses—as a Marxist—to the world about him. Conversely, the live nature of his politics informs the character of his personal life, tempering his daily judgments, widening the scope of his relationships, making all things human intensely interesting to him. In short: Lanzetti's Marxism is, indeed, not so much a political doctrine as it is a philosophical perspective, a piece of truth that lives inside him with such sure knowledge it is not necessary for him to sacrifice reality to theory.

Lanzetti is a man in constant motion. At the age of sixty-two he talks longer, harder, faster than anyone I've ever met. As he talks he smokes, drinks, cuts the air with his hands, leaps up from his chair, paces the floor, grasps the arm of his listener (you shouldn't disappear in the middle of the next very important point). His dark eyes grow darker, his brows come together in (mock) ferocity, his white spade beard makes him look now patriarchal, now intellectual, now satanic. This quicksilver quality of his is the objective correlative to Lanzetti's vital relation to the act of being. It is also the personification of his sense of Communism as a live, changing, responding force metaphorically akin to a force of nature.

Once, in the middle of a long conversation, I began to make a distinction between "real" Communists and fellow travelers or revolving-door Communists. Lanzetti turned on me and said: "*Real* Communists? What the hell does that mean, real Communists?" And he delivered to me the ultimate, mythic speech on what a Communist was.

"I'll tell you what a Communist is," Lanzetti said. "An organizer goes into a factory. He works with the men, begins giving them leaflets, points out what's happening at work, suggests relationships the workers didn't see before. A worker becomes interested in what the organizer is saying. He begins coming to a few meetings. He begins to read. He gets a little larger sense of things. He begins to think about capitalism. He learns about slavery and feudalism. He sees a pattern to this thing. He starts to feel history. Now he begins to see his life not only in terms of the corporation, or the sonofabitch over him, or just this lousy life that keeps pissing on him. He sees a system of oppression older than God and he feels himself part of something bigger than he ever knew existed. It eases his heart, gives him courage and stamina, he's politicized.

"All this time he belongs to the CP. Now, let's say he moves. Drops out of meetings, gets to a new town. Delays looking up the Party. They don't go looking for him. He doesn't pay his dues, he's dropped from the rolls, he's no longer in the Party. Time passes. He doesn't feel like going to meetings. Times change. He drifts away. Now, you tell me, what is that man? I'll tell you what he is. That man is a *Communist*! And for the rest of his *life* he's a Communist. Wherever some shitty thing is happening and he's anywhere near it he is going to respond in a certain way and act on a certain understanding. And men like him are everywhere. These are the Communists, these are my people, my children, my own. . . .

"And we're everywhere, everywhere. We *saved* this fucking country. We went to Spain, and because we did America understood fascism. We made Vietnam come to an end, we're in there in Watergate. We built the CIO, we got Roosevelt elected, we started black civil rights, we forced this shitty country into every good piece of action and legislation it has ever taken. We did the dirty work and the Labor and Capital establishments got the rewards. The Party helped make democracy work.

"We're the changing, shaping force that rears its head again and again. That's what a Communist is. If we reach a hundred or five hundred with any action, any pamphlet, our ultimate effect is a thousand-fold that. Because it's a way of feeling, a way of responding, a way of seeing the deeper meaning of this fucking profit system, and ultimately it's all of a piece."

It's all of a piece. Those are the operative words at the heart of Lanzetti's vision, and they include a host of actions, positions, attitudes inadmissible to the orthodox Communist's lexicon of correct revolutionary behavior. (They also include a host of *non*-actions: whenever a liberal or a conservative simply refuses to take part in "some shitty capitalist thing," Lanzetti counts it one for the socialist side.)

"You chip away, chip away at the fuckers," says Lanzetti. "Everytime somebody sees things just a little different than they did before say me or any other Communist talked to them, I figure it a gain. Me, I talk to everybody all the time. Doctors, janitors, cabdrivers. And anytime I do something or say something and somebody says to me, 'Gee, that was a nice thing you did or a good thing you said. Why'd you do that?' I say, 'Because I'm a Communist.' "

Lanzetti is the only American Communist I know whose mental set parallels that of European Communists. One way or another, he is continually organizing; in good times he organized New York's Lower East Side, in bad times he organized himself. He reads voraciously—books, journals, newspapers; left, right, and center. He takes part in community actions, supports fledgling movements, writes letters to the editor, has opinions on everything from ecology to feminism to the energy crisis. For him, the important thing is to stay alive inside yourself as a Marxist, keep the connections to the larger world open, and your eye on the long haul.

"Look at the Italian Communists," Lanzetti says. "For thirty years they lived in total eclipse. Well, what the hell do you think they were doing all that time nobody in the world knew they existed? They were *organizing*. For thirty years, in every town and village in Italy they kept a network of connections going. They never lost touch with the people. While the big shots were sneering at them in Washington, and in Rome, the Communists worked and waited. They never ossified, never became an anachronism, never became removed from the life of the country. Everywhere, they taught, they participated, they took positions. They wheedled, they compromised, they made concessions, they *stayed alive*. And now look at them. . . .

"There are a lot of American Marxists, people I've known for thirty years, who are panicked by the Italians. 'Revisionism,

revisionism,' they're yelling. Bullshit, I say. If there's a hope in the world for Western Communism the Italians are it."

Over the past twenty-five years—since his release from prison—Lanzetti has kept himself alive in a variety of ways: he worked for a labor union, he ran a left-wing publishing house, he rebuilt three houses in lower Manhattan (one of which is now his home). Throughout these years he has written continuously: books, pamphlets, articles. Only a fraction of what he has written has been published. Lanzetti says his work has been too left for the right, and too right for the left.

Why does he keep writing? "Because," he says, "what I'm saying is important, somebody's gotta say it, and eventually they've got to listen. It's the only way I know how to put my money where my mouth is. I'm a radical. I'm too old to organize so I write."

What is it, exactly, he thinks it so important to say? Lanzetti pours another drink, lights another cigarette, settles back in his chair, and says: "George Orwell left a legacy of despair. He came back from Spain and said Communism and fascism are the same. 'All revolution ends in totalitarianism. If you want to see a picture of the future imagine a boot forever stamping on a human face.'

"As far as I'm concerned, that was the worst thing that could have happened to the postwar world. It helped disintegrate the Left more than any government policy of the Cold War. And what happens when the Left disintegrates? The Right instantly moves to fill up the vacuum. Despair leads to anarchy, and anarchy leads to repression and fascism. In this country the despair of the Left led directly to Vietnam, Nixon, and Watergate.

"Look, let me explain it to you this way. You're a feminist, right? You hate what Freud said about women. You see the old man was wrong, wrong, wrong about women. But does that mean you wipe your ass with Freud? Of course not. That's like throwing the baby out with the bathwater. Freud was wrong on this, wrong on that, maybe wrong in every particular. But he was *right*!

"Well, it's the same in spades with Marx. He was wrong on this, wrong on that, wrong on a lot of things. But my God, he was *right*. And to throw out Marx along with totalitarianism is to spit on the future, dig our own graves, and fall right in.

"Now, I'm not talking revolution. Violent revolution, at least as far as the West is concerned, is a thing of the past, let's hope the Italians are going to prove that conclusively. But goddammit, we have *got* to move left. Look at this country—we won't even *mention* England—it's coming apart at the seams. What else can save it except an intelligent application of Marx?

"And besides, can you conceive of socialism coming to three-quarters of the world and not to America? It's ridiculous. This country *is* the greatest country in the world. No history of feudalism, no adoration of the state, a fluidity of society unknown anywhere else in the modern world. I love it. I love it better than the people who put me in jail love it. I shit on Europe. Europe is dead, finished, the past. But here in America there is hope, openness, a future still.

"And it will come, it will come. After all," Lanzetti finishes with a mocking grin, "it is no accident, comrade, that you and I are sitting here today, talking about these things."

CHAPTER FIVE

To End With

IN JULY of 1962 Murray Kempton spoke at a rally in New York City that had been called to protest the McCarran Act. The hall was packed with Communists. Kempton, a Cold War liberal and longtime antagonist of the Communists, said:

"I have known many Communists in my life. I have not known them as criminals. I knew them once as activists—and we had our quarrels. Someday, if you are ever put back on your feet again, I hope we may quarrel again. But in the interim I would like to say this: This country has not been kind to you, but this country has been fortunate in having you. You have been arrested, you have been followed, you have had your phones bugged, you have had your children fired, you have had everything done to you that can be done to make life as difficult as possible. Throughout this, I can think of numbers of you I have known who have remained gallant, and pleasant and unbroken. . . . Our children's children will someday walk together in the light and they will do so because numbers of you have done what you could to keep your courage and your patience. . . . I salute you and I hope for times to be better."

Having begun with a lengthy explanation of what the Communists meant to me in my early life it seems proper to end with an explanation of what they have come to mean to me now; of why, in fact, I felt compelled in the mid-1970s to "remember" them.

Between the ages of twenty and thirty-three, politics and a sense of the politicalness of life fell away from me. I, like most of my generation, became "silent," moving blindly and without cultural speech throughout a decade I experienced as formless and at an emotional distance from me as I struggled to make my own life cohere. The black civil rights movement did not strike a nerve in me; neither did the war in Vietnam. To be sure, I saw them as great and moving events in the life of American injustice, and I marched year after year in New York, Washington, and Berkeley along with thousands of others. But I did not feel that urgency, that sense of outraged innocence without which political partisanship is a sham. I felt rather the weary remove of the disengaged liberal. ("What does it all matter? It's hopeless. Nothing will ever change. We are beating with rubber hammers to break down a wall of stone.") I was profoundly depoliticized, unable to see my own image reflected in the history of my times.

In 1968 the second wave of American feminism broke over my head. Overnight, my inner life was galvanized. I "heard" the radical feminists as I had heard no other political voices in my adult life. The power and meaning of their insights sent that well-known shock of recognition coursing through me. I grasped instantly and whole what they were talking about: "Ah, yes. *That's* it. That is what our lives are all about." In the words of Arthur Koestler describing what it was like to suddenly feel Marxism: "To say one had 'seen the light' is a poor description of the intellectual rapture which only the convert knows. . . . The new light seems to pour from all directions across the skull." As Koestler first experienced Marxism, so I experienced feminism.

For me, feminism was a powerful new way of seeing what had always been there to be seen. It was as though the kaleidoscope of experience had been shaken and when the pieces settled into place an entirely new design had been formed. The new design was surrounded by a new space; the space created the distance necessary to "see" the larger meanings of our lives as women, as men and women together, as participants in a system of human sacrifice that served enormous social and political ends and was rooted in a common fear of life as old—older—than the very first act of man-made oppression.

What made contemporary feminism significant was its two-part nature: on the one hand, many of us saw clearly that the laws and institutions of our country discriminated ritually against women, unquestionably making of them second-class citizens; on the other hand, we saw equally clearly—and this was the heart of the matter—that we had, all of us, internalized the psychology of oppression, and that the psychology and the institutions formed a dynamic as old as history itself. Break the psychology, we posited, and the institutions would crumble. In short: In America in the second half of the twentieth century the power of feminism turned on the realization that social change had more to do with altered consciousness than with legislated law.

The necessity of squeezing the slave out of oneself drop by drop was, for me, *the* central insight. The idea that self-possession is a political act became rooted in me emotionally; it began to inform my work, my thought, my behavior. In the light of this insight I made connections between political repression, cultural anxiety, and existential terror I had never made before. The history of the world began to reshape itself through the idea of the patriarchy. Using the steady examination of my own experience as a source material I could reread the culture in terms of the oppression of women.

What was most exciting about this "rereading" in those early years was that I—and many others like me—experienced feminist consciousness as a perspective through which the sense of world and being was immeasurably enriched. To think in feminist terms was to feel intellectual promise and emotional discovery quickening to new life. For me, personally, the compelling insights of art and psychoanalysis with which I had long lived were deepened by feminist thought, and the renewed sense of the politicalness of life lightened my heart, put iron in my soul, and reduced my solitariness. The mere act of understanding my life again in historical terms induced in me a sense of human kinship.

And then the unthinkable happened to the woman's movement: feminist consciousness began to give way to feminist dogma. A militant rhetoric developed, an ideology began to form, a hard-edged theory of revolution flourished, "correct" and "incorrect" attitudes were defined, and bitter factional schisms occurred in the major feminist organizations. The "pro-woman" line became a party line, and feminists who objected to the line were denounced as the enemy. Rhetoric threatened to replace all thought: the word "sisterhood" became a club with which intellectual independence was beaten down. The great variety of women's experiences became politically inexpedient: in some quarters lesbians were declared agents of the CIA, in others married women were declared agents of the CIA.

I understood why this was happening. I saw daily the fear, rage, and frustration of women beginning to grasp the political meaning of their lives. I knew that a subjected people didn't emerge into clarity with proportion and generosity. I saw that the pull toward ideology was irresistible. It was a pull I experienced myself and had to fight daily; how alluring it was to simply explain the whole of things in one simple theory of victim and victimizer, how unappetizing to have to face the complex and contradictory truth of the experience we were up against. I saw also that the rhetoric was a powerful weapon "out there". . . . But I knew from the beginning that weapon was dangerous. I remember the first time I sat in a living room and heard a feminist use that rhetoric on a man sitting beside her. I thought, "One day she'll use this on another feminist—and that will be the death of us all."

I had written ardently about the rise of feminism. Now, I began to write just as ardently about the dangers of movement dogma. I wrote that feminist consciousness and feminist rhetoric were natural enemies. I wrote that political expediency was exercised in the name of some mythic tomorrow, but if we sacrificed each other today there would be no tomorrow. I wrote that when we had originally declared ourselves it had been as honest rebels speaking in the name of our common humanity, and then everything was permissible. If we now became revolutionary *apparatchiks* very soon nothing would be permissible, and the meaning of our original daring would be hopelessly distorted. I wrote that dogma was the kiss of death for all thought, and the whole point of the feminist movement was to *think*: honestly, clearly, freely about experience as we actually perceived it. Feminists were people who had said to the world, "For thousands of years you have described me thus. I tell you now there is an enormous discrepancy between what I am and what you describe." Would we now throw off one false and limiting description of ourselves only to put on another? I wrote and wrote and wrote.

It was during this time that the memory of the Old Left began to reassert itself in me. At first—and for quite a long time—I didn't realize what was happening, but it was the memory of the Communists beginning to work half-consciously in me that was giving me such a *detailed* vision of the horrors of dogma. I can remember as though it were yesterday how curiously calm I felt when this realization finally struck me. For the first time since 1956 I did not feel anger toward the Communists. I remember thinking: It's as though they've lain there all these years, deep inside me, chained to the wall of remote memory, waiting for the right psychic moment to be brought forward, waiting to let me understand. The thought was long and deep and amazingly quiet: It was simply that there was this enormous piece of human experience they had embodied, I had been close enough to observe it in its details, and now it was incumbent upon me to learn from it. I felt as though the Communists *wanted* me to learn.

Although feminist consciousness continued to explode in the country beyond the organized movement—and this, of course, was the great power of the second wave of feminism—within the movement itself feminist rhetoric flourished. One weekend during this time I attended a two-day meeting in Boston at which were gathered a group of radical feminists. I was desperately uncomfortable throughout the meeting. I found the language harsh and narrow, the papers presented filled with half-truths, the atmosphere charged with an anger that smelt badly of fear.

Toward the end of the meeting, having said relatively little throughout the two days, I rose to speak. A speaker had just announced that men were "by nature" oppressors. I said it was distressing to me to hear a feminist use those words against men, since these were the very words, used against us, that had made us feminists in the first place. If we had discovered that women were not women by nature but rather by culture how could it be otherwise for men? And of what possible use could it be to us, I continued, to want to go on declaring men the enemy in this simpleminded way when what was important was to keep our eyes on the ever-accumulating details of a system of relationships that was the true cause of our oppression?

A number of voices were instantly raised in an angry murmur. I felt myself surrounded by hostility. The speaker turned full face toward me. In a voice blazing with scorn she said to me: "You're an intellectual and a revisionist." I remained standing beside my seat, speechless. An intellectual and a revisionist. I hadn't heard those words used in this fashion since childhood. Did she realize what she had said? What did she think those words meant? I stared into her face. She stared back into mine. In her eyes, behind the anger, I saw an agony of confusion.

And there in that room, in Boston in the early 1970s, the memory of the Old Left surfaced like an underground spring bursting through encrusted earth, and it overran me, and I felt for the Communists what I had not felt in twenty years: compassion. "So *this* is how it all happened," I thought. "This is how all that treachery came about. Who on earth can deal with all this fear and anger? No one. Ever. Not then, not now."

I thought of the judgment I had handed down against the Communists: it was as though all these years I had been standing on the shore of a great body of water that looked like a calm sea. Out there, on the horizon where sea met sky, were a group of swimmers. Instead of swimming smoothly they were thrashing about in the water. How ridiculous they are, I thought. Clumsy, inept, dangerous to themselves and each other. How can they call themselves swimmers? A three-year-old could do better than that. And now I had left the shore and entered the water only to discover that it was an ocean rather than a sea, full of rocky currents and a treacherous undertow. Those who had been thrashing about on the horizon, I now saw, were doing admirably if they simply stayed afloat.

Feminism gave me a second, and even more moving, insight into the live meaning the history of American Communism held for me. It was this insight that pulled together in me those disparate strands of observation which, once woven into a whole, become a piece of empathetic understanding.

The second wave of American feminism never did become the property of the woman's movement. On the contrary: it proved to have a life of its own with the power to influence thought and behavior in the world far beyond the control of the movement. There are today thousands of people in the United States who do not call themselves feminists and do not know what's going on in feminist circles in New York, Boston, or Berkeley whose lives are nevertheless profoundly changed by feminist consciousness. They are asking questions they would never have asked before the rise of feminism, challenging old assumptions, demanding their "rights," observing social and political institutions in a new light. In short: feminism has become a radical perspective, a social influence, a way of seeing things rather than a movement as such. In the second half of the twentieth century it is a diffused piece of understanding rather than a structure of political leadership, speaking more deeply to the slowly altering process of social change than to political revolution in the classic sense.

One night two years ago a friend and I were speaking of the history of feminism. My friend recalled a story about Carrie Chapman Catt, the great suffragist who led the final struggle for the vote. Mrs. Catt, being taken to task by another suffragist for her formidable usage of political expediency and reminded of the bold eloquence of Elizabeth Cady Stanton, had replied: "Ah, yes. Elizabeth could say anything she wanted, we don't have that luxury."

My friend and I took off on that anecdote, speaking far into the night about its meaning for us today, at this moment, this hour. The observation we pieced together was this:

Elizabeth Cady Stanton belonged to that first generation of visionary feminists who, in the middle of the nineteenth century, stood alone, armed only with the clarity of original insight into the systematic nature of woman's oppression. They had nothing to lose and everything to gain by speaking a stirring rhetoric, radical to the core, alive with agitation. Their language sprang from the moral purity of their position, inspired by a vision of human humiliation in a blind, unfeeling world.

Sixty years later, the cause of women's rights had advanced

hardly one whit. The third generation of feminists had lost the revolutionary fervor of Elizabeth Stanton, Lucretia Mott, and Susan B. Anthony. Bitterly, they concluded that the large visionary sense of things must give way to narrow political action: all their efforts turned on suffrage.

Carrie Chapman Catt was the distilled essence of this third generation. A woman with an immense sense of politics, she built an amazingly effective organization and she ruled over that organization with an iron hand; dictatorial and singleminded, she cut down the opposition at every turn of the way, made deals, compromises, and coalitions with the most appalling elements and positions in American political life. It was generally felt she would have sold her grandmother on the auction block if by so doing she could have secured suffrage for women. It was also felt that Mrs. Catt was utterly convinced that authoritarianism alone could have built an effective political force.

Tens of thousands of feminists took part in that last struggle for suffrage. Many of these worshiped Carrie Catt and would gladly have laid down their lives for her. Many others hated her passionately and declared her methods every bit as much the enemy as the culture and government they were fighting. Out of this enmity there arose issues and questions of lasting value. In making the case against Mrs. Catt those feminists who were her declared enemies clarified and deepened feminist analysis, recovering and adding to the original insights of the nineteenth-century feminists.

I was born in 1935, fifteen years after Carrie Chapman Catt rode through the streets of Washington in an open car, her arms filled with flowers, accepting for the women of America the victory of suffrage. In our maturity, the women of my generation would come to think of Carrie Catt as a "battle-ax suffragist," a dominating party politician whose narrowness of vision had sold us out for a mess of pottage and left us where we were forty years later, as far from full citizenship as ever.

Fifty-five years after Carrie Catt rode through Washington in an open car, my friend and I sat speaking of her in voices crowded with conflict and contradiction. Although for us her figure was still swollen with everything we feared and hated in politics, grudgingly we admitted that she had, after all, done something remarkable, and if she hadn't done it we, the next generation of feminists, could never have gone forward. And we asked ourselves the oldest question in political life: Could it have been done in any other way? If Carrie Catt had not lived and worked in exactly the way she did live and work, would we now have the vote?

"And don't forget," my friend added softly, "after her came *us*." I understood instantly what she meant: from the visionary Elizabeth Cady Stanton to the fiercely political Carrie Chapman Catt to the broad-based feminist consciousness of today. They stood thus, three links on a historical chain, part of a forward-moving process that made each phase grow out of the last and, in the largest sense, made each generation of feminists know more than the last had known—but only because the last had lived.

That night I found myself thinking once more of the Communists. I felt deeply moved by the realization that they occupied a space on a similar and parallel historical chain: first had come the visionary socialists of the nineteenth century, then had come the fierce politicalness of the Communists, and now had come the unaffiliated Marxist consciousness of contemporary radicals. Was there anyone who could argue that each phase in its turn had not been necessary in the development of American radicalism? That one had not grown organically out of the other? If the nineteenth-century socialists had not been perceived as heart-breakingly ineffective, would the next generation of Marxists have become so ragingly political? And if the Communists had not embodied what is darkest and most terrifying in organized politics, would the current generation of Marxists know as much as it does know both of vision and of dogma? Would it have been able to recover with such sure knowledge the *idea* of socialism if the Communists had not lived out for them the bitter-as-gall lessons of a visionary idea subordinated to the political apparatus?

Thirty years have passed since Albert Camus wrote *The Rebel*. That brilliant and noble essay speaks more deeply to us today than it did when it was written; these thirty years have been filled with an ever-deepening consciousness of the agony at the heart of the book.

"The act of rebellion," wrote Camus, "affirms the value and the dignity common to all men." It is an act that breaks the morbid isolation of human life, binding men and women together: "I rebel, therefore we exist." But with rebellion, inevitably, comes stupefying rage: "So many injustices suffered, a sorrow so unrelieved, justify every excess." The consciousness of the rebel compels him to conquer the power that has been humiliating him; conquest can occur only through the use of force; force turns the rebel into a revolutionary; the revolutionary commits murder; murder breaks the solidarity forged by the original act of rebellion.

This is the agony at the heart of radicalism, an agony unbroken in modern history. And Camus asks in infinite sorrow: Must it ever be so? "When we have only just conquered solitude, must we then reestablish it definitively by legitimizing the act that isolates everything?"

The inborn need to defeat isolation, the perhaps equally inborn inability to do so: these are the warring elements in the struggle of the race to humanize itself. In this war there are two invariables: the elements are indissolubly linked, one growing organically out of the other; the act of struggle is everything. Dreading the worst, men and women must still act. For, knowing everything we know, yet we do not *know*, and in engagement alone lies all hope that new life may yet come out of life.

For better or worse, radical politics—full of sorrow and glory —embodies the stirring spectacle of human beings engaged, alive to the beauty and rawness of self-creation.

American Communists were caught up in the magnificent sorrow. They gave themselves to it passionately, with a wholeness of being. For this I honor them, and I am grateful to them.